BEHAVIOR DISORDERS

OHMER MILTON
ROBERT G. WAHLER

University of Tennessee
Knoxville

THE LIPPINCOTT COLLEGE PSYCHOLOGY SERIES
Under the Editorship of
Dr. Carl P. Duncan, Northwestern University
and Dr. Julius Wishner, University of Pennsylvania

ERSPECTIVES AND TRENDS

3EHAVIOR
)ISORDERS

THIRD EDITION

B. Lippincott Company

iiladelphia, New York, Toronto

ISBN 0–397–47277–3

Printed in the United States of America

Cover design by Michael Louridas
Interior design by Terry Reid

3 5 7 9 8 6 4 2

Library of Congress Cataloging in Publication Data

Milton, Ohmer, comp.
    Behavior disorders; perspectives and trends.

    Includes bibliographies.
    CONTENTS: Milton, O. and Wahler, R. G. Perspectives and
trends.—The medical model: Albee, G. W. The sickness model of
mental disorder means a double standard of care. Scheff, T. J. The
societal reaction to deviance. [etc.]
    1. Psychiatry—Addresses, essays, lectures. I. Wahler, Robert G.,
1936–   joint comp. II. Title. [DNLM: 1. Behavior—Collected works.
2. Mental disorders—Collected works. WM 5 M662b 1973]

RC458.M52   1973   616.8'9'008   73-660
ISBN 0–397–47277–3

To alert students who can help destroy professional myths and practices which continue to demean so many anguished souls.

Contents

Contents

Preface

WHILE THE EVIDENCE against the view that behavior disorders are an illness or disease has continued to mount since the first edition of this book in 1965, the editors believe that the fundamental ideology continues to dominate much of the thinking about and many of the programs for dealing with disordered behavior. Despite this fact, programs for helping people are much more flexible now, and the types are more numerous than a few years ago.

In this third edition, then, we continue to parade evidence against the "sickness" idea, give some indication of the variety of new approaches, and, perhaps most important of all, call to the attention of students, vividly, the plight of the institutionalized. At the same time, we have striven mightily in selection 1 to steer students away from peripheral issues and to direct them toward integrating points of view, which surely appear to them as disparate.

Grouping of materials and arranging them in some reasonable order is always a difficult problem and many times entails arbitrary decisions. The order of the three sections, however, is designed to correspond to the flow of selection 1; each individual selection elaborates problems, ideas, and concepts which have been introduced in selection 1. The particular arrangement of the selections within a section is not too important, and of course there is some unavoidable overlap. We do suggest, however, that certain of the selections be studied together: selections 3 and 4, selections 8 and 9, selections 13 and 14, and selections 18 and 19.

Once again, for this edition we scoured the literature for articles that would be readable by undergraduates (and interesting to them). During our search, we gained the impression that there is much less concern now by researchers than there was a few years ago about specific diagnostic labels. Thus there is even less emphasis in this edition than in former ones on discrete categories of disordered behavior.

In keeping with that portion of our title, "Trends," a major one we see on the horizon (and hope for fervently) is increasing concern about the civil rights of mental patients and about the cavalier manner in which our fellow citizens have been and are now being treated. We were dumbfounded by the spurious, simple, and unsubstantiated reasoning we encountered, even though we consider ourselves to be as enlightened and as shockproof as most psychologists. It was impossible for us to remain detached. It is for these reasons, especially, that we spoke as forthrightly as we did in selection 1 about these matters and included selections 3, 4, and 9. Further information about efforts to assist the presumed "mentally ill" can be obtained from the National Council on the Rights of the Mentally Impaired (1600 Twentieth Street, N.W., Washington, D.C. 20009, and 84 Fifth Avenue, New York, New York 10011).

OHMER MILTON
ROBERT G. WAHLER

Knoxville, Tennessee
January, 1973

Perspectives and Trends

By OHMER MILTON and ROBERT G. WAHLER

1

IT WAS AROUND 150 YEARS AGO that psychotic behavior—perhaps the only publicly or officially recognized form of deviancy at that time—was first thought of as a disease. In the ensuing years, what might be called the "disease" concept of psychosis has been extended to other forms of disorders of emotions, thought, and behavior. In recent years, a trend has been developing *away* from that concept as one appropriate for all behavior deviations; it is being led by critical and creative thinkers in all of the disciplines most directly concerned with human behavior.

Whatever basic views are maintained have major implications for the nation's approach to the problems which are labeled, depending upon their professional sources, as mental illness, mental and emotional disorders, or disorders of thought and behavior. The manner in which these difficulties are conceptualized, including what the causative and maintaining factors are presumed to be, helps to determine what our society does about them. Furthermore, the manner in which the members of a group view these problems may determine, to a large degree, the way in which an individual who experiences these problems perceives them and seeks resolutions.

THE DISEASE VIEW

Today many authorities believe that the "disease" view has limited usefulness both for the understanding and the alteration of most of the emotional and mental disorders (selections 2, 7, and 10). Whereas volumes would be needed to describe and explain the "medical model" for disease and all of its ramifications, this model as applied to physical matters (in an overly simplified way) is to the effect that pain or fever, for example, is a symptom of some disorder or malfunction in the body. The underlying cause of the symptom must be determined, and then the cause must be treated rather than the symptom. When the cause is treated properly, the symptom will subside or disappear; indeed, it is not only fruitless but may be harmful to treat only the symptom while ignoring the cause of it. Within this context a behavior deviation or peculiarity has been considered as a symptom of some internal mental or emotional disorder, and it has been reasoned that if the underlying cause is treated, the behavior deviation (symptom) will be altered. Diagnostic labels are one manifestation of the medical model. Briefly, a diagnosis is a word or few words at most, a shorthand description, if you will, conveying to professionals the cause(s) of an ailment, suggesting the treatment, and predicting the outcome.

The bewildering arrays of diagnoses or labels have not served their purposes well for most forms of deviant behavior, although there have been strenuous efforts to create very specific and discrete categories. These labels suggest special entities or things—something one has—to many people (particularly beginning students), as when one hears references to "a neurosis" or "the neurosis" or "schizophrenia." In reality, most of the labels are shorthand descriptive expressions for a variety of behavioral characteristics; a person does not have a neurosis; he behaves in a manner which we call neurotic. Moreover, there are very few objective criteria, and as a consequence, subjective opinions, and in some instances very distorted ones, operate in the examiner or diagnostician (selection 5). Furthermore, some psychiatrists have been known to assign labels to individuals, publicly, even without benefit of the usual examining procedures. A notorious example of such irresponsible professional behavior occurred during the presidential campaign of Senator Barry Goldwater (Boroson, 1964). Signed letters were published in which several of the most ominous diagnoses were ascribed to the senator; he later won a $75,000 libel suit against the publisher. Serious harm to persons often results when the labels are made public, and usually the aggrieved have no recourse (selection 4).

Many students may wish to see the particularly fulsome discussion of the "medical model" and a discerning analysis of its limitations in the "treatment" of psychological disorders as provided by Ullmann and Krasner (1965). Sarbin (1967) has presented a detailed historical analysis of the development of the model; he reasons that the label *illness* was first used as a metaphor and insists that "logical canons as well as humanistic value orientations direct us to delete 'mental illness' from our vocabulary." In an extension of his position Sarbin (1972) asserts flatly that the belief that "schizophrenia" (selection 11) is a disease is *false*. He documents his position carefully and in addition points out the damage caused to people by such labeling (selection 4).

Currently there are few "medical model" proponents who believe that all forms of deviant behavior are due to organic malfunction. Nevertheless, like their physically oriented forerunners, they still tend to look "inside" the person for the determinants of aberrations. True, the causes are not thought to be physical, but they are considered organic by virtue of the fact that they are part of the *internal* state of the individual. To attribute a criminal's stealing, for example, to an inadequate superego is little different, in a sense, from attributing it to an overly active reticular system; both of these presumed causal variables are hypothetical, and in both instances they are *internal*. Thus, while present-day advocates of the "medical model" tend to advance nonorganic causes for behavior deviations, the locus of their postulates is still the same—*inside* the person. The model was being utilized during the ordeal of Senator Thomas Eagleton in the summer of 1972 when numerous references were made to his "medical" problem and to "medical facts." The popular press in presenting discussions about the treatment of "depression" (apparently the label pinned to the senator) with drugs and electroshock quoted mental health professionals to the effect: "We're just treating symptoms."

One way of clarifying the "medical model" position on causality is to distinguish between *past* or *developmental* antecedents of behavior and immediate antecedents; the internal factors referred to in the model are those which are immediate and current.

Figure 1 presents a schematic illustration of the "medical model": As a result of certain historical experiences (e.g., a demanding and overly critical mother during early childhood), an individual may develop disturbances in his mental apparatus (e.g., an inadequate self-concept); the mental apparatus then becomes a here-and-now or present-day cause of adult deviant behavior (e.g., consumption of excessive amounts of alcohol to the point of being unable to keep a job). The long-range, developmental, or historical antecedents were *outside* the person, that is, within his social environment at one time.

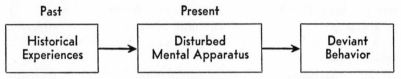

FIGURE 1   The "Medical Model" and Deviant Behavior

From the standpoint of altering the deviant behavior, the immediate, internal factors are those of prime importance—history is history, and the past cannot be changed. Psychoanalysis (Freud, 1949) is an especially good example of a "medical model" theory and exemplifies, too, a method of modifying the internally disturbed mental apparatus. In this approach, the disturbed mental apparatus is thought to be primarily the result of early interactions with the environment; the psychoanalyst's goal is to produce significant changes in this apparatus. How this is done is of interest since the method focuses almost exclusively on internal factors; the current environment or the here-and-now is rarely considered. Essentially the person is encouraged to describe his mental functioning, with particular emphasis upon the recall of early experiences. If the analysand is successful in uncovering those experiences which produced the disturbed mental apparatus, the road to change is near—or so goes the theory. It has been demonstrated clearly that the resulting insight is by no means always sufficient to bring about desired alterations in observable behavior. In fact, there is reason to believe that changes in deviant behavior can be produced without insight and that insight may be a product rather than a cause of such changes.

An example of the latter possibility is seen in a study by Wahler and Pollio (1968). These investigators utilized a learning theory approach to modify the extremely dependent behavior of an eight-year-old boy. The therapeutic techniques involved helping the boy's parents learn to react differently to his dependent behavior; no efforts were made to provide insight for the boy. In spite of this, as the youngster learned more independent behavior, his verbal awareness of his problems also changed. In a very real sense, he acquired insight concerning his dependency problems, but the insight came *after* not *before* the behavioral changes.

The psychoanalytic position and traditional psychotherapy tend to ignore other factors which often contribute to the maintenance of deviant behavior—factors which are environmental or external. As we shall see later in discussing recent views in the field, the current environment can be a powerful source of control, a source which can either support deviant behavior or modify it. That these other factors operate is illustrated, too, by comparisons between witch doctors and psychotherapists (selection 6).

The "disease" view appears to be prevalent and pervasive in the thinking of many individuals about most forms of deviant behavior. During the past fifteen or twenty years, there has been repeated emphasis upon the terms *mental illness* and *disease* in many publications; the National Association for Mental Health (1963) advertises, for example: "At least 50 percent of all the millions of medical and surgical cases treated by private doctors and hospitals have a mental illness complication." The terminology which is used to describe and explain mental and emotional disorders and other deviant behavior continues to consist of terms and words which have long been associated with physical disabilities: *patient, hospital, cure, therapy, diagnosis,* and *pathology;* a particular favorite is *psychopathology*. Although none of these words necessarily has a narrow technical meaning or definition which restricts its use to the physical realm, it is highly probable that their frequent utilization for reference to disorders of thought and behavior does connote disease to most students.

Still another line of evidence suggesting the prevalence of the "disease" view has been the ever-expanding application of the term *mental illness*. With increasing impetus since the late 1940s, it has become a catchall rubric for forms of behavior that in earlier times were called by other names, for example, *eccentric, shiftless, lazy, triflin', sinful, mean, trashy,* and *half-witted.* In other words, an increasing array of behavior is now being classified or labeled as mental illness or mental disorder that in former years was *not* thought of as sickness. Such problems in behavior as juvenile delinquency, marital strife, racial prejudice, alienation, alcoholism, and many others are all labeled by some authorities as *mental illness.* As you know, it is fashionable to talk about our "sick" society.

The rapidly changing estimates of its prevalence also illustrate the burgeoning of the "mental illness" category. Around 1940, the estimate was one person in every sixteen; around 1950, it was one in thirteen, and by 1960 or thereabouts, it was one in ten. The latter figure, of course, amounts to 10 percent of the population; one can easily conclude from these guesstimates that "mental illness" is increasing. In reality, the criteria are changing, and the term is becoming so broad as to approach meaninglessness; there are some who believe it has already reached that state.

Since the 1960 estimate of one in ten is cited without any qualification in many publications, some people have assumed that it is a well-established fact. Nothing could be further from the truth. Students, of course, should learn to be critical of such statistics and to question their origin and composition. It is difficult to tell where the one-in-ten figure originated, although it apparently was derived from a study conducted in Baltimore by the Commission on Chronic Illness (1957). The primary focus of the investigation was that of determining the prevalence of chronic and severe physical illness—arthritis, heart ailments, and so on—and identification of mental illnesses was of secondary or peripheral interest. Many rules of sampling the population of the city were violated; many standards of careful study of individuals were ignored; and the examining and labeling procedures were highly suspect.

You may have encountered or will encounter such propaganda statements as these:

The probability is one in twenty that any given individual will, at some time in his life, be a patient in a mental hospital [Kimble and Garmezy, 1963].

Estimates indicate that one out of every 10 babies born today will be hospitalized for mental illness at some time during his life [Hilgard and Atkinson, 1967].

The two sets of figures illustrate remarkable carelessness with data. The one-in-twenty statistic (the origin of which is unknown) is strikingly incompatible with well-documented data about mental hospital admissions; the number of persons admitted and readmitted each year has remained quite close to one-half of one percent of the total population ever since 1930—as far back as census data are available. The one-in-every-ten-baby statistic is a gross distortion of a carefully executed probability or actuarial investigation of babies born in New York State in 1940 (Goldhamer and Marshall, 1953). The expectation was one in ten that a baby would be admitted to a mental hospital by *age 75 provided* he lived to that age. The chances were predicted to be quite different for those living to other ages; for example, age 30, one in 100; age 45, one in 29; age 90, one in five. The predictions one in ten *at or after* age 75 and one in five *at or after* age 90 are not surprising in view of what is well known about the physical and mental ravages of old age. All of these estimates and predictions have been called to your attention in some detail because they are cited frequently without the necessary qualifications and because they are reflections of the "disease" position.

One of the most serious and neglected untoward effects of the "mental illness" era is the extent to which the civil rights of people have been ignored and violated under the banner of illness by the experts who make such judgments (selections 3 and 4). A recent legal study (Allen, Ferster, and Wiehofen, 1968) has revealed that in New York and Massachusetts, for example, there are departmental regulations which deny mental hospital patients the power to make a will, execute contracts or deeds, and even to sign a check. In some states there are statutes which provide that commitment to a mental hospital is conclusive evidence of incompetency. Such laws mean, among other things, that if a patient is discharged as "improved," for many years thereafter any of his legal transactions may be questioned.

The study also revealed that hospital commitment (incarceration) hearings are shams in many instances; by way of illustration, this one was observed in Texas:

The hearings I attended were conducted in . . . a lecture room at the . . . Hospital. Seated on a small stage at a long table were . . . the attorney ad litem,   and   [the judge and the chief clerk of the court]. While awaiting the various doctors, I asked [the attorney ad litem] if he had contacted any of the proposed patients. He had not. This was the first time he had served as an attorney ad litem. . . . The hearings began at 2:00 P.M.—an hour and five minutes for 40 persons; about a minute and a half per patient! All the doctors were sworn . . . prior to testifying. As each case was called the doctor would give the height, weight, and color of hair and eyes of the patient. These data are for the form sent to the Department of Public Safety concerning driver's licenses. Next, the Judge would read the patient's name and state the dates of medical examination. Without pausing or looking up he would then read to the doctors, apparently from the Order of Commitment, "Is it your opinion and both of you agree that [he] is a mentally ill person and needs medical care and treatment for his own welfare and protection or the protection of others and is mentally incompetent?" The doctor answered "yes" and the next case would be called in like fashion. . . . All of the proposed patients were ordered indefinitely committed and all were found to be incompetent [Allen, Ferster, and Wiehofen, 1968, p. 52].*

Contrast such regulations, laws, and procedures with the very elaborate ones which have been designed to protect the rights of alleged criminals. It seems that the mere presumption of illness results in the denial of basic and guaranteed freedoms. If you are locked up—a denial of a major freedom—and denied other fundamental freedoms, does it really matter whether the place is called a prison or a hospital? Note especially "all of the proposed patients were ordered indefinitely committed." Lieberman (1970) has charged that legislators have abdicated their responsibilities because incarceration is a legal decision: ". . . these agents in concert with deluded lawyers have been led to believe that certain restrictions on the liberty of citizens are medical problems" (Lieberman, 1970, p. 213).

Fortunately, there are a few rays of hope! Following a class action suit, *Wyatt* v. *Stickney* (1972), a judge in the United States District Court of the Middle District of Alabama, Northern Division, ordered such essentials for mental patients as the "right to privacy" and ruled "no person shall be deemed incompetent to manage his affairs, to contract, to hold professional or occupational or vehicle operator's licenses, to marry and obtain a divorce, to register and vote, or to make a will *solely* by reason of his admission or commitment to the hospital" (*Wyatt* v. *Stickney*, 1972, p. 9).

There were additional decrees about patients having the right to send and receive mail, to make telephone calls, and to wear

---

* From *Mental Impairment and Legal Incompetency* by Richard C. Allen, Elyce Z. Ferster, and Henry Wiehofen. By permission of Prentice-Hall, Inc.

their own clothes, but these were tempered by the fact that a qualified mental health professional could impose special restrictions under the guise of treatment. The court had certainly been persuaded by the "sickness" concept because the judge declared: "As is true in the case of any disease, no one is immune from the peril of mental illness" (*Wyatt v. Stickney,* 1972, p. 6).

One leading attacker of the disease view (Szasz, 1960) asserts that: (1) Mental illness can be thought of much more meaningfully as problems in living; (2) the notion of illness or disease has served to obscure the fact that life for most people is a continuous struggle to attain human values such as "peace of mind"; (3) adherence to the myth has allowed us to avoid tackling our personal, social, and ethical conflicts by placing the blame on factors beyond our control; and (4) the notion of mental illness has served to obscure man's responsibility for his own actions. Another critic (Mowrer, 1960) argues convincingly that the earlier notion of sin wherein the evil spirits invaded the lunatic or psychotic person because he had been bad was really better than the modern one of mental illness, because the notion of sin acknowledged individual responsibility and self-determination, whereas the idea of illness or disease did not.

THE CURRENT TREND

It is much easier to describe and criticize the "disease" view than it is to portray clearly the conceptual schemes which are gaining prominence. Basic to these schemes is a tendency to conceptualize the person and his current environment as interdependent systems; that is, the individual is not considered as an entity apart from the world in which he lives. For example, if one is to understand severe anxiety, one must know as much about the person's current situation as about him: What is his wife like? How about his children, his relatives, his boss? What is his economic position? Certainly historical experiences play a role in the development of the present-day behavior, but theorists now argue that current environmental factors support and maintain it (selections 8, 9, and 10).

Perhaps the term *psychosocial* best describes the current thinking about disordered behavior. That expression essentially implies an interaction between a person and his social environment—an interaction which may yield "normal" or deviant behavior. Just how these interactions occur and how they produce their effects have been the subjects of prolific research. Investigators have differed widely in their specific approaches to the problem, but all have shared the "psychosocial model." As an example, Bernal, Duryee, Pruett, and Burns (1968) trained a mother to control her eight-and-one-half-year-old emotionally disturbed boy (there had been serious parental strife since the child's infancy) who at the same time was a severe disciplinary problem. He regulated all family activities and even dictated when his mother could sit in the living room. By utilizing learning principles and providing behavioral feedback to the mother via closed-circuit television, her behavior was altered, and, in turn, the boy's abusive behavior was reduced. She began also to feel and show affection for him as he did for her.

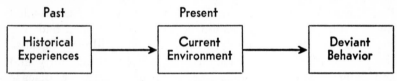

FIGURE 2   The "Psychosocial Model"

Figure 2 presents a schematic illustration of the current trend; this one should be contrasted with the illustration of the "medical model" in Figure 1. In both instances, historical experiences are important as developmental causes of deviant behavior (as was certainly true with the eight-and-one-half-year-old); however, such experiences have their primary influence on the current environment, *not* on the mental apparatus. In other words, the *function* of the current environment is determined by history. The present situation thus serves as an immediate cause of the deviant behavior; in a very real sense, the current environment may be seen as *maintaining* problems which were developed in the past. The critical difference between this view and that of the "medical model" is that of the locus of immediate causes; in the "medical model" the locus is *internal,* while in the newer trend the locus is *external.* To emphasize or focus upon outside causes of deviant behavior is not to deny that the individual has a mind; if the current environment is to influence behavior, it logically must do so through cognitive and emotional equipment. The intent of the newer approach is to produce a shift in our attention, a shift away from an exclusive concern with internal functioning and a shift toward examining those present variables which may elicit this functioning and thus produce or maintain deviant behavior.

Support for these positions is found in the fact that patterns of disordered behavior tend to be different in the various social classes. Hollingshead and Redlich (1958) demonstrated, in one of the most significant large-scale social studies in "mental illness" ever undertaken, that:

1. There is a relationship between the incidence of "mental illness" and social class—the incidence is higher in the lower class.
2. There is a relationship between the type of "mental illness" and social class—behavior labeled as neurotic tends to occur in the upper classes, while behavior labeled as psychotic tends to occur in the lower classes.
3. There is a relationship between type of care or treatment received and social class—people in the upper classes receive care which is based upon our most up-to-date notions; those in the lower classes receive largely custodial care. The fact that these latter people lack money is not the sole determinant of this discrimination; some of it is due to misperceptions or distortions by mental health experts. Similar or identical behavior by people in different social classes results in care that is drastically different. Two highly condensed descriptions of the almost identical behavior of two females illustrates that assertion:

An upper-class girl was involved in an automobile accident while drunk; this occurred following one of her frequent drinking and sexual escapades. Through family influence, no court action was taken, and the girl was returned to an exclusive boarding school. Within a few weeks, when it was realized that the girl was pregnant, she was placed in an expensive private psychiatric hospital in order to receive psychotherapy.

A lower-class girl was arrested after she was observed having intercourse with several men. Following a perfunctory trial, she was sent to a reform school. Two years later she was paroled but again was promiscuous and was then sent to the reformatory for women.

Another noteworthy feature of this investigation was the fact that the original sample of patients was studied over a ten-year period. Myers and Bean (1968) found that the higher the social class of the patients, the less the likelihood of their still being hospitalized ten years later, that the lower-class patients were continuing to receive custodial care, and that if the lower-class patient returns to his community, there are serious employment and financial problems and a high degree of social isolation. These authors emphasize: "In summary, social factors in the community, as well as in the treatment agency itself, operate to produce significant class differences in treatment outcome" (Myers and Bean, 1968, p. 211).

Other studies have tended to substantiate the results of these pioneering ones. A dramatic study that confirms the importance of external forces in schizophrenia (selection 11), the form of "mental illness" that constitutes the greatest puzzle of all of them, was that of Rogler and Hollingshead (1965). Carefully and highly trained investigators identified 40 families in San Juan, Puerto Rico, all of whom lived in the slums; all of the 80 spouses had been reared in abject, unbelievable poverty. In each of 20 families, at least one spouse (in a few cases, both) was diagnosed as schizophrenic; these 20 families were matched carefully on the basis of several criteria with 20 families in which both spouses were well. These 80 men and women were then studied by intensive and repeated interviews over a period of months and by frequent observations as they lived in their natural setting. To locate such subjects according to predetermined criteria and to study them in even a semi-objective fashion were staggering professional and personal tasks. In the slum section of San Juan, there is marked suspicion by everyone of all strangers, making it very difficult to obtain information, and it is not uncommon for the stranger to get a dog's teeth in his leg and a dagger in his back.

It was found that all of the 80 spouses had suffered extreme hardships, great economic deprivation, serious physical illness, and many personal dilemmas from the time of their birth until they entered the present marriage. There were, however, no essential childhood background differences between the spouses diagnosed as schizophrenic and the remaining ones who were well. This finding is at marked variance from those of many other investigations. Numerous studies in the past have suggested that the adult who becomes schizophrenic is one who experienced an abnormal childhood.

The onset of schizophrenia in each of the spouses so labeled was preceded by several extreme family crises during a 12- to 18-month period. These took the form of economic difficulties, severe physical deprivation, interspouse conflicts, and serious physical illnesses. Similar crises occurred in the well families, but there were fewer of them, and they were of milder degrees. This very condensed case history of one of the "sick" families will illustrate both the severity and the frequency of the problems the members faced during a very short span of time, referred to as the "problematic year."

The Gallardos

The problematic year, during which the Gallardos were beset by an intricate labyrinth of human misery, began when Mrs. Gallardo, at the age of 24, gave birth by Caesarian section for the third time. After a four-month period, since Mrs. Gallardo had not recovered, a partial hysterectomy was performed. Very shortly thereafter, the baby developed pneumonia, recovered, became asthmatic, and two months later had a recurrence of pneumonia and died. Illness was not a newcomer to the Gallardos: The oldest boy had had alternating bouts of tonsillitis, severe colds, asthma, and measles since he was three months old. The second child, a girl, had a hernia at 15 days of age and pneumonia at 25 days, complicated by asthma and bronchitis. At one year she had pneumonia for the second time.

Six weeks after the baby died, the little girl, age three, had pneumonia for the third time. After being kept at the clinic three days, she was sent home, where she remained bedfast for approximately two months. Meanwhile, the little boy, age six, developed a cold and had trouble breathing. The clinic doctors diagnosed ulcerated tonsils, and an operation was scheduled. On the morning of the operation, the family arrived at the hospital to find the child anesthetized and on a table ready for surgery. "The parents noticed that the child, although unconscious, was vomiting; a hand lying outside the blanket was red, they rushed to the child, felt his hand, and decided he was feverish. They insisted that the nurse take the child's temperature, and, according to Mr. Gallardo, the boy had '6 degrees of fever'" [Rogler and Hollingshead, 1965, p. 201].* They forbade the operation, but the boy was

---

* From *Trapped: Families and Schizophrenia* by L. H. Rogler and A. B. Hollingshead. Copyright © 1965 by John Wiley and Sons, Inc. By permission of John Wiley and Sons, Inc.

kept at the clinic until his temperature subsided; he subsequently recovered without further treatment.

Just before the experience with the tonsils, and while the daughter had pneumonia, Mr. Gallardo arose one morning to find he had developed a facial paralysis. His left cheek was twisted, his mouth partially open, and his eye staring off at an angle. The paralysis was actually a muscle spasm, but Mr. Gallardo thought it was caused by a cerebral hemorrhage and the doctors were keeping it from him. He refused to go to his job on the docks for several weeks, brooded about his family's problems, and became weak and ill. Shortly after his return to work, where he was ridiculed about his appearance, his co-workers went out on strike—more severe hunger, illness, nervousness, anxiety for himself and his family. Mrs. Gallardo's father and other relatives helped to feed them. They did what they could, but there simply was not enough food; Mr. and Mrs. Gallardo ate only enough to keep alive and gave the rest to the children.

When Mr. Gallardo returned to work, he was very thin and weak as a result of lack of food. In this condition, it was difficult for him to perform manual labor. Also, his favorite brother appeared to be quite thin and ill, and Mr. Gallardo kept prodding him to go to the clinic; the brother became angry and hostile, threatening Mr. Gallardo with a knife. A few days later the brother dropped on the docks—dead from tuberculosis. Mr. Gallardo felt responsible for his death, feeling that he should have insisted his brother go to the clinic much sooner. He immediately decided he had tuberculosis; although chest X-rays were negative, he continued to be convinced he was tubercular and had only a short time to live. He began to drink heavily, had trouble with his neighbors, whose uncomely conduct and squalor were difficult to contend with, and moved continuously from one slum shack to another. His stomach ached; Mrs. Gallardo had pain in her ovary and legs; the daughter had a high fever and inflamed tonsils. Four more months of no work because he thought he had cancer, ulcers, and tuberculosis brought continued hunger, fear, and "ideas" that commanded him to do things. His relationship with his wife and family and neighbors worsened.

At this juncture, another series of untoward events took place. Mrs. Gallardo's sister's husband left her with nine children to support; she sent to Mrs. Gallardo for help. A niece went to the hospital with a high fever; a nephew had to have a serious operation; Mrs. Gallardo's 14-year-old brother set fire to an 11-year-old boy and was paroled to Mrs. Gallardo's father, but she kept the boy for two weeks to give her father a rest. Mrs. Gallardo experienced a partial paralysis. A hammer began beating on her middle finger and then on her hand. Soon her left hand and arm became paralyzed from the imaginary beating.

(How would you cope with such an intricate labyrinth of human misery?)

Ryan (1969) has documented the fact that in Boston, which is especially well supplied with mental health specialists, care is not provided for the poor; instead it is rendered primarily for the benefit of an educated group of young adults—mostly females. Indeed traditional psychotherapy has always tended to be restricted to a select group of anxious people.

As might be expected, approaches to care or treatment are being modified and are becoming increasingly flexible. For example, Project Re-ED (selection 15) is demonstrating that a learning approach to emotionally disturbed children is more effective than traditional ones. In one follow-up study (Weinstein, 1969), it was found that the children were more relaxed, less aggressive, and more dominant, and that they improved substantially in school. Other programs for children involve nonprofessionals and family intervention (selection 16). New approaches to adults include Gestalt therapy (selection 17) and behavior modification (selections 18 and 19).

The expanding field of family therapy (Haley, 1971) is a further illustration of a decreasing concern for intrapsychic forces and an increasing focus on the milieu in which the individual with an emotional or behavior problem operates. As the name implies, efforts are made to change an entire family rather than one individual. There is no one specific technique; instead there are numerous ones.

TWO FORMULATIONS OF THE PSYCHOSOCIAL MODEL

Within the last ten years, what appears, on the surface, to be two radically different strategies have become evident features of the psychosocial model. Upon closer examination of basic assumptions underlying the two approaches, their unity as psychosocial formulations of human behavior becomes apparent. Unfortunately, their various proponents are presently divided into two isolated camps—behaviorists and humanists. The effort is warranted to see the commonalities between these two warring groups because both offer important conceptualizations and because both have abandoned the medical model.

BEHAVIORISM

Behavioral formulations for the understanding and alleviation of human problems extend well into ancient history. For example, the Romans developed a crude approximation to today's "aversion therapies" for the treatment of alcoholism. The alcoholic was presented a brimming cup of specially prepared wine. As the drinker began to drain the cup, he discovered to his horror that a number of ferocious-looking eels were contained therein. Despite this fact, he was required to drink the potion; supposedly then, the taste, smell, and appearance of wine would become aversive to him. Demosthenes is said to have suffered from a shoulder tic. He suspended a sharp pointed sword above his shoulder so that each time it twitched upward, there was a painful prick.

Precise formulations of behaviorism as a treatment strategy are much more recent (Watson, 1919; Skinner, 1953; Bandura, 1969; Wolpe, 1958). Although several different behaviorist views have resulted, all are tied together by two premises: (1) behavior, normal or deviant, is learned; and (2) concentration on observable features of the person's behavior and of his environment is necessary.

These premises lend an attractive simplicity to behavior therapy (also called behavior modification). Learning has specific reference to a few simple paradigms—operant learning, classical conditioning, and modeling—and since there is focus on what the patient does and says (observable events), complex hypothetical constructs are unnecessary. Such simplicity not only eases the task of evaluating therapeutic effectiveness, it also permits nonprofessionals to become competent practitioners of the technique. If it is assumed that deviant behavior is learned, then the teacher and the teaching process must be identified. Most behavior therapists believe that anyone or anything can set the conditions for learning. While parents, schoolteachers, and peers are the obvious human teachers for children, physical location in the community and income level also provide powerful day-to-day contingencies of reward and punishment. In other words, the structure of events in a child's social and physical environment will determine the learning experiences—experiences that can lead to the development of adaptive or maladaptive behaviors.

Perhaps the most important feature of behavior therapy (and the psychosocial model in general) is the assumption about the role of current events in the maintenance of behavior disorders. Much of a person's deviant behavior is thought to be tied directly to conditions within the present environment. That is, regardless of the history of learning experiences, continued deviance depends on the presence (or absence) of relevant environmental contingencies. For example, would the dependent adult continue to cling to others if others did not reward such behaviors? Would the isolate adolescent continue his solitary existence if he were not punished for his few social approaches? Would the unmotivated fifth-grader continue to ignore his schoolwork were he suddenly rewarded for brief attempts in that direction? Within the framework of behavior therapy, these answers are all "no"; if the environmental contingencies change, so will the behavior. As you will recall, a principal tenet of the psychosocial model is that history determines the *function* of events within the person's current environment. In order for these events to influence the person continually, they must continue to occur; if they cease to occur, or if new events are created with competing functions, the person is bound to change.

Behavior therapy thus depends on the ability of the "patient" and therapist to identify and modify stimulus contingencies in the "patient's" real world—his home, his school, and other relevant community settings. In the past ten years, a wide variety of ingenious assessment and intervention techniques has been created to accomplish these tasks. All involve a series of carefully planned encounters between "patient," therapist, and often people in the "patient's" natural environment. Terms such as *baseline sampling, stimulus hierarchies, differential attention, desensitization,* and *token economies* all have reference to such planning. A behavior therapist might best be described as a "clinical ecologist"—one who is knowledgeable about how real-life social and physical events control human behavior and what options are available to modify this control.

HUMANISM

While it is relatively easy to describe behavior therapy and its historical antecedents, such is not the case for humanistic approaches to behavior disorders. In large part, this is due to a lack of clarity in the clinical strategies and techniques shared by humanists; such ambiguity, though, is purposeful. Man is so infinitely complex that any well-defined model of human behavior is artificial; thus, humanists resist the cataloguing of behaviors, environments, and techniques. Rather their approach to behavior disorders is highly subjective and speculative; in some ways the humanistic strategy falls more within philosophy and religion than psychology.

Humanistic strategies in the understanding and alleviation of human problems extend into the past at least as far as those considered to be behavioristic; the writings of early philosophers often touched on the miseries of man and speculated about an ideal world. In a more directly clinical vein, Phillipe Pinel, although trained in the eighteenth-century medical model view of behavior disorders, introduced concepts of freedom and kindness into the treatment of disturbed people. His work involved no "techniques" or carefully mapped out strategies; rather it reflected his philosophical belief about the rights and considerations due any human being, regardless of behavior peculiarities. Indeed, a type of care developed in mental hospitals around 1850 was called "moral treatment." As Bochoven (1972) has pointed out, one of its greatest assets was the attention given to the physical setting and social influences of hospital life. Recovery rates were higher than they are at the present time.

Like behavior therapy, humanism did not become a formal clinical strategy until recently. The works of Rogers (1951) and Maslow (1954) are usually associated with the initial conceptual developments; these writers and many following them were instrumental in formulating current notions. One assumption fundamental to humanistic views of behavior disorders concerns the concept of freedom. The argument is that man has a very large number of choices available to him in the determination of his behavior, but is "free" only to the extent that he recognizes this fact and becomes able to select from the options. Disturbed people have few choices in life because they are locked into a pattern of interaction with their environment, and they are unaware of and/or unwilling to select other patterns.

Man's potential freedom of choice suggests a second oft-mentioned feature of humanism, namely, personal awareness. "Choice," as seen from the individual's perspective, is a phenomenological experience in which man is aware of and can describe those options that are available to him. As an example, an adolescent is often teased by his peers in the school lunchroom. Typically, he laughs when the teasing occurs, although his internal reaction is intense anxiety. Eventually, he begins to sit away from his peers but feels lonely and frustrated. When asked about this isolate behavior, the boy says that nobody likes him and that his feelings toward others are mutual. In essence, his phenomenological experience is one of pain, anger, and helplessness; he sees no other choice but to withdraw. In actuality many other options are available to him when he enters the lunchroom: He could confront the teasers; he could seek out new friends; or he could refuse to enter the lunchroom. He feels trapped, though, because he does not perceive any of the alternatives.

It is most important to recognize that the humanistic therapist does not *plan* new experiences for the patient. He may be quite directive in trying to make the patient aware of environmental constraints that seem to maintain the problem behavior, and he may actively foster the patient's effort to describe and sample new environmental options, but it must be the patient alone who makes choices concerning these new options. He can become "free" only to the extent that he becomes aware that new interactions are possible *and* if he can choose from these options and act accordingly.

DIFFERENCES AND SIMILARITIES

One obvious difference between these two approaches to behavior disorders is the language used to communicate. The behavioristic language is composed of terms that refer directly to observable events (e.g., *response frequency*); the humanistic language is more figurative, and thus its terms refer to a much broader class of events (e.g., *self growth*). Undoubtedly, the language difference makes the two approaches seem more different than they actually are. Clearly, both behaviorism and humanism focus on man and his present environment. Both approaches assume that behavior disorders are a function of conditions within man's social and material surroundings. While one approach describes surroundings in terms of *positive and negative reinforcers*, the other uses terms such as *choices and options*. From both viewpoints, disordered behavior is seen as undesirable patterns of interaction between man and his environment. The role of treatment is to change these patterns, or, more appropriately, to make possible new interactions between the patient and his environment.

Much of the disagreement between behaviorists and humanists centers on the means by which new interactions are determined. Humanists contend that these ought to be determined solely by the patient; since adaptation is equated with one's freedom to choose, the therapist must avoid choosing for the patient. Behaviorists, on the other hand, believe that both patient and therapist must contribute to the decision-making process. While the patient must state his eventual decision concerning the direction of change, the therapist might believe that such a direction would result in environmental outcomes that the patient would find undesirable. Therefore, the therapist must serve as consultant in the decision. Probably much of this disagreement has to do with beliefs of humanists and behaviorists on the ultimate functioning of man. Behaviorists believe that man's behavior is always tied to environmental conditions, albeit these conditions can encompass a very wide spectrum of events. Humanists are less clear on this issue but seem to argue that man can transcend these conditions and ultimately determine his own behavior.

Thus, both behaviorism and humanism are oriented to an understanding of man and his environment. In this shared orientation, both are psychosocial. Their differences lie both in language and basic beliefs on the perspective used in describing the behavior-environment relationships.

While the following case history (Bachrach, Erwin, and Mohr, 1965) is a particularly dramatic one, it will serve to highlight the inapplicability of the medical model and some of the conflicts therapists face in attempting to help people in trouble.

Mrs. A. N.

At age 18, Mrs. A. N.'s usual weight was 120 pounds. Over a period of five or six years, her weight decreased to 65 pounds, and during the next 11 years, or until her admission to the University of Virginia Hospital, it decreased to 47 pounds. The formal diagnosis was "anorexia nervosa." This means "loss or severe diminishment of appetite." The weight loss was due to the fact that Mrs. A. N. consumed less and less food.

Elaborate physical studies were conducted at the hospital, and no organic explanations were forthcoming for the loss of appetite. Of course there were many and severe secondary physical problems: "The physical examination revealed a creature so cachetic and shrunken about her skeleton as to give the appearance of a poorly preserved mummy suddenly struck with the breath of life. Her pasty white skin was mottled a purple hue over her feet and stretched like so much heavy spider webbing about the bony prominences of her face. Edematous ankles and feet ballooned out grotesquely from the margins of her slippers. Cavernous ulcers opened up over the right buttock, pubis and back of the skull while smaller ulcers stood out over the knees, elbows and ankles. Delicate silky threads of hair hung lifelessly from her skull. Broken, gray teeth peered out between thin, white lips through which there weakly issued forth a high pitched distant voice. . . ." [Bachrach, Erwin, and Mohr, 1965, p. 154]*

The usual medical and psychiatric care brought no changes, and Mrs. A. N. was *at the point of death* when operant conditioning techniques were introduced. Mrs. A. N. was transferred from a cheerful and pleasant hospital room, which contained the routine comforts such as television, flowers, and magazines, to a barren room containing only a bed, nightstand, and chair. The ordinary privileges for patients, such as having visitors, were eliminated, and the nursing personnel agreed to cooperate by never speaking to her when it was necessary that they be in the room.

These isolation steps were part of a regime whereby the three investigators could control the environment of the patient and reenforce eating responses. Each of them ate one meal with her each day and at those times verbally reenforced movements associated with eating. As the weeks passed, and as the food intake increased, there was postgrandial reenforcement in the form of Mrs. A. N. being allowed to watch television for a specified period of time, in having visitors, and so on. In other words, the ordinary comforts of living were made contingent upon the patient's eating. Over a period of six weeks, Mrs. A. N.'s weight increased 14 pounds. The rigid regime was relaxed somewhat at that time, and a few weeks there-

---

* From *Case Studies in Behavior Modification* edited by L. P. Ullmann and L. Krasner. By permission of Holt, Rinehart, and Winston, Inc.

after, she was discharged from the hospital. Mrs. A. N. was followed for several months, and some 18 months after admission, her weight was 88 pounds. There continued to be informal contacts with the hospital for several years. Mrs. A. N. held a job, and her weight was maintained at between 85 and 90 pounds. Whatever caused the loss of appetite was never determined.

In the final analysis, was the ultimate approach to Mrs. A. N. a behaviorist or humanist one?

REFERENCES

Allen, R. C.; Ferster, E. Z.; and Wiehofen, H. 1968. *Mental impairment and legal incompetency.* Englewood Cliffs, N.J.: Prentice-Hall.

Bachrach, A. J., et al. 1965. The control of eating behavior in an anorexic by operant conditioning techniques. In *Case studies in behavior modification,* ed. L. P. Ullmann and L. Krasner. New York: Holt, Rinehart, and Winston.

Bandura, A. 1969. *Principles of behavior modification.* New York: Holt, Rinehart, and Winston.

Bernal, M. E., et al. 1968. Behavior modification and the brat syndrome. *Journal of Consulting and Clinical Psychology* 32(4): 447–455.

Bochoven, J. S. 1972. *Moral treatment in community mental health.* New York: Springer.

Boroson, W. 1964. What psychiatrists say about Goldwater. *Fact,* vol. 1, no. 5 (September-October), pp. 24–64.

Commission on Chronic Illness. 1957. *Chronic illness in a large city.* Vol. 4 of *Chronic illness in the United States.* Cambridge: Harvard University Press.

Freud, S. 1949. *An outline of psychoanalysis.* New York: Norton.

Goldhamer, H., and Marshall, A. 1953. *Psychosis and civilization.* Glencoe, Ill.: Free Press.

Haley, J., ed. 1971. *Changing families: A family therapy reader.* New York: Grune and Stratton.

Hilgard, E. R., and Atkinson, R. C. 1967. *Introduction to psychology.* 4th ed. New York: Harcourt, Brace, and World. P. 570.

Hollingshead, A. B., and Redlich, F. C. 1958. *Social class and mental illness.* New York: Wiley.

Kimble, G., and Garmezy, N. 1963. *Principles of general psychology.* 2d ed. New York: Ronald Press. P. 523.

Lieberman, J. K. 1970. *The tyranny of the experts.* New York: Walker.

Maslow, A. H. 1954. *Motivation and personality.* New York: Harper and Row.

Mowrer, O. H. 1960. "Sin": The lesser of two evils. *American Psychologist* 15:301–304.

Myers, J. K., and Bean, L. L. 1968. *A decade later.* New York: Wiley. P. 211.

National Association for Mental Health. 1963. *Facts about mental illness, fact sheet.*

Rogers, C. R. 1951. *Client-centered therapy.* Boston: Houghton Mifflin.

Rogler, L. H., and Hollingshead, A. B. 1965. *Trapped: Families and schizophrenia.* New York: Wiley.

Ryan, W. 1969. *Distress in the city: A summary report of the Boston Mental Health survey.* Cleveland: Case Western Reserve University Press.

Sarbin, T. R. 1967. On the futility of the proposition that some people be labeled "mentally ill." *Journal of Consulting Psychology* 31(5):447–453.

Sarbin, T. R. 1972. Schizophrenia is a myth, born of metaphor, meaningless. *Psychology Today* 6(1):18–27.

Skinner, B. F. 1953. *Science and human behavior.* New York: Macmillan.

Szasz, T. 1960. The myth of mental illness. *American Psychologist* 15(2):113–118.

Ullmann, L. P., and Krasner, L. 1965. *Case studies in behavior modification.* New York: Holt, Rinehart, and Winston.

Wahler, R. G., and Pollio, H. R. 1968. Behavior and insight: A case study in behavior therapy. *Journal of Experimental Research in Personality* 3(1):45–50.

Watson, J. B. 1919. *Psychology: From the standpoint of a behaviorist.* Philadelphia: Lippincott.

Weinstein, L. 1969. Project Re-ed schools for emotionally disturbed children: Effectiveness as viewed by referring agencies, parents, and teachers. *Exceptional Children,* May, pp. 703–711.

Wolpe, J. 1958. *Psychotherapy by reciprocal inhibition.* Stanford: Stanford University Press.

Wyatt v. Stickney. 1972. Civil No. 3195-N (N.D. Alabama). April 13.

PART I:
THE MEDICAL MODEL

The Sickness Model of Mental Disorder Means a Double Standard of Care

2

By GEORGE W. ALBEE

Dr. Albee, president of the American Psychological Association in 1970 and currently professor of psychology at the University of Vermont, is bombastic in this paper in his criticisms of the medical model and the limitations it has imposed upon manpower for the staffing of institutions. The disease notion helped also to promote an operating philosophy in mental hospitals of dehumanization and an atmosphere in which a self-fulfilling prophecy is rampant.

Dr. Albee is especially critical of the Big Four—the psychiatrist, clinical psychologist, psychiatric social worker, and psychiatric nurse—and argues that we do not need more of them than we now have. Rather, he insists on the need for mental health workers who have received types of training vastly different from the traditional.

LET ME BEGIN by arguing that the explanatory *model* used to account for disturbed and deviant human behavior determines the kind of *institutions* which society supports to provide intervention, and the nature of these institutions in turn determines the *kind of manpower* required for their staffing.

The explanatory model occupying the center of the stage today insists on the fiction that "mental illness is an illness like any other." It trims the stage with institutional trappings of sickness, beds, hospitals, and clinics. As a consequence, our manpower problems are defined as shortages of medical and

This paper is based on a talk presented in September, 1969, at Ypsilanti State Hospital (Michigan). The paper appeared in the Michigan Mental Health *Research Bulletin*, vol. 4, no. 1 (Winter, 1970), and is reprinted by permission of the author and the *Bulletin*.

Dr. Albee has written extensively on mental health manpower problems and served from 1957 to 1959 as director of the Task Force on Manpower for the Joint Commission on Mental Illness and Health.

paramedical professionals, which include the four major actors in the drama—the psychiatrist, clinical psychologist, psychiatric social worker, and psychiatric nurse. The bit players, or extras, we are seeking in large numbers include all the ancillary paramedical professionals needed to fill the depleted ranks in our "treatment institutions."

There is an ever-widening gap between the growing manpower needs of our tax-supported treatment institutions and the shrinking supply of high-level professional workers. Partly this is due to an unwillingness to forego the benefits of status agency or private practice to take underpaid jobs in public agencies serving those most in need of help. As a result there is a great deal of talk today about training a new group of non-professionals, or semiprofessional people, to staff the places serving primarily the numerous emotionally distressed poor. This third-rate idea, combined with a large dose of expert public relations, has almost convinced the public that there will soon be enough intervention to go around. Many people actually believe that a large number of housewives actually are being trained to be counselors, that hundreds of storefront intervention centers already exist, and that highly successful intervention is being accomplished in the new comprehensive mental health centers. Actually, this whole show is going to fold in Boston, long before it reaches the Big Time!

What is required in this field is a whole reconceptualization of causation. Once the *sickness model* is replaced with a more valid *social-learning* explanation (which attributes most emotional disturbance to the dehumanized environment rather than to biological defect) there will follow a redefinition of intervention institutions as re-educational or rehabilitative centers which will call for a very different sort of manpower.

I want to develop the argument that this reconceptualization will lead to the establishment of centers staffed primarily by people educated at the bachelor's level or less, with nursing, education, and social work as strong contenders for responsibility and leadership.

A GLOOMY FORECAST

One of the several major myths which we must abandon before we can make any progress in closing the manpower gap suggests that somehow, someday, we will have enough traditional mental health professionals, and, therefore, the need for nonprofessional, or middle-level, mental health workers is a temporary situation. This myth leads to all sorts of inconsistent behavior in approaching the training of these people. We hesitate to change our civil service requirements. We even fear that if we train too many they may organize, take over, and shut us out. The latter situation may come to pass, but we should welcome it.

Actually, there is no chance that psychiatry and psychology, as these disciplines are now defined, will ever provide the necessary amount of manpower for effective intervention (Albee, 1968). Indeed, the number of people in these precious, highly specialized disciplines will decrease rather than increase over the next couple of decades in proportion to population.

Let us take the field of psychiatry as an example. During the past two decades, as a result of an enormous financial investment in psychiatric training by the National Institute of Mental Health, together with the massive importation of foreign physicians, the membership of the American Psychiatric Association has quadrupled. But during this same period, *the number of psychiatrists employed in tax-supported mental institutions has declined in absolute numbers!*

Today we have some 2,000 psychiatric clinics scattered throughout our land. However, more than two-thirds of these clinics do not have a single full-time psychiatrist on their staff! Obviously something at least equal to the miracle of the loaves and fishes will be required to staff the 2,000 comprehensive community mental health centers that are to be built by NIMH in the next decade.

Nor would a crash program to increase the number of psychiatrists trained have much effect. In the first place, the long-time policy of the American Medical Association to hold down medical school enrollments has resulted in a shortage of physicians which grows steadily greater. Each year we are at least 3,000 new M.D.'s behind the number that would be required simply to hold our own in ratio of physicians to population. And psychiatry must draw most of its recruits from the same limited pool where all the other medical specialties, equally hungry for residents, are seeking their neophytes (Albee, 1967).

But suppose by some magic we could double the output of our medical schools and thereby double the number of young

M.D.'s going into psychiatric residencies. It would still be a hopeless situation. When we look at the *distribution* of psychiatrists, we find that more than 50 percent of our nation's total are to be found in the five favored (is that the right word?) states of Massachusetts, Pennsylvania, New York, Illinois, and California. Within these states, of course, the psychiatrists are concentrated in suburbia, where 80 percent of psychiatry is practiced in private offices (with a white, middle-class, largely female, non-Catholic clientele) (Albee, 1967).

I will not take time to recite comparable statistics for other mental health professions except to make it quite clear that I have no hidden agenda which intends somehow to advance *psychology* in the care-delivery field. Let me tell you quite bluntly that clinical psychology is going to disappear from the marketplace for the next 10-20 years, as the relative handful of people we are able to produce is recruited into academic teaching, where serious shortages are developing, and where the psychologist is not a second-class citizen but breathes the air of academic freedom. It is also worth noting that there are 20 vacant positions for every graduate of social work, and that qualified psychiatric nurses are as close to extinction as the blue whale.

TRAINING FOR NEW OR OLD?

Psychiatrist Moody Bettis (1969) recently raised the crucial question when he asked whether solutions to "the manpower problem" involve training people for where we are trying to go, or for where we have been! Do we want to train people for new community programs or old institutional programs? Do we want to reconsider the adequacy of many of the institutions of the past or continue to regard them as somehow sacred and above change?

Generally we think of action programs aimed at reducing emotional disturbance in our society in terms that have traditionally been associated with institutional programs. We think of highly trained mental health professionals—medical and paramedical—intervening on a one-to-one basis in some specific physical place (clinic or hospital) in the community. It is very difficult for us to get over our belief that the things we have been doing for so long (and so ineffectively) in our clinics and public hospitals are wrong or worthless. Many programs achieve sanctification through use, a sacred cow status which requires that they continue to be used in the community.

Perhaps the most entrenched and pervasive attitude that influences our thinking about approaches to the preparation of new mental health workers has it that they are to be employed in existing agencies and institutions. Most of the accounts I have read of new training programs for various new kinds of workers imply that they will be used to help relieve senior people—"under careful supervision." The implication is quite clear that many of these workers are to fit into the conventional care-delivery structures as "assistants."

Behind this assumption, of course, lurks that old devil, the *sickness model*. Without beating further what is at least a sickening horse, if not a dead one, I think it is still important to point out that our profession's adherence to the sickness explanation of disturbed behavior ("mental illness is an illness like any other") puts us into a Procrustean model which binds us to hospitals (Procrustean beds?) and clinics as our primary intervention centers.

I would emphasize that a significant component of the enthusiasm for training middle-level workers originates among those seeking a solution for the glaringly inadequate staffing of our tax-supported public facilities. These new people are sought to staff, primarily, state hospitals, county-run child centers, retardation centers, etc. A cynical way of viewing this situation would be to suggest that there will always be just enough high-class, highly trained mental health professionals to work in psychiatric wards in general hospitals, university hospitals and clinics, and in high-prestige agencies, as well as private practice. We have known for years that the shortages become more and more acute in the facilities that serve the poor—the public agencies, public clinics, and public hospitals. Recently Mike Gorman (1966) pointed out that in well over a third of the state hospitals in this country, little or no psychiatric time is available. My guess is that even this is a minimum estimate.

THE ROLE OF THE CCMHC

The Comprehensive Community Mental Health Centers (CCMHC) movement, originally conceived as a shining hope for the poor, and described as small, intensive, community-based centers in the heart of our cities, where the largest number of disturbed people is to be found, has now been captured and used to increase the resources of middle-class-serving general hospitals. The regulations for CCMHCs were written in such a way that a general hospital with a psychiatric unit could qualify for construction funds if it agreed to use even 10 percent of the beds for the indigent, beds newly built with tax dollars. This means that in a majority of the CCMHCs now being built in general hospitals, the poor will be largely excluded.

As a matter of fact this probably also means that middle-level mental health workers will be excluded too. General hospitals are not known for their eagerness to hire salaried people whose services are not billable. Indeed, most CCMHCs get by with a very minimum of psychological and social work help (Glasscote et al., 1964). The whole emphasis in the funding of the CCMHC program has been on the granting of construction funds to add beds. General hospitals make their income from the use of beds, and the fortunate few psychiatrists who control bed privileges have a good thing. Does this sound cynical? Listen to the psychiatrist-director of the Los Angeles County Department of Mental Health (Harry R. Brickman, M.D.):

Those responsible for mental health programs must soon decide whether they wish to build a vast new social machinery which will paradoxically "create" illness under the banner of health or whether they wish to grasp a real opportunity to help build a more humanistic community which is emotionally nutritive and which is increasingly tolerant and constructively helpful to social deviation in all forms [Brickman, 1967].

Dr. Brickman goes on to argue that the CCMHCs must not be considered an end in themselves. Rather they should be a means toward achieving a better and more humanistic society with intervention primarily carried out "by non-psychiatric agents." There is little evidence that this will happen.

Somehow as our society becomes more dehumanized, more consumption-oriented, and more and more inbred with the philosophy: "I'll get mine, Jack," the more we seem to need "helping" professionals. For most of the world the mental health professions are unknown or unwanted. The Peace Corps does not receive requests for psychiatrists or clinical psychologists. In societies where families, neighborhood, religious institutions, and tradition provide comfort and support, relationship therapy is unneeded or unknown. It is only as we move toward a society of strangers, highly mobile, without roots, with little tradition, and few stable relationships that we develop a market for "the purchase of friendship" (William Schofield's apt name for psychotherapy). I would not argue against the fact that there are large numbers of lonely and lost people in our society who need help. It is simply that we can never solve our human problems by trying to put these people into hospitals or clinics, by calling them patients, and by giving them individual treatment by our traditional methods.

EFFECTIVE INTERVENTION

From one perspective the most effective interventionists responsible for increasing and improving the mental health of millions of citizens need not be conventionally trained mental health workers at all. If we could reach newspaper publishers, TV advertisers, and disc jockeys—who have more input than most professional organizations—we might cause really effective intervention.

Let me suggest an example of what I have in mind.

Recently two black psychiatrists, Grier and Cobbs (1968), spelled out in searing and stark detail the tragic consequences of our racist white society's behavior for the mental health of black citizens.

Millions of black children grow up in a racist white society which thoughtlessly and chauvinistically equates attractiveness in children and adults with fair, straight hair and regular features. The damaged self-concepts and damaged interpersonal relationships which result for black children might be eliminated very quickly if, for example, the federal government (Federal Communications Commission) were to order that at least 20 percent of all commercial advertisements use black models, that all actors in television dramas be employed without regard to skin color, and that our vast communication industry be rewarded with tax credits for effective techniques it develops to transmit the message that beauty and attractiveness can take many colors and forms.

As a matter of fact I find myself continually falling into the bad habit of thinking our mental health problems involve primarily schizophrenic and other serious conventional disorders. When I stop to consider, I do *not* believe that the most significant mental health problems of our society today are to be found in the population of our state hospitals, *nor* in the clientele of our outpatient psychiatric clinics, *nor* do I believe that our most serious mental health problems are to be found in the psychiatric wards of our general hospitals.

Our most significant mental health problems exist in middle-class people who rarely end up in a clinic or mental institution. I speak of the white racists identified in the Kerner Report, and their dehumanized fellows—perhaps most of us—who accept institutions that do not strengthen people but dehumanize them. It follows that a significant number of the mental health workers that I believe must be recruited and educated will hardly be identified as such, but rather as a cadre who may provide future leadership in combatting and reducing the amount of dehumanized aggression in our society and in our world, and increasing the amount of responsible human interaction of which humans are capable. These recruits are available in significant numbers in our undergraduate colleges. I believe the Kerner Report is right in reporting white racism to be the major cause of the social unrest in our society. I believe also that we are moving (often with maddening delays and detours), toward an integrated society in which all human beings will be able to live and love more freely. The consequences of achieving such a society, in mental health terms, will far exceed any new treatment techniques, or new psychotropic drug discoveries, or any number of new mental health workers trained as interventionists.

The morally destructive forces in our society—forces that have polluted our environment, destroyed our lakes and streams, deforested our national parks, strip-mined our hills and fields, and turned our cities into a hideous blight—the same forces that have supported meaningless wars and have poured billions down the rat hole of accelerating militarism—they are also responsible for the dehumanization of our social environment. Our society is proselytized and propagandized into thinking that wasteful, meaningless consumption is the highest end of living. We are told that human sexuality is obscene, but murder, violence, and aggression are entertaining. This obscene philosophy, which negates the importance of social relationships, produces dehumanized and irrational consumers unresponsive or refractory to violence and suffering whose fragmented emotional lives lead increasing numbers to go out of control.

Then the Establishment (the military-industrial complex that President Eisenhower warned us against) proceeds to explain away the increasing social pathology as being a result of individual defect (mental illness is an illness like any other) and escapes responsibility by well-publicized support of biochemical research aimed at discovering "causes and cures."

MOST NEEDED MENTAL HEALTH WORKERS

While a major contribution to the problems in our society originates in white racism, a significant amount of the actual resulting damage is done to the poor and the black. While we are trying to change the pattern of racist behavior, our society must also develop interventionists to ameliorate the damage already done. These interventionists should be drawn largely from the disadvantaged groups themselves. I think they should be essentially BA-level people, and we should make urgent efforts to recruit and train special interventionists from black and from other disadvantaged groups. It is more and more difficult to separate mental health problems from welfare problems and from educational problems. The most needed middle-level mental health workers may turn out to be specially selected teachers.

We also need bachelor-level social welfare workers in our public agencies serving the inner-city to do something about such problems as the high rate of "mental deficiency" revealed there by epidemiological studies. Most of these cases of retardation are not due to organic factors but are due to impoverished and demoralized conditions of life. Olshansky and Sternfield (1963) studied 1,000 children in Boston whose families were receiving Aid for Dependent Children and discovered that nearly 7 percent were functionally retarded. I believe that social welfare workers and preschool teachers and visiting nurses (all primarily black) must be the interventionists until we can reform our cities and eliminate slums and ghettoes.

I am not convinced that we need a new generic, all-purpose, middle-level mental health worker to work in institutions. We need a number of different kinds of mental health workers, trained primarily at the bachelor's level, but many of them could develop out of existing professions.

A profession is distinguished from other occupations primarily by the fact that it has *theory* which the aspiring young professional must learn before he begins practice. There is also a sense of lifetime *career choice*, together with the learning of a special language, and ultimate responsibility for the indoctrination of the neophyte. With 40-50 percent of our college-age youngsters enrolled in some kind of higher education, the new mental health workers are going to have to be professionals, or we are not going to recruit them.

One problem arises immediately. Bachelor-level professionals have high status when they run their own show. They have low status when they work as assistants to other higher status professions. Look, for example, at the profession of schoolteaching. It is a nice respectable BA profession because teachers control the schools and have clear-cut upwardly mobile paths available. On the other hand, bachelor-level people in hospitals are far down the pecking order and are recruited only with difficulty.

I would propose that some of our existing service professions should move quickly to take over or develop their own *care delivery institutions* which they would own and operate. The profession of nursing, for example, lacks just one thing to become a major force. It does not have a *care delivery setting* which it owns and controls. Many of the individuals in institutions for the insane and many of those in institutions for the mentally deficient could be cared for much better in institutions owned and operated by the nursing profession. (So could persons with any of the other chronic organic diseases.) As soon as nursing learns that it must have a setting of its own in which to train its own neophytes, and in which upward-bound career patterns are available, I anticipate that nursing will take over and do a much more effective job for the people now cared for in our antiquated state hospital program.

Psychiatric social work is another field that is on the verge of developing an effective independent service delivery system. Social group work is already intervening more frequently and more effectively with the emotionally disturbed poor than any other profession. As soon as psychiatric social workers free themselves from the psychiatric setting and establish their own crisis intervention centers that blend mental health and welfare programs, and that recruit staff from the inner-city people served—or better still as soon as they go to work with group workers in settlement houses located close to where the people are who need help—the sooner good care will be available. In truth, social work is doing most of the psychiatric care in the so-called mental hygiene clinics today. How long will it sit still and see the clinics directed by persons who give a few hours a week and take home high salaries for this limited service to the wrong target groups?

CLERGY, POLICE, AND STUDENTS

In ranging over some of the current literature on mental health training for new groups of professional workers we frequently encounter mental health training for the clergy. Certainly it is true, as we discovered in William Ryan's survey of Boston's mental health services, that the clergy actually provide more counseling and psychotherapy within the American city than do the more traditional mental health professions. [Ryan [1969] found that in Boston clergymen were doing more counseling than psychiatrists despite the fact that greater Boston is practically overrun with psychiatrists.] Mental health training for clergymen has usually come to mean training in psychodynamics and individual one-to-one intervention. But because most of the important, well-funded, and heavily supported churches and synagogues have moved to suburbia with the rest of the middle-class population, the one-to-one counseling of clergymen tends to be largely limited to middle-class parishioners. In talking with clergymen in my own neighborhood I discover that their counseling is most frequently with people with "drinking problems" and with families trying to cope with pregnant unmarried teenagers.

These clergymen could provide far more significant mental health intervention by leading their congregations toward a firm stand on fair housing and neighborhood integration, perhaps with an emphasis that prejudice and discrimination are grounds for excommunication from the church. This sort of "intervention" will require some significant breakthroughs in religious dogma!

Let me cite another existing profession that, with a little change, might become more relevant.

This potential source of new and effective mental health professional workers is the police. I would suggest that we find ways to recruit to the urban police forces some of the same brave and socially motivated young people now attracted to the Peace Corps or the VISTA program. Most police forces are having trouble finding qualified recruits. Instead of such nonconstructive activities as many of our young people have engaged in vis-à-vis the police, why not find ways to help them volunteer to spend a few years on the police force trying to help teach the principles of democracy and respect for individual human dignity in this setting.

While on the subject of the police why not use what we know about operants, and reinforcement theory, to single out those policemen who exhibit human relations skills? Policemen who complete training in human relations courses could be given a salary increment, and a further increment or bonus each time they demonstrate that they practice behaviorally what they have learned.

Still another innovative source of people for intervention is the pool of high school students who could be spending time in the elementary school or even in kindergarten classes. In a few pilot projects around the country, high school students are spending as much as one day a week working with one, two, or three children in a kindergarten or elementary school in their own district. High school boys, particularly, may be led to discover and experience the universal satisfaction to be derived from a consistent helping relationship with a young child. High school girls, too, may find new skills and satisfactions not available in conventional courses.

Under appropriate reinforcement conditions high school boys and girls can help younger children to learn, but can also serve (self-consciously) as role models. I find no convincing reason why a country that is able to spend $80 million a day in Southeast Asia cannot find a way to pay high school students to work with younger students.

CLOSE STATE MENTAL HOSPITALS

We cannot limit our attention, either, to the pathology of our society and to preventive efforts without paying some attention to the unfortunate who have been damaged or destroyed by our system and who now sit out their empty lives in our "state institutions." What is to be done, and who is to do it? Obviously not the present Big Four mental health professions.

Two years ago (Albee, 1968) I suggested that our state hospitals and mental hygiene clinics should be closed and torn down—taken apart piece by piece and stone by stone and then, like the city of Carthage, plowed three feet under and sowed with salt. This proposal was widely reported by the press, and as a consequence I received many letters, some highly supportive and some highly critical. A number of the writers were psychiatrists. Some of them were angry because my suggestion would eliminate their jobs in state hospitals, while others were angry (although they themselves were in private practice and knew relatively little about the state hospitals system) because it was inappropriate for a psychologist to butt into what was essentially a medical problem.

I continue to think the state hospitals should be abandoned, and I cite as supporting participants in this movement two recent presidents of the American Psychiatric Association, Harry C. Solomon (1958) and Daniel Blain (1965), both of whom suggested in their presidential addresses to their association that the state hospitals are obsolete and should be eliminated.

The important point is that the state hospitals have come to be a dumping ground for the emotionally disturbed poor, for those who don't have Blue Cross insurance or some kind of labor union coverage to pay for occupancy of a bed in a general hospital psychiatric ward.

Why bring up this whole matter of state hospitals and the double standard of care? Because much of the demand for the new mental health workers results from the need for such people to work in the state hospitals where medical and paramedical professionals refuse to work. State hospitals and clinics are tax-supported, and that makes them socialized medicine, and we all know how bad that is! So let's train a host of nonprofessionals to work in these places where we will dump the uninsured poor. Thus we neatly separate our free-enterprise medical intervention with the affluent from our salaried subprofessional services for the poor. Training a corps of subprofessionals to staff the state hospitals would serve to prolong the existence of these antiquated institutions and perpetuate the double standard of care. One way of blocking this neat but chauvinistic solution would be to close the state hospitals, thereby forcing the community, with good planning, into more effective nonmedical programs which might indeed be under the control of BA-level professional workers.

If the state hospitals are eliminated, what would happen to all of the present unfortunate inmates, and to those first-admission cases who now wind up in the state hospital? It is instructive to look carefully at the poor people in these places now, and those entering them for the first time.

First of all, there is evidence that the unfortunate state hospital inmates are afflicted more by the desocialization that comes from the training these places give them in the role of inmate than from any real disease process. What has happened for years to people in state hospitals is an almost perfect example of the self-fulfilling prophecy. When we admit them, we predict that their condition is hopeless, and then we proceed to take away every vestige of humanity, self-respect, and pride, thus creating cases without hope. Then we congratulate ourselves that our original predictions were right.

We know now that at least half the first admissions really do not belong in a "mental hospital." Let me just cite the results of a recent study done by Moody C. Bettis and Robert E. Roberts of the Texas Research Institute of Mental Sciences (1969). Drs. Bettis and Roberts did a systematic study of more than 500 "proposed mentally ill patients" referred to an evaluation center for possible commitment. These people were studied for as much as a week at the center, after which they were sent to a local state hospital or discharged back to the community. These scientists found that considerably more than half did not need mental hospital commitment, or would not have if community services had been available. It turns out that only about one-third of the precommitment group should have been put in a mental hospital if their need had been the major consideration. As it turns out three-quarters of the group studied were actually committed to the state hospital, because no other solution was available. In a related study the same group of investigators found a significantly large number of persons trapped in the state hospital system who clearly did not belong there but for whom no appropriate intervention was available in the community.

If we were to close the state hospitals, what would happen to the people who presently are entering through their front door?

It is instructive to look at the nature of our first-admission group in the state hospitals across the country. As indicated above, the majority of them should not be admitted ever to a state hospital. Half the first admissions are nonpsychotic but represent a mixed group of alcoholics, character disorders, neurotics, and lonely people who might be better dealt with in the community.

Of the remaining 50 percent who are admitted for the first time to state hospitals with the diagnosis of psychosis, half of them are diagnosed "chronic brain syndrome," which means that they are primarily elderly, senile individuals who certainly do not deserve the horrible fate of being locked up in a state hospital. Again, better ways of dealing with elderly, senile cases can be developed in the community, and in the case of those who require intensive care, general hospitals or nursing homes offer better solutions.

The remaining 25 percent of first admissions are functionally psychotic. But clearly a significant number of these could be dealt with in foster homes, halfway houses, day or night facilities, and with effective means of community support.

Ordinarily we tell legislators that we need our state hospitals for persons who are "dangerous to themselves or others." But when we look at our first admissions, we find that the proportion that is dangerous is a very small number indeed.

We should develop small, tax-supported, comprehensive community mental health centers in the heart of the urban blight. But these centers cannot be medical or paramedical. They may take several forms—some owned and operated by nursing, some by social work, some by special education, and some by new child care professions. Most of the staff should be drawn from the same disadvantaged groups served. The rest of us should be working to bring about the social revolution we need to arrest our nation's pell-mell rush toward disaster.

REFERENCES

Albee, G. W. 1968. Myths, models, and manpower. *Mental Hygiene* 52:2.

Albee, G. W. 1967. The relation of conceptual models to manpower needs. In *Emergent approaches to mental health problems*, ed. E. L. Cowen, E. A. Gardner, and M. Zax, pp. 63–73. New York: Appleton-Century-Crofts.

Bettis, M. 1969. Personal communication.

Bettis, M. C., and Roberts, R. E. 1969. Mental health manpower—the dilemma. *Mental Hygiene.*

Blain, D. 1965. Presidential address. *American Journal of Psychiatry.*

Brickman, H. R. 1967. Community mental health—means or end? *Psychiatric Digest* 28:43–50.

Glasscote, R., et al. 1964. *The community mental health center: An analysis of existing models.* Washington, D.C.: Joint Information Service of the American Psychiatric Association and the National Association for Mental Health.

Gorman, M. 1966. *What are the facts about mental illness in the United States.* National Committee Against Mental Illness.

Grier, W. H., and Cobbs, P. M. 1968. *Black rage.* New York: Basic Books.

Olshansky, S., and Sternfield, L. A. 1963. A study of suspected cases of mental retardation in families receiving aid to dependent children. *American Journal of Public Health* 53:793.

Ryan, W. 1969. *Distress in the city: A summary report of the Boston mental health survey.* Cleveland: Case Western Reserve University Press.

Solomon, H. 1958. Presidential address to American Psychiatric Association. *American Journal of Psychiatry.*

The Societal Reaction to Deviance: Ascriptive Elements in the Psychiatric Screening of Mental Patients in a Midwestern State Hospital

3

By THOMAS J. SCHEFF

Legal concepts are applied often in instances of major mental illness (few textbooks for beginning students make this point appropriately clear); sometimes the legalities play a determinative role in the fate of the "patient." One conclusion to draw from this paper by Scheff, of the University of California at Santa Barbara, is that the civil rights of people suspected of being psychotic are often denied because of the presumption of "illness." That pre-judgment also leads to decisions being made in a cavalier and untenable manner (confinement is confinement and a loss of freedom whether the place is called a prison or a mental hospital). It is poor people or those from the lower classes who are most likely to be the subjects of such victimization. Under these circumstances, "treatment" in the classical sense is of little moment.

Note carefully the assumptions which underlie these commitment practices—many of which stem from the "illness" notion. For a more thorough discussion than is contained in this paper see Dr. Scheff's book *Being Mentally Ill: A Sociological Theory* (Aldine).

Fortunately, a few states have begun to modify the laws and procedures which govern commitment. What are the laws governing commitment, and how are the procedures carried out in your state? Read selection 4 after you have completed this selection.

This report is part of a larger study, made possible by a grant from the Advisory Mental Health Committee of Midwestern State. By prior agreement, the state in which the study was conducted is not identified in publications. Published in *Social Problems*, vol. 11 (Spring, 1964), pp. 401–413. Reprinted by permission of the author, the journal, *Social Problems*, and the Society for the Study of Social Problems. The author was assisted in this study by Daniel M. Culver.

THE CASE FOR MAKING the societal reaction to deviance a major independent variable in studies of deviant behavior has been succinctly stated by Kitsuse:

A sociological theory of deviance must focus specifically upon the interactions which not only define behaviors as deviant but also organize and activate the application of sanctions by individuals, groups, or agencies. For in modern society, the socially significant differentiation of deviants from the non-deviant population is increasingly contingent upon circumstances of situation, place, social and personal biography, and the bureaucratically organized activities of agencies of control.[1]

In the case of mental disorder, psychiatric diagnosis is one of the crucial steps which "organizes and activates" the societal reaction, since the state is legally empowered to segregate and isolate those persons whom psychiatrists find to be committable because of mental illness.

Recently, however, it has been argued that mental illness may be more usefully considered to be a social status than a disease, since the symptoms of mental illness are vaguely defined and widely distributed, and the definition of behavior as symptomatic of mental illness is usually dependent upon social rather than medical contingencies.[2] Furthermore, the argument continues, the status of the mental patient is more often an ascribed status, with conditions for status entry external to the patient, than an achieved status with conditions for status entry dependent upon the patient's own behavior. According to this argument, the societal reaction is a fundamentally important variable in all stages of a deviant career.

The actual usefulness of a theory of mental disorder based on the societal reaction is largely an empirical question: to what extent is entry to the status of mental patient independent of the behavior or "condition" of the patient? The present paper will explore this question for one phase of the societal reaction: the legal screening of persons alleged to be mentally ill. This screening represents the official phase of the societal reaction,

---

1 John I. Kitsuse, "Societal Reaction to Deviant Behavior: Problems of Theory and Method," Social Problems 9 (Winter, 1962): 247–257.
2 Edwin M. Lemert, Social Pathology (New York: McGraw-Hill, 1951); Erving Goffman, Asylums (Chicago: Aldine, 1962).

which occurs after the alleged deviance has been called to the attention of the community by a complainant. This report will make no reference to the initial deviance or other situation which resulted in the complaint, but will deal entirely with procedures used by the courts after the complaint has occurred.

The purpose of the description that follows is to determine the extent of uncertainty that exists concerning new patients' qualifications for involuntary confinement in a mental hospital, and the reactions of the courts to this type of uncertainty. The data presented here indicate that, in the face of uncertainty, there is a strong presumption of illness by the court and the court psychiatrists.[3] In the discussion that follows the presentation of findings, some of the causes, consequences, and implications of the presumption of illness are suggested.

The data upon which this report is based were drawn from psychiatrists' ratings of a sample of patients newly admitted to the public mental hospitals in a midwestern state, official court records, interviews with court officials and psychiatrists, and our observations of psychiatric examinations in four courts. The psychiatrists' ratings of new patients will be considered first.

In order to obtain a rough measure of the incoming patient's qualifications for involuntary confinement, a survey of newly admitted patients was conducted with the cooperation of the hospital psychiatrists. All psychiatrists who made admission examinations in the three large mental hospitals in the state filled out a questionnaire for the first ten consecutive patients they examined in the month of June, 1962. A total of 223 questionnaires were returned by the 25 admission psychiatrists. Although these returns do not constitute a probability sample of all new patients admitted during the year, there were no obvious biases in the drawing of the sample. For this reason, this group of patients will be taken to be typical of the newly admitted patients in Midwestern State.

The two principal legal grounds for involuntary confinement in the United States are the police power of the state (the state's right to protect itself from dangerous persons) and *parens patriae* (the state's right to assist those persons who, because

---

[3] For a more general discussion of the presumption of illness in medicine and some of its possible causes and consequences, see the author's "Decision Rules, Types of Error, and Their Consequences in Medical Diagnosis," *Behavioral Science* 8 (April, 1963): 97–107.

of their own incapacity, may not be able to assist themselves).[4] As a measure of the first ground, the potential dangerousness of the patient, the questionnaire contained this item: "In your opinion, if this patient were released at the present time, is it likely he would harm himself or others?" The psychiatrists were given six options, ranging from Very Likely to Very Unlikely. Their responses were: Very Likely, 5 percent; Likely, 4 percent; Somewhat Likely, 14 percent; Somewhat Unlikely, 20 percent; Unlikely, 37 percent; Very Unlikely, 18 percent. Three patients, or 1 percent, were not rated.

As a measure of the second ground, *parens patriae*, the questionnaire contained the item: "Based on your observations of the patient's behavior, his present degree of mental impairment is: None ———; Minimal ———; Mild ———; Moderate ———; Severe ———. The psychiatrists' responses were: None, 2 percent; Minimal, 12 percent; Mild, 25 percent; Moderate, 42 percent; Severe, 17 percent. Three patients, or 1 percent, were not rated.

To be clearly qualified for involuntary confinement, a patient should be rated as likely to harm self or others (Very Likely, Likely, or Somewhat Likely) and/or as Severely Mentally Impaired. However, voluntary patients should be excluded from this analysis, since the court is not required to assess their qualifications for confinement. Excluding the 59 voluntary admissions (26 percent of the sample), leaves a sample of 164 involuntarily confined patients. Of these patients, 10 were rated as meeting both qualifications for involuntary confinement; 21 were rated as being severely mentally impaired, but not dangerous; 28 were rated as dangerous but not severely mentally impaired; and 102 *were rated as not dangerous nor as severely mentally impaired*. [Italics added by editors.] Three patients were not rated.

According to these ratings, there is considerable uncertainty connected with the screening of newly admitted involuntary patients in the state, since *a substantial majority (63 percent) of the patients did not clearly meet the statutory requirements for involuntary confinement*. [Italics added by editors.] How does the agency responsible for assessing the qualifications for confinement, the court, react in the large numbers of cases involving uncertainty?

---

4 Hugh Allen Ross, "Commitment of the Mentally Ill: Problems of Law and Policy," *Michigan Law Review* 57 (May, 1959): 945–1018.

On the one hand, the legal rulings on this point by higher courts are quite clear. They have repeatedly held that there should be a presumption of sanity. The burden of proof of insanity is to be on the petitioners; there must be a preponderance of evidence, and the evidence should be of a "clear and unexceptionable" nature.[5]

On the other hand, existing studies suggest that there is a presumption of illness by mental health officials. In a discussion of the "discrediting" of patients by the hospital staff, based on observations at St. Elizabeth's Hospital, Washington, D.C., Goffman states:

[The patient's case record] is apparently not regularly used to record occasions when the patient showed capacity to cope honorably and effectively with difficult life situations. Nor is the case record typically used to provide a rough average or sampling of his past conduct. [Rather, it extracts] from his whole life course a list of those incidents that have or might have had "symptomatic" significance. . . . I think that most of the information gathered in case records is quite true, although it might seem also to be true that almost anyone's life course could yield up enough denigrating facts to provide grounds for the record's justification of commitment.[6]

Mechanic makes a similar statement in his discussion of two large mental hospitals located in an urban area in California:

In the crowded state or county hospitals, which is the most typical situation, the psychiatrist does not have sufficient time to make a very complete psychiatric diagnosis, nor do his psychiatric tools provide him with the equipment for an expeditious screening of the patient. . . .
In the two mental hospitals studied over a period of three months, the investigator never observed a case where the psychiatrist advised the patient that he did not need treatment. Rather, all persons who appeared at the hospital were absorbed into the patient population regardless of their ability to function adequately outside the hospital.[7]

---

[5] This is the typical phrasing in cases in the *Dicennial Legal Digest*, found under the heading "Mental Illness."
[6] Goffman, op. cit., pp. 155, 159.
[7] David Mechanic, "Some Factors in Identifying and Defining Mental Illness," *Mental Hygiene* 46 (January, 1962): 66–75.

A comment by Brown suggests that it is a fairly general understanding among mental health workers that state mental hospitals in the U.S. accept all comers.[8]

Kutner, describing commitment procedures in Chicago in 1962, also reports a strong presumption of illness by the staff of the Cook County Mental Health Clinic:

> Certificates are signed as a matter of course by staff physicians after little or no examination. . . . The so-called examinations are made on an assembly-line basis, often being completed in two or three minutes, and never taking more than ten minutes. Although psychiatrists agree that it is practically impossible to determine a person's sanity on the basis of such a short and hurried interview, the doctors recommend confinement in 77% of the cases. It appears in practice that the alleged-mentally-ill is presumed to be insane and bears the burden of proving his sanity in the few minutes allotted to him. . . .[9]

These citations suggest that mental health officials handle uncertainty by presuming illness. To ascertain if the presumption of illness occurred in Midwestern State, intensive observations of screening procedures were conducted in the four courts with the largest volume of mental cases in the state. These courts were located in the two most populous cities in the state. Before giving the results of these observations, it is necessary to describe the steps in the legal procedures for hospitalization and commitment.

STEPS IN THE SCREENING OF PERSONS ALLEGED TO BE MENTALLY ILL

The process of screening can be visualized as containing five steps in Midwestern State:

1. The application for judicial inquiry, made by three citizens. This application is heard by deputy clerks in two of the courts (C and D), by a court reporter in the third court, and by a court commissioner in the fourth court.

---

8 Esther Lucile Brown, *Newer Dimensions of Patient Care*, part I (New York: Russell Sage, 1961), p. 60, fn.
9 Luis Kutner, "The Illusion of Due Process in Commitment Proceedings," *Northwestern University Law Review* 57 (Sept., 1962): 383–399.

2. The intake examination, conducted by a hospital psychiatrist.
3. The psychiatric examination, conducted by two psychiatrists appointed by the court.
4. The interview of the patient by the guardian *ad litem*, a lawyer appointed in three of the courts to represent the patient. (Court A did not use guardians *ad litem*.)
5. The judicial hearing, conducted by a judge.

These five steps take place roughly in the order listed, although in many cases (those cases designated as emergencies) step No. 2, the intake examination, may occur before step No. 1. Steps No. 1 and No. 2 usually take place on .the same day or the day after hospitalization. Steps No. 3, No. 4, and No. 5 usually take place within a week of hospitalization. (In courts C and D, however, the judicial hearing is held only once a month.)

This series of steps would seem to provide ample opportunity for the presumption of health, and a thorough assessment, therefore, of the patient's qualifications for involuntary confinement, since there are five separate points at which discharge could occur. According to our findings, however, these procedures usually do not serve the function of screening out persons who do not meet statutory requirements. At most of these decision points, in most of the courts, retention of the patient in the hospital was virtually automatic. A notable exception to this pattern was found in one of the three state hospitals; this hospital attempted to use step No. 2, the intake examination, as a screening point to discharge patients that the superintendent described as "illegitimate," i.e., patients who do not qualify for involuntary confinement.[10] In the other two hospitals, however, this examination was perfunctory and virtually never resulted in a finding of health and a recommendation of discharge. In a similar manner, the other steps were largely ceremonial in character. For example, in court B, we observed twenty-two judicial hearings, all of which were conducted per-

---

[10] Other exceptions occurred as follows: the deputy clerks in courts C and D appeared to exercise some discretion in turning away applications they considered improper or incomplete, at step No. 1; the judge in Court D appeared also to perform some screening at step No. 5. For further description of these exceptions see the author's "Social Conditions for Rationality: How Urban and Rural Courts Deal with the Mentally Ill," *American Behavioral Scientist* 7 (March, 1964): 21–24.

functorily and with lightning rapidity. (The mean time of these hearings was 1.6 minutes.) The judge asked each patient two or three routine questions. Whatever the patient answered, however, the judge always ended the hearings and retained the patient in the hospital.

What appeared to be the key role in justifying these procedures was played by step No. 3, the examination by the court-appointed psychiatrists. In our informal discussions of screening with the judges and other court officials, these officials made it clear that although the statutes give the court the responsibility for the decision to confine or release persons alleged to be mentally ill, they would rarely if ever take the responsibility for releasing a mental patient without a medical recommendation to that effect. The question which is crucial, therefore, for the entire screening process is whether or not the court-appointed psychiatric examiners presume illness. The remainder of the paper will consider this question.

Our observations of 116 judicial hearings raised the question of the adequacy of the psychiatric examination. Eighty-six of the hearings failed to establish that the patients were "mentally ill" (according to the criteria stated by the judges in interviews).[11] Indeed, the behavior and responses of 48 of the patients at the hearings seemed completely unexceptionable. Yet the psychiatric examiners had not recommended the release of a single one of these patients. Examining the court records of 80 additional cases, there was still not a single recommendation for release.

Although the recommendation for treatment of 196 out of 196 consecutive cases strongly suggests that the psychiatric examiners were presuming illness, particularly when we observed 48 of these patients to be responding appropriately, it is conceivable that this is not the case. The observer for this study was not a psychiatrist (he was a first-year graduate student in social work), and it is possible that he could have missed evidence of disorder which a psychiatrist might have seen. It was therefore arranged for the observer to be present at a series of psychiatric examinations, in order to determine whether the examinations appeared to be merely formalities or

---

11 In interviews with the judges, the following criteria were named: appropriateness of behavior and speech, understanding of the situation, and orientation.

whether, on the other hand, through careful examination and interrogation, the psychiatrists were able to establish illness even in patients whose appearance and responses were not obviously disordered. The observer was instructed to note the examiners' procedures, the criteria they appeared to use in arriving at their decision, and their reaction to uncertainty.

Each of the courts discussed here employs the services of a panel of physicians as medical examiners. The physicians are paid a flat fee of ten dollars per examination, and are usually assigned from three to five patients for each trip to the hospital. In court A, most of the examinations are performed by two psychiatrists, who went to the hospital once a week, seeing from five to ten patients a trip. In courts B, C, and D, a panel of local physicians was used. These courts seek to arrange the examinations so that one of the examiners is a psychiatrist, the other a general practitioner. Court B has a list of four such pairs, and appoints each pair for a month at a time. Courts C and D have a similar list, apparently with some of the same names as court B.

To obtain physicians who were representative of the panel used in these courts, we arranged to observe the examinations of the two psychiatrists employed by court A and one of the four pairs of physicians used in court B, one a psychiatrist, the other a general practitioner. We observed 13 examinations in court A and 13 examinations in court B. The judges in courts C and D refused to give us the names of the physicians on their panels, and we were unable to observe examinations in these courts. (The judge in court D stated that he did not want these physicians harassed in their work, since it was difficult to obtain their services even under the best of circumstances.) In addition to observing the examinations by four psychiatrists, three other psychiatrists used by these courts were interviewed.

The medical examiners followed two lines of questioning. One line was to inquire about the circumstances which led to the patient's hospitalization; the other was to ask standard questions to test the patient's orientation and his capacity for abstract thinking by asking him the date, the president, governor, proverbs, and problems requiring arithmetic calculation. These questions were often asked very rapidly, and the patient was usually allowed only a very brief time to answer.

It should be noted that the psychiatrists in these courts had access to the patient's record (which usually contained the application for judicial inquiry and the hospital chart notes on the patient's behavior), and that several of the psychiatrists stated that they almost always familiarized themselves with this record before making the examination. To the extent that they were familiar with the patient's circumstances from such outside information, it is possible that the psychiatrists were basing their diagnoses of illness less on the rapid and peremptory examination than on this other information. Although this was true to some extent, the importance of the record can easily be exaggerated, both because of the deficiencies in the typical record and because of the way it is usually utilized by the examiners.

The deficiencies of the typical record were easily discerned in the approximately one hundred applications and hospital charts which the author read. Both the applications and charts were extremely brief and sometimes garbled. Moreover, in some of the cases where the author and interviewer were familiar with the circumstances involved in the hospitalization, it was not clear that the complainant's testimony was any more accurate than the version presented by the patient. Often the original complaint was so paraphrased and condensed that the application seemed to have little meaning.

The attitude of the examiners toward the record was such that even in those cases where the record was ample, it often did not figure prominently in their decision. Disparaging remarks about the quality and usefulness of the record were made by several of the psychiatrists. One of the examiners was apologetic about his use of the record, giving us the impression that he thought that a good psychiatrist would not need to resort to any information outside his own personal examination of the patient. A casual attitude toward the record was openly displayed in six of the 26 examinations we observed. In these six examinations, the psychiatrist could not (or in three cases, did not bother to) locate the record and conducted the examination without it, with one psychiatrist making it a point of pride that he could easily diagnose most cases "blind."

In his observations of the examinations, the interviewer was instructed to rate how well the patient responded by noting his behavior during the interview, whether he answered the orientation and concept questions correctly, and whether he denied and explained the allegations which resulted in his hospitalization. If the patient's behavior during the interview obviously departed from conventional social standards (e.g., in one case the patient refused to speak), if he answered the orientation questions incorrectly, or if he did not deny and explain the petitioners' allegations, the case was rated as meeting the statutory requirements for hospitalization. Of the 26 examinations observed, eight were rated as Criteria Met.

If, on the other hand, the patient's behavior was appropriate, his answers correct, and he denied and explained the petitioners' allegations, the interviewer rated the case as not meeting the statutory criteria. Of the 26 cases, seven were rated as Criteria Not Met. Finally, if the examination was inconclusive, but the interviewer felt that more extensive investigation might have established that the criteria were met, he rated the cases as Criteria Possibly Met. Of the 26 examined, 11 were rated in this way. The interviewer's instructions were that whenever he was in doubt, he should avoid using the rating Criteria Not Met.

Even giving the examiners the benefit of the doubt, the interviewer's ratings were that in a substantial majority of the cases he observed, the examination failed to establish that the statutory criteria were met. The relationship between the examiners' recommendations and the interviewer's ratings is shown in the following table.

TABLE 1 Observer's Ratings and Examiners' Recommendations

Observer's Ratings		Criteria Met	Criteria Possibly Met	Criteria Not Met	Total
Examiners' Recommendations	Commitment	7	9	2	18
	30-day Observation	1	2	3	6
	Release	0	0	2	2
	Total	8	11	7	26

The interviewer's ratings suggest that the examinations established that the statutory criteria were met in only eight cases, but the examiners recommended that the patient be retained in the hospital in 24 cases, leaving 16 cases which the interviewer rated as uncertain, and in which retention was recommended by the examiners. The observer also rated the patient's expressed desires regarding staying in the hospital and the time taken by the examination. The ratings of the patient's desire concerning staying or leaving the hospital were: Leave, 14 cases; Indifferent, 1 case; Stay, 9 cases; and Not Ascertained, 2 cases. In only one of the 14 cases in which the patient wished to leave was the interviewer's rating Criteria Met.

The interviews ranged in length from five minutes to 17 minutes, with the mean time being 10.2 minutes. Most of the interviews were hurried, with the questions of the examiners coming so rapidly that the examiner often interrupted the patient, or one examiner interrupted the other. All of the examiners seemed quite hurried. One psychiatrist, after stating in an interview (before we observed his examinations) that he usually took about thirty minutes, stated:

It's not remunerative. I'm taking a hell of a cut. I can't spend 45 minutes with a patient. I don't have the time, it doesn't pay.

In the examinations that we observed, this physician actually spent 8, 10, 5, 8, 8, 7, 17, and 11 minutes with the patients, or an average of 9.2 minutes.

In these short time periods, it is virtually impossible for the examiner to extend his investigation beyond the standard orientation questions and a short discussion of the circumstances which brought the patient to the hospital. In those cases where the patient answered the orientation questions correctly, behaved appropriately, and explained his presence at the hospital satisfactorily, the examiners did not attempt to assess the reliability of the petitioner's complaints or to probe further into the patient's answers. Given the fact that in most of these instances the examiners were faced with borderline cases, that they took little time in the examinations, and that they usually recommended commitment, we can only conclude that their decisions were based largely on a presumption of illness. Supplementary observations reported by the interviewer support this conclusion.

After each examination, the observer asked the examiner to explain the criteria he used in arriving at his decision. The observer also had access to the examiner's official report, so that he could compare what the examiner said about the case with the record of what actually occurred during the interview.

This supplementary information supports the conclusion that the examiner's decisions are based on the presumption of illness and sheds light on the manner in which these decisions are reached:

1. The "evidence" upon which the examiners based their decision to retain often seemed arbitrary.
2. In some cases, the decision to retain was made even when no evidence could be found.
3. Some of the psychiatrists' remarks suggest prejudgment of the cases.
4. Many of the examinations were characterized by carelessness and haste.

The first question, concerning the abritrariness of the psychiatric evidence, will now be considered.

In the weighing of the patient's responses during the interview, the physician appeared not to give the patient credit for the large number of correct answers he gave. In the typical interview, the examiner might ask the patient fifteen or twenty questions: the date, time, place, who is president, governor, etc., what is 11 x 10, 11 x 11, etc., explain "Don't put all your eggs in one basket," "A rolling stone gathers no moss," etc. The examiners appeared to feel that a wrong answer established lack of orientation, even when it was preceded by a series of correct answers. In other words, the examiners do not establish any standard score on the orientation questions, which would give an objective picture of the degree to which the patient answered the questions correctly, but seem at times to search until they find an incorrect answer.

For those questions which were answered incorrectly, it was not always clear whether the incorrect answers were due to the patient's "mental illness," or to the time pressure in the interview, the patient's lack of education, or other causes. Some of the questions used to establish orientation were sufficiently difficult that persons not mentally ill might have difficulty with them. Thus one of the examiners always asked, in a rapid-fire manner: "What year is it? What year was it seven years ago? Seventeen years before that?" etc. Only two of the five patients who were asked this series of questions were able to answer it correctly. However, it is a moot question whether a higher percentage of persons in a household survey would be able to do any better. To my knowledge, none of the orientation questions that are used have been checked in a normal population.

Finally, the interpretations of some of the evidence as showing mental illness seemed capricious. Thus one of the patients, when asked, "In what way are a banana, an orange, and an apple alike?" answered, "They are all something to eat." This answer was used by the examiner in explaining his recommendation to commit. The observer had noted that the patient's behavior and responses seemed appropriate and asked why the recommendation to commit had been made. The doctor stated that her behavior had been bizarre (possibly referring to her alleged promiscuity), her affect inappropriate ("When she talked about being pregnant, it was without feeling,") and with regard to the question above:

> She wasn't able to say a banana and an orange were fruit. She couldn't take it one step further, she had to say it was something to eat.

In other words, this psychiatrist was suggesting that the patient manifested concreteness in her thinking, which is held to be a symptom of mental illness. Yet in her other answers to classification questions and to proverb interpretations, concreteness was not apparent, suggesting that the examiner's application of this test was arbitrary. In another case, the physician stated that he thought the patient was suspicious and distrustful, because he had asked about the possibility of being represented by counsel at the judicial hearing. The observer felt that these and other similar interpretations might possibly be correct, but that further investigation of the supposedly incorrect responses would be needed to establish that they were manifestations of disorientation.

In several cases where even this type of evidence was not available, the examiners still recommended retention in the hospital. Thus, one examiner, employed by court A, stated that he had recommended 30-day observation for a patient whom he had thought *not* to be mentally ill, on the grounds that the patient, a young man, could not get along with his parents, and "might get into trouble." This examiner went on to say:

> We always take the conservative side [commitment or observation]. Suppose a patient should commit suicide. We always make the conservative decision. I had rather play it safe. There's no harm in doing it that way.

It appeared to the observer that "playing safe" meant that even in those cases where the examination established nothing, the psychiatrists did not consider recommending release. Thus in one case the examination had established that the patient had a very good memory, was oriented, and spoke quietly and seriously. The observer recorded his discussion with the physician after the examination as follows:

When the doctor told me he was recommending commitment for this patient too (he had also recommended commitment in the two examinations held earlier that day) he laughed because he could see what my next question was going to be. He said, "I already recommended the release of two patients this month." This sounded like it was the maximum amount the way he said it.

Apparently this examiner felt that he had a very limited quota on the number of patients he could recommend for release (less than 2 percent of those examined).

The language used by these physicians tends to intimate that mental illness was found, even when reporting the opposite. Thus in one case the recommendation stated: "No gross evidence of delusions or hallucinations." This statement is misleading, since not only was there no gross evidence, there was not any evidence, not even the slightest suggestion of delusions or hallucinations, brought out by the interview.

These remarks suggest that the examiners prejudge the cases they examine. Several further comments indicate prejudgment. One physician stated that he thought that most crimes of violence were committed by patients released too early from mental hospitals. (This is an erroneous belief.)[12] He went on to say that he thought that all mental patients should be kept in the hospital at least three months, indicating prejudgment

---

[12] The rate of crimes of violence, or any crime, appears to be less among ex-mental patients than in the general population. Henry Brill and Benjamin Maltzberg, "Statistical Report Based on the Arrest Record of 5354 Ex-patients Released from New York State Mental Hospitals during the Period 1946–48." Mimeo available from the authors; Louis H. Cohen and Henry Freeman, "How Dangerous to the Community Are State Hospital Patients?" *Connecticut State Medical Journal* 9 (Sept., 1945): 697–700; Donald W. Hastings, "Follow-up Results in Psychiatric Illness," *American Journal of Psychiatry* 118 (June, 1962): 1078–1086.

concerning his examinations. Another physician, after a very short interview (eight minutes), told the observer:

On the schizophrenics, I don't bother asking them more questions when I can see they're schizophrenic because *I know what they are going to say.* You could talk to them another half-hour and not learn any more.

Another physician, finally, contrasted cases in which the patient's family or others initiated hospitalization ("petition cases," the great majority of cases) with those cases initiated by the court:

The petition cases are pretty *automatic.* If the patient's own family wants to get rid of him, you know there is something wrong.

The lack of care which characterized the examinations is evident in the forms on which the examiners make their recommendations. On most of these forms, whole sections have been left unanswered. Others are answered in a peremptory and uninformative way. For example, in the section entitled Physical Examination, the question is asked: "Have you made a physical examination of the patient? State fully what is the present physical condition."; a typical answer is "Yes. Fair." or "Is apparently in good health." Since in none of the examinations we observed was the patient actually physically examined, these answers appear to be mere guesses. One of the examiners used regularly in court B, to the question "On what subject or in what way is derangement now manifested?" always wrote in "Is mentally ill." The omissions and the almost flippant brevity of these forms, together with the arbitrariness, lack of evidence, and prejudicial character of the examinations, discussed above, all support the observer's conclusion that, except in very unusual cases, the psychiatric examiner's recommendation to retain the patient is virtually automatic.

Lest it be thought that these results are unique to a particularly backward midwestern state, it should be pointed out that this state is noted for its progressive psychiatric practices. It will be recalled that a number of the psychiatrists employed by the court as examiners had finished their psychiatric residencies, which is not always the case in many other states. A still common practice in other states is to employ, as members of the "lunacy panel," partially retired physicians with no psychiatric training whatever. This was the case in Stockton, California, in 1959, where the author observed hundreds of hearings at which these physicians were present. It may be indicative of some of the larger issues underlying the question of civil commitment that, in these hearings, the physicians played very little part; the judge controlled the questioning of the relatives and patients, and the hearings were often a model of impartial and thorough investigation.

DISCUSSION

Ratings of the qualifications for involuntary confinement of patients newly admitted to the public mental hospitals in a midwestern state, together with observations of judicial hearings and psychiatric examinations by the observer connected with the present study, both suggest that the decision as to the mental condition of a majority of the patients is an uncertain one. The fact that the courts seldom release patients and the perfunctory manner in which the legal and medical procedures are carried out suggest that the judicial decision to retain patients in the hospital for treatment is routine and largely based on the presumption of illness. Three reasons for this presumption will be discussed: financial, ideological, and political.

Our discussions with the examiners indicated that one reason that they perform biased "examinations" is that their rate of pay is determined by the length of time spent with the patient. In recommending retention, the examiners are refraining from interrupting the hospitalization and commitment procedures already in progress, and thereby allowing someone else, usually the hospital, to make the effective decision to release or commit. In order to recommend release, however, they would have to build a case showing why these procedures should be interrupted. Building such a case would take much more time than is presently expended by the examiners, thereby reducing their rate of pay.

A more fundamental reason for the presumption of illness by the examiners, and perhaps the reason why this practice is allowed by the courts, is the interpretation of current psychiatric doctrine by the examiners and court officials. These officials make a number of assumptions, which are now thought to be of doubtful validity:

1. The condition of mentally ill persons deteriorates rapidly without psychiatric assistance.
2. Effective psychiatric treatments exist for most mental illnesses.
3. Unlike surgery, there are no risks involved in involuntary psychiatric treatment; it either helps or is neutral; it can't hurt.
4. Exposing a prospective mental patient to questioning, cross-examination, and other screening procedures exposes him to the unnecessary stigma of trial-like procedures, and may do further damage to his mental condition.
5. There is an element of danger to self or others in most mental illness. It is better to risk unnecessary hospitalization than the harm the patient might do himself or others.

Many psychiatrists and others now argue that none of these assumptions is necessarily correct.

1. The assumption that psychiatric disorders usually get worse without treatment rests on very little other than evidence of an anecdotal character. There is just as much evidence that most acute psychological and emotional upsets are self-terminating.[13]
2. It is still not clear, according to systematic studies evaluating psychotherapy, drugs, etc., that most psychiatric interventions are any more effective, on the average, than no treatment at all.[14]
3. There is very good evidence that involuntary hospitalization and social isolation may affect the patient's life: his job, his family affairs, etc. There is some evidence that too hasty

---

[13] For a review of epidemiological studies of mental disorder see Richard J. Plunkett and John E. Gordon, *Epidemiology and Mental Illness* (New York: Basic Books, 1960). Most of these studies suggest that at any given point in time, psychiatrists find a substantial proportion of persons in normal populations to be "mentally ill." One interpretation of this finding is that much of the deviance detected in these studies is self-limiting.

[14] For an assessment of the evidence regarding the effectiveness of electroshock, drugs, psychotherapy, and other psychiatric treatments, see H. J. Eysenck, *Handbook of Abnormal Psychology* (New York: Basic Books, 1961), part 3.

exposure to psychiatric treatment may convince the patient that he is "sick," prolonging what might have been an otherwise transitory episode.[15]

4. This assumption is correct, as far as it goes. But it is misleading because it fails to consider what occurs when the patient who does not wish to be hospitalized is forcibly treated. Such patients often become extremely indignant and angry, particularly in the case, as often happens, when they are deceived into coming to the hospital on some pretext.

5. The element of danger is usually exaggerated both in amount and degree. In the psychiatric survey of new patients in state mental hospitals, danger to self or others was mentioned in about a fourth of the cases. Furthermore, in those cases where danger is mentioned, it is not always clear that the risks involved are greater than those encountered in ordinary social life. This issue has been discussed by Ross, an attorney:

A truck driver with a mild neurosis who is "accident prone" is probably a greater danger to society than most psychotics; yet, he will not be committed for treatment, even if he would be benefited. The community expects a certain amount of dangerous activity. I suspect that as a class, drinking drivers are a greater danger than the mentally ill, and yet the drivers are tolerated or punished with small fines rather than indeterminate imprisonment.[16]

From our observations of the medical examinations and other commitment procedures, we formed a very strong impression that the doctrines of danger to self or others, early treatment, and the avoidance of stigma were invoked partly because the officials believed them to be true, and partly because they provided convenient justification for a preexisting policy of sum-

---

15 For examples from military psychiatry, see Albert J. Glass, "Psychotherapy in the Combat Zone," in *Symposium on Stress* (Washington, D.C.: Army Medical Service Graduate School, 1953), and B. L. Bushard, "The U.S. Army's Mental Hygiene Consultation Service," in *Symposium on Preventive and Social Psychiatry* 15-17 (April, 1957), Washington, D.C.: Walter Reed Army Institute of Research, pp. 431–443. For a discussion of essentially the same problem in the context of a civilian mental hospital, cf. Kai T. Erikson, "Patient Role and Social Uncertainty—A Dilemma of the Mentally Ill," *Psychiatry* 20 (August, 1957): 263–275.

16 Ross, op. cit., p. 962.

mary action, minimal investigation, avoidance of responsibility, and, after the patient is in the hospital, indecisiveness and delay.

The policy of presuming illness is probably both cause and effect of political pressure on the court from the community. The judge, an elected official, runs the risk of being more heavily penalized for erroneously releasing than for erroneously retaining patients. Since the judge personally appoints the panel of psychiatrists to serve as examiners, he can easily transmit the community pressure to them, by failing to reappoint a psychiatrist whose examinations were inconveniently thorough.

Some of the implications of these findings for the sociology of deviant behavior will be briefly summarized. The discussion above, of the reasons that the psychiatrists tend to presume illness, suggests that the motivations of the key decision-makers in the screening process may be significant in determining the extent and direction of the societal reaction. In the case of psychiatric screening of persons alleged to be mentally ill, the social differentiation of the deviant from the nondeviant population appears to be materially affected by the financial, ideological, and political position of the psychiatrists, who are in this instance the key agents of social control.

Under these circumstances, the character of the societal reaction appears to undergo a marked change from the pattern of denial which occurs in the community. The official societal reaction appears to reverse the presumption of normality reported by the Cummings as a characteristic of informal societal reaction, and instead exaggerates both the amount and degree of deviance.[17] Thus, one extremely important contingency influencing the severity of the societal reaction may be whether or not the original deviance comes to official notice. This paper suggests that in the area of mental disorder, perhaps in contrast to other areas of deviant behavior, if the official societal reaction is invoked, for whatever reason, social differentiation of the deviant from the nondeviant population will usually occur.

---

[17] Elaine Cumming and John Cumming, *Closed Ranks* (Cambridge, Mass.: Harvard University Press, 1957), p. 102; for further discussion of the bipolarization of the societal reaction into denial and labeling, see the author's "The Role of the Mentally Ill and the Dynamics of Mental Disorder: A Research Framework," *Sociometry* 26 (December, 1963): 436–453.

CONCLUSION

This paper has described the screening of patients who were admitted to public mental hospitals in early June, 1962, in a midwestern state. The data presented here suggest that the screening is usually perfunctory and that in the crucial screening examination by the court-appointed psychiatrists there is a presumption of illness. Since most court decisions appear to hinge on the recommendation of these psychiatrists, there appears to be a large element of status ascription in the official societal reaction to persons alleged to be mentally ill, as exemplified by the court's actions. This finding points to the importance of lay definitions of mental illness in the community, since the "diagnosis" of mental illness by laymen in the community initiates the official societal reaction, and to the necessity of analyzing social processes connected with the recognition and reaction to the deviant behavior that is called mental illness in our society.

Psychiatric Justice: The Case of Mr. Louis Perroni

By THOMAS S. SZASZ

4

Even introductory psychology texts exercise great care in emphasizing that the psychological world of a person is publicly available only through his behavior. Terms such as *mental health, emotional disorder*, and *psychosis* are global inferences based on what people *do*. Experts who use these terms in their judgments about patients must be careful to document those patient behaviors which support usage of the expressions; unfortunately, not all experts take the time and effort to do so. Some of them are incredibly haphazard and unreasonable in the assertions they make about other human beings. The case of Mr. Louis Perroni is a shocking example of two such experts; the two authorities, testifying in court, offered sweeping inferences about Mr. Perroni, based on completely inadequate behavioral data. The consequences of their utterances were quite terrible for Mr. Perroni.

We present this case to demonstrate that mental health professionals have no magical and infallible powers which enable them to judge others; their judgments are always open to question. Students should become accustomed to questioning psychological and psychiatric inferences. If we are to settle for abstractions as facts in and of themselves, we allow the Perroni case to be repeated again and again. Dr. Thomas Szasz, a psychiatrist of the State University of New York, Upstate Medical Center, has often described the injustices that result from unauthenticated psychological terms—particularly when they are made public. His discussion of the injustices suffered by Mr. Perroni will elaborate this point.

As you read Dr. Szasz's comments about the damage which results when the label pinned on a person is made public (see page 103), recall the very recent and unwarranted damage to the Democratic vice-presidential candidate, Senator Thomas

Chapter 4, "The Case of Mr. Louis Perroni," pp. 85–119, pp. 121–136, pp. 140–143. Reprinted with permission of the Macmillan Company from *Psychiatric Justice* by Thomas S. Szasz. Copyright © Thomas S. Szasz, 1965; and by permission of McIntosh and Otis, Inc.

Eagleton, in the summer of 1972. Following publicity that he had received psychiatric care and was, therefore, "mentally ill," an inference that was totally unjustified (see selection 5), he was removed from the ticket.

You may wish also to see the book *Prisoners of Psychiatry*, by a lawyer, Bruce Ennis (Harcourt Brace Jovanovich, 1972).

I

UNTIL MAY 5, 1955, Mr. Louis Perroni* operated a filling station in Glenview, a Syracuse suburb. On that day his world fell apart.

The events that led up to this fateful day, though rather trivial, are typical of the Kafkaesque webs in which the small man gets caught in a big bureaucracy; and how, once caught, the more he struggles, the more firmly he is held.

Early in 1955, Perroni was informed that the lease on his filling station, which was to expire on July 1, was not going to be renewed. The station he had operated for approximately ten years was in an area that was to be razed in preparation for a new shopping center.

During the winter, Perroni was approached by agents of the real estate developer with a request that he vacate his premises early, preferably no later than May 1. Although offered compensation, Perroni refused.

As Mr. Perroni tells it, the real estate developer went to court and obtained permission to take possession of Perroni's filling station on May 1. Perroni was the last occupant on the property, and therefore the only obstacle in the way of proceeding with the building of the new shopping center. After urging Mr. Perroni to move and offering him bonuses for doing so, the agents of the real estate developer allegedly threatened him with court action. He, on the other hand, began to feel that he was being "pushed around," and resolved not to give an inch from what he considered his "legal rights."

On May 2, 1955, representatives of the real estate developer erected a sign on what Mr. Perroni considered his gas station. He remonstrated with them and removed the sign. At last,

---

* The dates and the names of persons, places, and institutions (except mine, the Onondaga County Court's, and the Matteawan State Hospital's) are fictitious; otherwise, the account is factual.

when two men appeared on May 5 and proceeded to erect another sign, Mr. Perroni took a rifle from his station and fired a warning shot into the air. The men departed. Soon Mr. Perroni was arrested by the police.

This was Perroni's first brush with the law. Nor had he had any previous contact with psychiatry. During the Second World War, Perroni had served for nearly five years in the army as a mechanic and received an honorable discharge. Until his arrest, when he was forty years old, he was a responsible, self-supporting citizen.

Mr. Perroni was arraigned but was not indicted. Instead, at the request of the district attorney, the Onondaga County Court judge before whom he appeared ordered him to undergo pretrial psychiatric examination to determine his fitness to stand trial. He was examined by two court-appointed psychiatrists, found incapable of standing trial, and committed to the Matteawan State Hospital.

Aided by his brothers, Perroni tried by every means possible, including an appeal to the United States Supreme Court, to secure his right to be tried. At long last, in June, 1961—six years after Perroni was committed to the Matteawan State Hospital—a writ of habeas corpus was heard and sustained by the State Supreme Court judge in Dutchess County (where the hospital is located). Perroni was ordered to be tried or discharged. Nevertheless he was not immediately released. "The wheels of justice moved slowly," reported the Syracuse *Post-Standard,* "and only when officials of Matteawan State Hospital were faced with contempt charges did they send Perroni back to Onondaga County."

Perroni was returned to Syracuse on Thursday, August 31, and held incommunicado in the county jail. "His relatives," according to the newspaper, "have not been allowed to visit him." Perroni was to be arraigned in County Court, Tuesday, September 3. His arraignment was adjourned to the following day. On September 4, however, he was neither indicted nor released. Instead, he was ordered to submit to a fresh pretrial psychiatric examination.

A month later, on October 1, 1961, the Syracuse *Herald-Journal* reported that the court issued a new order for "mental tests" on Perroni. "For the fourth time since his arrest—and the second in less than a month—Louis Perroni, 46, former operator of a Glenview gasoline station, has been ordered to a hospital for mental tests. Perroni, who has been in and out of County Court more than a half a dozen times since his arrest in 1955, was in court again yesterday. And again, County Judge Francis T. Kirby ordered mental tests."

In due course, Perroni was committed to the Oakville State Hospital near Syracuse to determine once more whether he was competent to stand trial.

In anticipation of the hearing to be held in Onondaga County Court concerning Mr. Perroni's fitness to stand trial, the defendant's family and his attorney, Mr. Jerome Gross, sought my help. They requested that I furnish psychiatric testimony to support the claim—shared by the defendant, his family, and his attorney—that Mr. Louis Perroni was mentally competent to stand trial. It must be noted that in the course of the past seven years, while Mr. Perroni tried to gain his freedom, he had never had the help of a psychiatrist retained by himself and his attorney. Thus no psychiatric testimony favorable to him was ever presented in court.

After conferring with Mr. Perroni's relatives and his attorney, I interviewed the defendant at the Cedar Street Jail in Syracuse. I considered him competent and agreed to testify on his behalf.

The hearing was held on April 12, 1962, in Onondaga County Court before a judge and without a jury. It lasted for two full days. The following excerpts from the hearing are taken from the official records of the court stenographer. Much of the testimony was, of course, repetitious and trivial, and, for the sake of readability, I have omitted the larger part of it. I have tried to retain only enough to convey the atmosphere of the proceedings and the sorts of information elicited from the witnesses.

II

Proceedings before Honorable Francis T. Kirby, County Court House, on April 12, 1962, at 10 a.m.
Appearances:
For the People: Robert Jordan, Esq., Assistant District Attorney
For the Defendant: Jerome Gross, Esq.
[Defendant and both attorneys present in Court]
   The Court: This is the time set for a hearing to controvert the findings of the psychiatrists in the matter of The People of the State of New York versus Louis Perroni. Is the defendant ready, Mr. Gross?

Mr. Gross: The defendant is ready, Your Honor.

Mr. Jordan: The People are ready, Your Honor.

The Court: You may proceed, Mr. Jordan.

James B. Roscoe, having been called and duly sworn, testified as follows:

Direct Examination by Mr. Jordan

Q Dr. Roscoe, can you tell us where you live, please?

A I live at Oakville State Hospital, Oakville, New York.

Q And what is your present employment, sir?

A I am Assistant Director, Clinical, of Oakville State Hospital.

Q And in what field are you engaged in at Oakville State Hospital?

A I am engaged in the practice of psychiatry.

Q And for how long, sir, have you been a psychiatrist?

A I have been a psychiatrist for fifteen years.

Q Now, Doctor, during the course of your career as a psychiatrist have you had occasion either in your employment or with any mentally ill person to be in contact with the alleged criminal insane?

A On very many occasions I have examined cases under the Code of Criminal Procedure.

Q Now, would you tell the Court and the defense, please, approximately how many people you have seen pertaining to the criminal insane and according to the Code of Criminal Procedure?

A I have examined approximately 200 individuals under the Code of Criminal Procedure.

Q Doctor, let me ask you, have you ever had occasion to talk or meet an individual by the name of Louis Perroni?

A Yes, I have.

Q Now, if you can recall, when was the first time you examined Mr. Perroni?

A I examined Mr. Perroni on February 24, 1962.

Q Now, can you tell us what your examination consisted of?

A It consisted of an interview of an hour and a half's duration, proceeding in the usual form of a psychiatric interview in order to ascertain the individual's mental state. I determined his attitude and general behavior. I determined his stream of mental activity, his emotional reaction, his content of thought, and his sensorium.

Q Now, Doctor, as a result of your examinations of Mr. Perroni were you able to form an opinion whether this patient was in such a state of idiocy, imbecility, or insanity as to be able to understand the nature of the charge against him and to make his defense?

A Yes.

Q What is that opinion, Doctor?

A It is my opinion that Mr. Perroni is in such a state of idiocy, imbecility, or insanity as to be unable to understand the charges against him, the procedures, or of aiding in his defense.

. . .

Q Did you at any time, Dr. Roscoe, inquire or discuss with the patient the charges against him?

A I attempted to talk with him about the charges against him.

Q Can you tell us the conversation about that, sir?

A He refused to discuss the charges against him. As I recall, he maintained that under the Fifth Amendment he did not have to discuss the nature of the charges against him.

Q And did you ask him anything further pertaining to the charges against him?

A I asked him whether he felt he had been dealt with fairly under the laws dealing with these charges.

Q And let me ask you, Doctor, was the fact that he didn't discuss the charges against him, was that decisive in determining whether this man was in such a state of idiocy, insanity, or imbecility as not to be able to understand the charges against him?

A It was not.

Q Then you say this was part of the interview, but it wasn't decisive, is that correct?

A It was not decisive.

. . .

Mr. Jordan: You may inquire, Mr. Gross.

Cross-examination by Mr. Gross

. . .

Q Dr. Roscoe, can you tell us what Mr. Perroni is charged with—what the charge is?

A I believe it is a charge under the Penal Law having to do with carrying a gun.

Q Do you know whether or not he is charged with assault?

A That I do not know.

Q I see. And is he charged with anything else, Doctor?

A To my knowledge, no.

Q And do you know, Doctor, whether carrying a gun is a violation of law?

A I do not know. I'm not a lawyer.

Q I see. Doctor, in order to defend against a charge of carrying a gun what does a defendant have to know in order to aid his attorney in the trial of the case?

Mr. Jordan: I will object to that, if Your Honor please.

The Court: No, overruled.

Mr. Gross: It is the meat of the case, Your Honor. It is the very basis of it.

The Court: The witness may answer.

Mr. Jordan: I don't know if a proper foundation has been laid for the witness to be qualified to answer.

The Court: He may so state if he is not.

Mr. Gross: I will withdraw that question, Your Honor.

The Court: All right.

Q Doctor, you have stated as a conclusion and as the result of your examination of this defendant Perroni under Court order, you have come to the conclusion that Perroni is not able to understand the charges or to assist with his defense. Now, Doctor, is it not true that in order to come to that conclusion, whether you be a psychiatrist or a man on the street, that it is first necessary to know what a defendant has to know in order to understand the charges against him and to aid his attorney? Is it not necessary first to know what capacity he must have in order to cooperate with his attorney?

A I would say that he had to be capable of judgment, capable of sufficient thinking capacity to be able to cooperate.

Q Is it not true, Doctor, that the defense of different charges would require different capacities for the purpose of defense?

A I am not a lawyer. I don't believe I can answer that question.

Q Doctor, I do not mean from a legal standpoint, but I mean from a layman's standpoint and a psychiatrist's standpoint.

A From a psychiatric standpoint again a person must have demonstration of judgment, intelligence, contact with reality to be able to cooperate in defending any charge.

Q Any charge? Would there be a different capacity required between defending a murder charge and a speeding charge?

A From a psychiatric point of view, no.

Q No difference at all? In other words, the simplicity of the charge and the simplicity of the defense makes absolutely no difference?

A That would be my opinion.

Q And is that a psychiatric conclusion, Doctor?

A Yes.

. . .

Q All right. Now, when you first examined Mr. Perroni—that was, you say, on February the twenty-fourth?—did you have any reason to believe that he was abnormal at that time?

A I did.

Q Why was that, Doctor?

A Because of the attitude the patient had, the inappropriateness of his emotional affect, the evasive manner in which he discussed things—nondirect way—

Q (Interrupting) Excuse me, Doctor. I want to cut off your answer for this reason. I don't think you understand my question. When he first came in for the interview on February twenty-fourth, as you started that interview did you have any conclusion of his normalcy or abnormalcy?

A I had none.

Q What you are testifying to now is what your conclusion was at the conclusion of that first interview; is that right?

A Yes.

Q Now, you say he was evasive, Doctor. Is that what you said?

A Yes.

Q In what way? Can you give us some specifics, Doctor; how was he evasive?

A To my questions he answered with a response "That is a good question."

Q Well, which question was it? Give us one question he answered that to.

A I do not recall specifically.

Q Well, Doctor, February twenty-fourth isn't long gone. It is just two months. Can't you remember a single solitary question that he so responded to with "That is a good question"?

A I do not. There were a number of them on that occasion.

Q But you cannot remember a single solitary question?

A I cannot specifically remember a question.

Q You didn't make a single note of any question you asked him?

A I did not write up the results of this interview on a question-and-answer basis.

Q And is there anything abnormal, Doctor, for any person to respond "That is a good question"—anything abnormal about that?

A When this is a response to a number of different questions it has significance psychiatrically.

Q How many times did he repeat that phrase, Doctor? How many times on February twenty-fourth did he use that phrase "That is a good question"?

A At least half a dozen.

Q At least half a dozen times in an hour and a half, is that right?

A Yes.

Q By your standards and your judgment you think the phrase "That is a good question" during an hour-and-a-half interrogation, that indicates in some fashion to you, does it, Doctor, that that is an abnormality?

A It does.

Q Do you remember, Doctor, to what type of question he so responded?

A To certain questions relative to his marriage, to certain questions relative to his confinement, and to other questions which I don't clearly recall.

Q Isn't it true, Doctor, that those responses "That is a good question" were to questions in the area only of his marriage and of the circumstances that happened on the day he was arrested, isn't that true?

A No, that is not true.

Q What other area did he refuse to answer in?

A I cannot recall specifically, but there definitely were other areas.

Q But you don't remember a single one of them?

A I don't remember.

. . .

Q Now, Doctor, I understand you to say this man was untidy?

A Yes.

Q Can you describe in detail for me what that untidiness was?

A On every occasion that I examined Mr. Perroni the upper button or two of his shirt was unbuttoned, his sleeves were not buttoned, and his shoelaces were untied.

. . .

Q Have you brought with you in Court, Doctor, the records of Oakville State Hospital pertaining to Louis Perroni?

A Yes.

Q And those records go back how far as far as Oakville is concerned?

A They go back to his first admission in Oakville State Hospital, which I believe was in September of 1961.

Q Have you ever examined those records, Doctor?

A I have.

Q Part of those records are clinical notes, are they not, Doctor?

A What do you mean by clinical notes?

Q What are clinical notes? You are a doctor.

A I am asking your definition. It may be different.

Q Do you have a form in your hospital that is printed and marked "Clinical Notes"?

A I believe you refer to what we commonly call nurses' notes.

Q Is there not in your hospital—Oakville State Hospital— where you say you have been a doctor for fifteen years, a printed form called "Clinical Notes"? You answer that question. Tell me if you have such a form.

A I believe there is.

Q You believe or you know, Doctor?

    Mr. Jordan: Just a moment. I believe the witness answered
       the question.

    Mr. Gross: This is cross-examination.

    The Court: Overruled, Mr. Jordan. Proceed. (To witness)
       You may answer the question.

Q Do you have such a form in your hospital printed in black type—bold black type "Clinical Notes"?

A Yes.

. . .

Q Now, taking the very first clinical note that you have, will you tell us the first entry—the date of the first entry?

A September 3, 1961. 9:30 p.m.

Q All right. Tell us what that clinical note is.

A Middle-aged, white male admitted to ward by Mrs. Mason.

Quiet and cooperative to admission care. Nutrition good. Cleanliness good. Vermin, none noted. Patient states he has been in the State Prison and does not want to talk about it. Small round scar upper left leg. Pimple on right hip. No skin diseases noted. Vaccination left arm. Temperature 100. Pulse 80. Respiration 20.

Q Read the date and the next clinical note.

A The next clinical note is on the same date at 10 p.m. Quiet and cooperative.

Q Is that all?

A That's all.

Q What is the next date and the next note?

A The next note is the same date. Twelve midnight. Sleeping.

Q Will you continue on, Doctor, reading the dates and the clinical notes? Give the date and then give the note opposite.

A September Fourth. Twelve midnight. Asleep all night. Cooperative. Quiet. Urine specimen to lab.

Q I want you to keep going, Doctor. Read the dates. Give the date on each occasion and give the clinical note.

A Twelve noon. Temperature 98.6. Pulse 84. Respiration 20. Regular diet. This patient remains quiet and cooperative. Ate well. Offers no complaints. Reads. Watches TV. Patient seems uninterested in ward routine.

. . .

Q Will you go on with your clinical notes?

A Five p.m. September 5, 1961. Regular diet. Appetite good. Quiet. Cooperative. Watching TV. Twelve. Sleeping. Another note, the time not given. Patient sleeps well at night. Quiet. Cooperative. Ate good breakfast in the morning. This is on September Sixth.

Q Keep going.

A Again September Sixth. Eight a.m. Regular diet. Patient quiet, cooperative. Ate good dinner. Four p.m. Patient reads. Watches TV. Is somewhat seclusive. Offers no complaints.

Q Doctor, what do you mean by somewhat seclusive? What does that mean?

A I didn't make that note.

Q I see. But it is an official record of your hospital?

A Yes.

Q You wouldn't know what that meant?

A I know what the term seclusive means in psychiatry.

Q What does it mean, Doctor?

A It means the patient stays by himself and aloof from others.

Q Is that a significant indication in schizophrenia?

A It is one of the symptoms that is frequently found in schizophrenia.

. . .

Q You mean he doesn't socialize with other people?

A He does not socialize or mingle.

Q Tell us, how is he supposed to mingle? What is a normal person supposed to do when he is in an institution?

A There are no normal people in institutions.

Q There are no normal people in institutions? I see. Doctor, as a matter of psychiatry, when a person comes to you to be examined does he bring a presumption with him—and I mean a presumption in regards to his normalcy?

A Many patients come to the hospital of their own volition desiring help.

Q That is not my question. Please try to understand it. I will repeat it. When a person comes to you for a psychiatric examination, is there any presumption on your part as to his sanity or lack of sanity?

A Not at the time he comes in.

Q Does a person psychiatrically carry a presumption of normalcy?

A When a patient comes to the hospital it is a matter of their coming for examination and treatment—a determination of whether they are normal or mentally sick is made after they have had this examination.

Q That is not my question, Doctor. I am asking about a presumption. Is there in psychiatry a presumption whether a person is normal or not normal?

A Yes, people would be classified generally as either normal or ill.

. . .

Q Now, let me make the question just a little more specific. A person off the street, whom you have never seen before, who has absolutely no history that you know of, is that person—does that person have with him a presumption of sanity?

A Yes.

Q So that, Doctor, when you took the oath to determine for the Court whether Perroni was normal or not normal, you at that time knew that he had been at Oakville before, and did that in your mind—in your own mind carry a strike against Perroni? By that I mean was there already a presumption in your mind that this man was not normal?

A There was not. This did not occur.

Q Did you not a moment ago tell me that if a person came from another institution transferred to your institution, that there was a presumption of abnormality?

A Mr. Perroni came to us from jail.

Q But he had been at Oakville State Hospital and you knew that he had been at Oakville in September and again on a separate commitment in October, is that true?

A That's true.

Q So that knowing that he had been in your institution twice before, did that in your own mind, Doctor, carry a presumption of mental illness?

A It did not.

Q And why, Doctor, was there an exception in this case to the rule that you stated a moment ago, that when a patient with a history of prior illness or prior confinement, that they carry a presumption of insanity?

A I said if the individual is transferred directly from another mental hospital to us.

Q But if a patient had been in your own hospital before, the rule would be different?

A Not necessarily. The situation would be that there could be a change from the time that Mr. Perroni had been in Oakville State Hospital before.

Q But Doctor, that is not what I am asking you at all. I am asking you whether when a patient comes from another hospital transferred directly to you—you said that there was a presumption of abnormality, right? Isn't that what you said?

A I did.

Q All right. I am asking you did Perroni, having been at Oakville in September and October of 1961, and the records at your hospital so showing, and you knowing that these were the records, did that in your own mind carry any presumption?

A It did not carry a presumption.

Q Why the exception to the rule that you stated a moment ago—that when a person is transferred directly from another institution he is presumed to be abnormal?

A As I explained a moment ago, Mr. Perroni was away from the hospital for a period of time in jail.

Q Are you talking about remission, Doctor?

A No.

Q When a patient is out of a hospital for three months or six months, is it possible that he is improved?

A It could be possible, yes.

. . .

Q Doctor, I want you at this point, please, to go on reading your clinical notes.

A Eight o'clock on the sixth of September. Temperature 99. Pulse 78. Respiration is 18. Regular diet. Quiet and cooperative. Appetite good. No complaints. September Eighth. Asleep all night. Cooperative. Appetite good. Eight in the morning. Ambulatory. Quiet and cooperative. Shaved this morning.

Q Go ahead.

A At noon. Temperature 98.4. Pulse 86. Respiration is 20. Regular diet. Ate well. Regular diet. Appetite good. Quiet. Cooperative. Watching TV. Twelve. Sleeping.

Q Keep going.

A September Ninth—8 a.m. Ambulatory. Quiet and cooperative. Regular diet. Ate well. Noon. Temperature was 98. Pulse 92. Respiration was 20. Watched TV this afternoon.

Q Doctor, instead of pulse and temperature and that, will you read only what is on the extreme right-hand side of the page—those notes—rather than the physical status of the patient?

A No complaints. Sleeping.

Q Give us the dates and what is on the extreme right hand.

A Twelve. Slept all night. Quiet. Cooperative. Friendly and conversational. Appetite good. Do you wish me to omit the time and date?

Q No, I just want the date. I don't care about the time. And the note on the extreme right hand side of that sheet.

. . .

A September Tenth. Early in the morning. Nine a.m. Chart closed as of today. This patient seems to have come along quite well on this ward. He is quiet, cooperative. He is friendly. Will do some ward work if asked. He is oriented in all spheres.

Q What does that mean, that he is oriented in all spheres?

A That would refer to his orientation as far as time, place, and person.

Q Go ahead.

A He eats and sleeps well, offers no complaints, regular diet, no medication. September Seventeenth. Mr. Perroni is oriented in all spheres. His recent and remote memory is good. He is an ambulatory patient who is clean in toilet and personal habits. Eats well and sleeps without complaints. His conversation is rational and coherent. However, he is very suspicious and will tell you that he will talk only to his lawyer as to why he is here. He is quiet and cooperative towards routine. He mingles well with some of the ward cases. Today Mr. Perroni is going to Court at 9:30 a.m. He plays cards, watches TV, and listens to the radio. He does some ward work. He weighs 160 pounds. No medication or treatment.

Q The next day, Doctor? Go ahead.

A September Twenty-first. This patient has adjusted well to ward routine. He is quiet and friendly and sociable. He will assist with ward routine willingly. Neat and clean. Showed no abnormal tendencies so far. Mingles well. Plays cards and watches TV. Eats and sleeps regularly. Receives no medication. September Twenty-sixth. This patient discharged into care of Sheriff of Onondaga County. September Twenty-sixth at 9 p.m. Unimproved.

Q It is marked "Unimproved," isn't it?

A Yes.

Q What kind of improvement could there have been, Doctor, when the day before he mingles well, was adjusted well to ward routine, quiet, friendly, sociable, would assist in ward willingly, neat, and clean, shows no abnormal tendencies so far, plays cards, watches TV, eats and sleeps regularly? What do you mean he is unimproved? Unimproved what for?

A I don't know. I didn't place that note there.

. . .

Q How do you account, Doctor, for the continuous notes in your official records to the effect that this man was neat and clean, shaved and showered and so forth? How do you account for that, Doctor?

Mr. Jordan: I object to the question. It is improper in form.

The Court: Overruled. If the Doctor knows, he may answer.

A It was my opinion on the occasions I examined the patient that I would call him untidy in his dress.

Q Was he shaved at the time you saw him?

A I can't clearly recall. I recall that on one occasion he had a growth of beard.

. . .

Q And Doctor, at the time that you examined him were

you, yourself, acquainted with the Fifth Amendment to the Constitution?

A I believe that is the amendment that has to do with a person making statements tending to incriminate himself.

Q You are aware of that right of a citizen not to talk regarding facts surrounding crimes that he is alleged to have committed?

A Yes.

Q Did you want him, Doctor, at the times you examined him, to forego that right, Doctor?

A I asked for his cooperation in order that we could better ascertain the facts as he presented them.

Q Doctor, when he refused to answer those questions pertaining to the facts of that particular day that he got into trouble, did you hold that against him in any way?

A I did not.

Q Did you feel he was well within his rights in not answering your questions?

A I did as far as the situation on the date that he was arrested.

. . .

Q You said there was no spontaneity on his part. What do you mean by that?

A At no time did he enter into conversation except in response to a question.

Q Doctor, isn't that normal, rational procedure, when somebody examines somebody else, that he only answers questions and doesn't become enthusiastic in his conversation?

A Many of the patients that I examine spontaneously enter into the conversation.

Q But the fact that this patient, Mr. Perroni—this defendant —merely answered your questions, and did not shoot his mouth off, so to speak—is that any sign of his abnormality?

A Not in and of itself.

Q Did you, Doctor, expect him to pour his heart out to you, is that it, after seven years of confinement?

A I did not.

Q Did you, Doctor, see a note in the clinical records, or read a note—a short time ago that he was spontaneous?

A Yes, I believe there was such a note.

Q Do you know whether or not he is spontaneous with other people on the ward?

A I do not.

...

Q Now Doctor, none of those things alone that you had mentioned would cause you to arrive at the conclusion that Mr. Perroni cannot stand trial, would they?

A None of them individually.

Q And taken together, Doctor, could you tell us what the magic ingredient is that cements these things together and leads you to the conclusion that this man cannot stand trial?

A Any illness, mental or physical, is marked by a combination of symptoms and signs. The things that I have mentioned are symptoms or, rather, signs of an emotional mental illness that would indicate in my opinion that this man is incapable of—suffering—is in such a state of insanity as to be incapable of understanding the charges, or the procedure, or aiding in his defense.

Q Doctor, did you at any time note any action or any word on the part of this patient or defendant that you could tag as abnormal?

A Any action?

Q Yes, any physical action or word or phrase?

A On occasion he demonstrated a particular mannerism involving his left palpebral fissure.

Q His what?

A His left palpebral fissure.

Q What is that?

A The left eye.

Q What do you mean, he twitched his eye?

A Twitched or looked upwards in a manneristic way.

Q What does that indicate, Doctor?

A In itself possibly nothing, but it is an additional thing that added to the other things is frequently, if not commonly, seen in certain mental illnesses.

Q How many times did you see him twitch his eye?

A I could not say.

...

Q Now, the diagnosis that you make that this man Perroni cannot stand trial, is that made purely on a medical basis, Doctor?

A That is made on a medical basis.

Q Purely on a medical basis?

A Yes.

Q Have you, yourself, ever been a party to a lawsuit?

A I have not.

Mr. Jordan: I am going to object to that as being immaterial.

The Court: Overruled.

Q Have you ever been engaged in litigation, civil or criminal?

A No.

Q Do you know, Doctor, what it takes, practically speaking as a layman, to assist an attorney in the defense of a case?

A I can speak as a psychiatrist.

Q And speaking as a psychiatrist, where do you get your knowledge from as to what it takes in the courtroom to assist an attorney?

A It would take judgment, understanding, it would take a memory, it would take a good contact with reality.

Q All right. What in the clinical notes of your hospital that you read at length into the record—what in those notes do you find contrary to good memory, to orientation—is there anything in those notes that is contrary to this man's ability to understand and help in his defense? I am referring specifically now to the clinical notes of your institution.

Mr. Jordan: If Your Honor please, I am going to object to it.

The Court: Overruled.

A These notes were made by people who are not psychiatrists, who are not even college graduates. Their ability to ascertain clearly and completely as to the memory, the orientation of an individual is not entirely clear.

Q In other words, Doctor, it is your contention—your conviction—that only a man trained in psychiatry, and only a person who has gone through college, can determine whether a person is able to understand a charge against him and to participate in his defense. Is that your conclusion, Doctor?

A I believe that is it under the law. (To the Court) Is it not, Your Honor?

The Court: I don't think you understood counsel's question. (To Reporter) Would you read it?

Question read by Reporter as follows:

Q In other words, Doctor, it is your contention—your conviction—that only a man trained in psychiatry, and only a person who has gone through college, can determine whether a person is able to understand a charge against him and to participate in his defense. Is that your conclusion, Doctor?

A I don't believe that these people who made these notes

had any determination to make as to whether or not the man could stand trial or participate in his defense.

...

Q Let me ask you, Doctor, can Mr. Perroni handle his every-day affairs?

A I would say no.

Q All right. Now, as I understand it, you based your answer on the supposition that his judgment is not good?

A That's correct.

Q Will you please tell us, Doctor, in what realm his judgment is not good?

A His judgment in—may I refer to my notes, please?

Q Yes.

A I feel that his judgment is affected by his illogical thinking processes.

Q Doctor, can you give me a single example from the records, from your interview with Mr. Perroni—a single example of any illogical thinking processes?

A When it was explained to Mr. Perroni the desirability of his cooperating fully for the examinations that we asked him to cooperate in taking, his comment was "What good is that—how is that going to help me?"

Q Is that the only remark, Doctor, in the entire proceedings?

A This is one that I clearly recall. There were others.

Q I see. And can you think of one other, Doctor—just a single one?

A I cannot recall another one that I am sure of.

Q Well, Doctor, it is a fact, is it not, that there is such a thing as despair?

A Yes.

Q And wouldn't you say, Doctor, that after a man has been incarcerated for seven years, attempting to get out for the purpose of standing trial, that he may feel "What is the use of answering questions"?

A But it was fully explained to Mr. Perroni that this would add to the objectivity and the completeness of his examination. We very clearly explained to him we had no bias one way or the other. We were trying to determine the state of his mental processes in order to help the Judge in making his decision. We made this very clear to him.

...

Q Doctor, does a person suffering from schizophrenia ever recover?

A A person suffering from schizophrenia may recover socially.

Q But not beyond socially?

A That's correct.

Q So that once a person suffers from schizophrenia he can never defend a lawsuit, right?

> Mr. Jordan: I am going to object unless we know what kind of lawsuit is concerned. In other words, is it under the Code of Criminal Procedure?

> The Court: If the Doctor has an opinion on it I will let him express it. Overruled.

A I don't believe I can answer that question.

Q You can't answer the question? Is it too broad, Doctor?

A It seems very broad.

Q Is there any type of a lawsuit a person suffering from schizophrenia can defend?

A I don't feel I am competent to get into that area.

Q You are not competent?

A I don't feel I can answer that question.

Q From your examination of Mr. Perroni, will he, in your opinion, ever be able to defend himself against the charges that were placed against him approximately seven years ago?

A I do not know.

Q What information must you know, Doctor, in order to form an opinion? What information must Mr. Perroni give you, what questions must he answer for you in order for you to determine whether he will ever be able to defend himself against the charges that were brought against him?

A It would be necessary for me to find on examination that he had sufficient awareness of reality, ability to reason, and to show absence of the signs that I found on my previous examination of his inability to at the present—

Q (Interrupting) Doctor, what specific symptoms or signs would he have to rid himself of, or what would he have to acquire or accumulate, in order for you to declare that he was able to stand trial?

A He would have to demonstrate a more logical process of reasoning than I was able to ascertain previously on my examinations.

Q What specifically—what would he have to improve in?

A I tried to, as best I can, indicate some of the specific things that I recall, specific questions. His thought processes when I examined him appeared illogical. Again I go back to the testimony I have given before that he appeared self-absorbed.

. . .

Q Now, Doctor, is there such a thing as remission in a schizophrenic case?

A Some individuals suffering from schizophrenia are felt to have remissions.

Q Do you know whether Mr. Perroni at any time has had any remission, any time in the last seven years?

A I do not know.

Q Do you know whether he is in a state of remission at the present time?

A When I examined him last in March, on March Twenty-fifth, in my opinion he was not.

Q Now, Doctor, you said the word *insanity* was not a medical term, right?

A It is not used commonly in medicine. The term that is used is another type.

Q When you reported to Judge Kirby on March Twenty-seventh, when you signed a written report that Mr. Perroni was in a state of insanity, that is not a medical conclusion, right?

A It is a translation of a medical conclusion into accepted legal terminology.

Q And what is the equivalent, Doctor, of insanity in medical terminology?

A As close as I could come to it would be that of psychosis.

Q What you are saying to the Court today is that Mr. Perroni is in a state of psychosis, is that right?

A I am saying today that the last time I examined Mr. Perroni he was in such a state of imbecility, idiocy, or insanity as to be incapable of understanding the charges, procedures, or making his defense.

Q Do you mean he was in a state of psychosis?

A Yes.

Q Do you have any conception, Dr. Roscoe, of what the defense of Mr. Perroni's case will entail?

A Not being a lawyer, I am afraid I don't understand the full possibility.

Mr. Gross: That's all.

. . .

Dr. Martin T. Lipsky, having been called and duly sworn, testified as follows:

Direct Examination by Mr. Jordan

Q Dr. Lipsky, where do you live, sir?

A Oakville State Hospital.

Q And where do you carry on your duties?

A At Oakville State Hospital.

Q And in what capacity?

A As Assistant Director, Administrative.

. . .

Q Now, Doctor, during the course of your career as a psychiatrist, have you had occasion to have contact with people that are mentally ill?

A Oh yes, sir.

Q And have you had occasion to come into contact with people who are mentally ill as far as the criminal law is concerned?

A Yes, sir.

Q And will you tell the Court, please, approximately how many people have you come in contact with as far as being criminally insane?

A On examinations, over three hundred.

Q And as a result of these examinations you made various conclusions as to whether a person was criminally insane or not, is that correct?

A That is correct.

Q Now, Doctor, did you have an occasion to come in contact with Mr. Perroni?

A Yes, sir.

Q Where was that, sir?

A At Oakville State Hospital.

Q Do you know when?

A I was designated by the Director as one of the qualified psychiatrists to make an examination for the Court and to report my results of the examination to the Court. . . . My first examination after the oath was on February the twenty-third.

Q Where did that take place?

A That took place in the visitor's room on the sixth floor of the ward where the defendant was presently lodged.

. . .

Q And can you tell us what the examination consisted of?

A It was a complete mental examination.

Q Well, will you please tell me what it consisted of?

A By observing the defendant, watching his behavior, noting his method of talk, noting his content of thought, noting from the things just related his insight, judgment, and reasoning.

Q Now, was part of this derived by the interview method, Doctor?

A Yes.

Q You asked various questions and he made or did not make various responses, is that correct?

A That's correct.

Q Now, what was the length of that examination, if you recall?

A May I refer to my notes?

Q If you have no independent recollection you may.

A The examination on February the twenty-third was fifty minutes.

. . .

Q What did you observe about him that made you come to a conclusion?

A Generally, my observations were as follows: His general attitude showed aloofness, an air of superiority, a fixation of posture—he sat erect, arms folded, in most part staring into space. He showed a mannerism—the mannerism being a dilatation in the opening of the left palpebral fissure. He showed personal neglect, suspiciousness, and a psychomotor retardation.

Q What was that last statement?

A A psychomotor retardation.

Q What does that mean?

A When a question was asked, if an answer was given it was given after a delayed period. It was a definite delayed period before an answer was given to a question. And part of the time there was no answer given.

Q Was there any time when there was no delay as far as the answers being given?

A If I recall correctly, only with reference to when he spoke about the judge and the doctors, that the doctors had lied, and "Why doesn't the judge give me a fair trial—a trial by jury?"

. . .

Q Now, you tell the Court approximately how long in cumulative time your examination took—all the examinations which you had as a result of being a qualified psychiatrist.

A As a psychiatrist designated by the Director, 135 minutes.

. . .

Q Now, as a result of your examinations and the other aids that are used, do you have an opinion of reasonable medical certainty as to whether Mr. Perroni is in such a state of idiocy, imbecility, or insanity as to know or understand the charges against him, and to assist counsel in his defense? Do you have an opinion?

A Yes.

Q What is that opinion?

A It is my opinion that Mr. Perroni is in such a state of idiocy, imbecility, and insanity as to be incapable of understanding the charges against him, or the proceedings, or of making his defense.

. . .

Mr. Jordan: You may inquire.

Cross-examination by Mr. Gross

Q Dr. Lipsky, with what is the defendant Perroni charged? With what crime?

A I was told yesterday it was carrying a gun.

Q At the time of the examination, what was it?

A I don't know. All I know is that he was sent in on a Code of Criminal Procedure, under Section 658.

Q At the time you made your examinations at Oakville, and at the time you signed your opinion on March twenty-seventh of this year, you did not know with what Mr. Perroni was charged?

A No, I did not.

Q Did you have any idea at all?

A No.

Q Doctor, does it make any difference in your medical opinion with what a man is charged in order to be able to determine whether he can understand such a charge and can help defend such a charge?

A No. The answer is no.

Q The answer is no?

A No. It doesn't matter what he is charged with. My psychiatric examination and opinion would be the same whether he was charged with murder or a misdemeanor.

Q Would it be the same whether the psychiatric examination is for the purpose of defending a case or whether it is for the purpose of drawing a will, or opening a bank account—it would make no difference, would it?

A Your previous question related to charge. Your present question is related to—you are intermingling will with charge. I can't answer the question. Will you break your question up?

Q I want an answer to the question I just asked.

A Would you read it?

Question read by Reporter as follows:

Q Would it be the same whether the psychiatric examination is for the purpose of defending a case or whether it is for the purpose of drawing a will, or opening a bank account—it would make no difference, would it?

A It certainly would.

Q It would make a difference?

A It certainly would.

Q All right. Now, is Mr. Perroni—as of March 27, 1962—in a position to draw a will?

A No, sir.

Q Is he in a position to open a bank account?

A I do not know the legal aspects of banking. I cannot answer.

Q Is it necessary to know the legal aspects of banking?

A I don't know. I don't know the legal aspects.

Q I say, is it necessary for you to know, to answer the question?

A Yes.

Q Is it necessary for you to know the process that is gone through in making a will in order to answer the question?

A Yes. I know that.

Q You know that?

A That I know.

Q Do you know the process that is necessary in defending a criminal case?

A Yes.

Q I see. And you say that it makes no difference to you whatever the charge is, just so long as it is a criminal case, is that right?

A If we keep category within category it makes no difference—the examination would be the same. If you are changing categories there is a difference in our determination.

Q When you say category, Doctor, what do you mean by category?

A If a defendant is up on a charge of misdemeanor or felony, the examination in one or the other would be exactly the same, and would give the same weight for both. When it is a determination for a will—for money determination—the question is whether the patient is psychotic. There is a difference between psychosis and mental illness. If the patient is going to open a bank account, I cannot relate. I do not know the laws of banking.

Q Doctor, would it make any difference whether the crime was a crime that was *mala in se* or a crime which was *mala prohibita?* A crime which is *mala in se* is a crime which is bad in itself. For instance, an act that we don't have to be told by the legislature that the bad act is a crime—for instance, murder, larceny, robbery, arson. On the other hand, we have the type of crime which is *mala prohibita.* In other words, you can't travel more than sixty miles an hour with your automobile just because the lawmakers have said you can't travel any faster, but there is nothing bad in it itself. Now, does it make any difference to you, Doctor, in diagnosing a defendant's ability to defend a case whether it falls into the one category of an act that is bad in itself or an act because it is prohibited?

A With the illustration as you have cited, thinking of a vehicle as a dangerous weapon, I would say there would be no difference.

Q Well, Doctor, if Mr. Perroni were charged with speeding, would you say that he isn't able to come into Court, either with or without a lawyer, and say to the Judge—or help his attorney —and say "I was speeding" or "I wasn't speeding"? Would he be able to do that much?

A If he is mentally well or mentally ill?

Q As Mr. Perroni has been during the months of February and March of 1962 under your observation—and if he were charged with speeding—could he come into Court and tell the Judge "I am guilty of speeding" or "I am not guilty of speeding"?

A It depends on his reaction at the time. . . . At times going into Court he may not be able to—at other times, he may be able to.

Q Now, as of March 27, 1962, when you signed the report for Judge Kirby, would you say that at that time and for a few weeks previous that Mr. Perroni would have been able to come into a Traffic Court and tell the Judge "I am guilty of speeding" or "I am not guilty of speeding"?

A I would not, no.

Q You say he was unable to do so?

A That's correct.

Q Now, is it a fact, Dr. Lipsky, that Mr. Perroni regularly during February and March at Oakville State Hospital played cards?

A I don't know.

Q Well, I mean from the clinical notes.

A Of all the notes written that I have inspected, to my best recollection there were several occasions that he had played cards.

Q Would he have been in a position to play cards, Doctor, mentally?

A Yes. Oh, yes.

Q He can understand that?

A Oh, yes.

Q Does that take any intelligence at all, Doctor?

A A degree of intelligence.

Q A higher degree than to plead guilty to a traffic charge, Doctor?

A Well, I don't believe the two are analogous or can be compared. The playing of cards—we find mentally defective children playing cards. It is according to the game they are playing. We find that the two categories cannot be compared. You are trying to compare two categories.

Q Doctor, you said that one of the reasons that you came to the conclusion that Mr. Perroni could not defend himself was the fact that when a question was put to him he thought out his answer—he delayed his answer and thought about it before he answered, is that so?

A No, sir.

Q You didn't say that?

A I did not say he thought out his answer.

Q What did you say?

A I said there was a delayed reaction in answering.

Q When you say "delayed reaction" what do you mean? A lapse of time?

A A lapse of time in answering.

Q Now, you have sat here all day, Dr. Lipsky, until now and you heard Dr. Roscoe testify, did you not?

A That is correct.

Q Now, did Dr. Roscoe delay in any of his answers when I put questions to him?

A At times he did.

Q At times they were rather lengthy delays, would you not say?

A Well, you would have to define lengthy.

Q At times half a minute went by, did it not?

A No.

Q Not a half a minute?

A No.

Q Thirty seconds did not go by at any time?

A No, I don't think so.

Q Doctor, you have delayed answering some of my questions, have you not?

A That's correct.

Q Without any personal reflection, does that in any way show a mental aberration on your part?

A No, sir. The situation is different.

Q Why is it different, Doctor, between you and me and Judge Kirby and this gentleman here, as to a delay in time in answering a question?

A When you ask a question some of your questions contain clauses that require figuring out from the past record. When Mr. Perroni was asked a question, he was asked a simple question like "When were you married?"

. . .

Q You did ask him, Doctor, about the circumstances that transpired on the day that Mr. Perroni was arrested—didn't you ask him that?

A I asked him what the charges were.

Q What did he say?

A "Ask my lawyer" or words to that effect.

Q Didn't he also tell you the records were downstairs at the office of Oakville State Hospital?

A That is what he said.

Q He told you that?

A Yes.

Q Isn't that an intelligent answer?

A Taken out of context it would be considered an intelligent answer, but we are not considering taking a statement out of context.

Q No, Doctor, we are not talking about taking a statement out of context. You asked the man "What were you charged with?" So the man says to you "The records are downstairs in the office of the Oakville State Hospital." Is that an intelligent answer?

A As I said, taking a question out of context does not make an answer an intelligent answer. We have got to look at the entire bird's-eye view of the questioning and answers.

Q I am taking the specific case of your having examined Mr. Perroni on a given date in February or March. I am asking you when you put that specific question to him on that specific date, you asked him what the charges were against him, and Mr. Perroni answered you, "The records downstairs in the office in Oakville will give you what the charges are." Was that an intelligent answer?

A No, it is an evasive, negativistic answer from a psychiatric point of view.

Q It is an evasive, negativistic answer from a psychiatric point of view?

A This is a negativistic evasive answer. . . .

Q I see. Did you go downstairs to the records room at Oakville State Hospital and try to find out what the charges were against this man?

A I did not.

Q You didn't care what the charges were against this man?

A At the time of my examination I was going to be as objective as possible, and not refer to the previous examinations until my examination was over.

Q During your examination you did not care what this man was charged with?

A I did not say that. I said I was going to be as objective as possible and not let the other records influence me in any way.

. . .

Q Doctor, did you attempt to find out in any other way what the charges against this man are other than by looking at old records?

A I did not.

Q You didn't think it was important?

A I knew that the man was charged—he was in the hospital under 658 because that is what the Court order stated, and this is an indictment, and that is all I was concerned about.

. . .

Q Now, Doctor, will you tell us why Mr. Perroni can't stand trial?

A Would you want me to elaborate?

Q No, not elaborate. Be specific in telling us why. Give specifics rather than general psychiatric terms.

A We are psychiatrists. I must use psychiatric terms.

Q No, I don't want psychiatric terms. I want plain everyday English.

A If I can without using psychiatric terms. If I do use them you stop me and I will define it. I found the patient to be in general attitude and general behavior aloof, having an air of superiority.

Q May I stop you there, Doctor, please? When you say a man is aloof, would you try to narrow that down so we can understand in what fashion Mr. Perroni was aloof?

A I would use a synonym there of a lordly type—a lordly type of behavior reaction.

Q What did he say or do that gave you that impression?

A His method of walk, method of talk, his sitting fixed, head high.

Q He was belligerent?

A No.

Q Defiant?

A No. No, negativistic would be the term.

Q What does negativistic mean, Doctor?

A A reaction opposed to a normal reaction expected in a situation.

Q Expected by whom?

A By the psychiatrist who is doing the examination.

. . .

Q It is necessary to have training in psychiatry in order to understand whether a man is able to stand trial or not, is that right?

A No. If a man knows human behavior. For example, an outright psychotic—one does not have to be a psychiatrist to recognize.

Q Is Mr. Perroni an outright psychotic?

A I would say he is psychotic.

Q But not outright?

A Not in the gross, overt fashion that could be recognized by all lay people, no.

Q I see. And you have typed him in what type, did you say?

A Schizophrenia.

...

Q Doctor, what makes you come to the conclusion that all these separate factors, as you call them—a snicker in one instance, an inappropriate grin—what makes you come to the conclusion that these things added together constitute or add up to an inability to defend himself in a courtroom?

A When we have a person who shows symptoms of this type, as Mr. Perroni has shown, we can only draw one conclusion, and that is that this man is in such a state of insanity that he cannot defend himself, that he cannot make his own defense or understand the charges against him.

Q Regardless of the nature of the charges?

A Would you be specific on the nature of the charges?

Q Of a criminal charge.

A You are taking a generalized point of view here. I would like to be more specific.

Q I say regardless of what the criminal charge is?

A More or less, yes.

Q Do you take into consideration at all the clinical notes that were read into evidence this morning?

A Yes, I do.

Q Is there a single thing in those clinical notes that indicate any mental illness on the part of Mr. Perroni?

A There was an observation of seclusiveness in some of the notes.

...

Mr. Gross: That's all, Doctor.

Thomas S. Szasz, having been called and duly sworn, testified as follows:

Direct Examination by Mr. Gross

> *The Court:* Gentlemen, at this point, for the record, have The People rested?
>
> *Mr. Jordan:* Yes, Your Honor.

Q Dr. Szasz, what is your profession?

A I am a psychiatrist.

Q And you reside in the City of Syracuse, do you?

A That's correct.

...

Q Now, Doctor, at my request and at the request of the brothers of Louis Perroni, the defendant in this case, did you make contact with Louis Perroni sometime in the recent past?

A I did.

Q And can you tell us when you first saw Mr. Perroni?

A I saw Mr. Louis Perroni first on Monday, April third.

Q And where did you see him, Doctor?

A At the Cedar Street Jail, in Syracuse.

Q And could you tell us approximately what time of day it was, morning or afternoon?

A It was at three-fifteen in the afternoon.

Q And did you interview or communicate with Mr. Perroni at that time for any length of time?

A I interviewed him, I talked with him then for one hour and forty-five minutes.

Q And were you alone with him?

A I was alone with him, locked in the cell.

Q And what was the purpose, Doctor, of your interview and communication with him?

A The purpose of my visit was to ascertain whether or not in my opinion he understood the charges pending against him and could assist counsel. In other words, whether he was fit to stand trial.

Q And did you arrive at a conclusion after this hour and forty-five minutes, or did you not at that time arrive at any conclusion?

A I arrived at the conclusion that satisfied me.

Q I see. Now, did you at any time thereafter, after April the seventh, communicate with Mr. Perroni?

A I requested that I be given access to the full records in the case, which I wanted to study, and after which I wanted to examine him once more.

. . .

Q And you told me you wanted to get an order of the Court for the purpose of getting these records?

A Correct.

Q That was done, Doctor? Judge Kirby signed an order for that purpose?

A Correct.

Q You were given some 120 sheets of records which had been copied with a picture machine at the Oakville State Hospital?

A Correct.

Q And did you study those records, Doctor?

A Yes.

Q And could you estimate the length of time that you took in studying those records?

A It was in excess of two hours.

Q I see. And after you studied those records, Doctor, did you again interview Mr. Perroni?

A I did.

Q Where?

A At the Cedar Street Jail.

Q And do you remember the date of that visit, Doctor?

A That was last Saturday, which I believe was the eighth. This past Saturday.

Q And how long a time did you spend at the Cedar Street Jail with Mr. Perroni at that time approximately?

A Half an hour.

Q And when you came away, Doctor, from your second and last visit with Mr. Perroni, did you then have an opinion of Mr. Perroni's ability to understand the charges and to help counsel in his defense?

A I did.

Q And then, Doctor, you sat in Court all day yesterday, did you not, at counsel table?

A I did.

Q And during the nearly six or seven hours that you sat here did you observe Mr. Perroni who also sat at counsel table?

A I did.

Q Now Doctor, do you at this time have an opinion whether or not Louis Perroni, the defendant here, is in such a state of idiocy, imbecility, or insanity as to be incapable of understanding the charge against him, or the proceedings, or of making his defense?

> *Mr. Jordan:* I am going to object to the question, if Your Honor please. I don't believe a proper foundation has still been laid for the answer to that question.
>
> *The Court:* In what respect?
>
> *Mr. Jordan:* I don't think we have been told what the examination consisted of. We have heard that he saw him for an hour and forty-five minutes one day, and some other time another day, but we have no testimony in the record as to what the examination consisted of.
>
> *The Court:* Yes, I think I will sustain the objection on that ground.

Mr. Gross: Counselor, do you mean the mechanics of the examination?

Mr. Jordan: Well, just what the examinations consisted of.

Q Doctor, will you please relate for us and for the record what you did the first time that you visited Mr. Perroni? Did you talk with him?

A I conversed with him, yes.

Q And what else—did you ask him questions?

A I asked him questions.

Q And what else did you do? You didn't give him a physical examination, did you?

A I didn't give him a physical examination.

Q You tell us professionally what you did.

A I conversed with him.

Q In other words, did you question Mr. Perroni for the purpose of determining whether or not he was able to stand trial and help in his defense, is that what you did?

A That is what I did.

Q Now, when you examined the records that were put into your possession, what did you do in examining those records, did you read them?

A I read them.

Q Did you analyze them?

A I read them.

. . .

Q Now, Doctor, may I repeat my original question. In your opinion, Doctor, is or is not Louis Perroni, the defendant here, in such a state of idiocy, imbecility, or insanity as to be incapable of understanding the charge against him, or the proceeding or of making his defense?

Mr. Jordan: I am going to renew my objection, if Your Honor please. As I understand it, the only thing that the reply was as to what his examination consisted of, was that he conversed with the defendant and he also read the record. If that allows the psychiatrist to make an opinion, all right, but just pure conversation—I don't know what the conversation consisted of.

Mr. Gross: I will ask that question.

Q Doctor, what you did—was that the approved psychiatric method of determining and arriving at a conclusion?

Mr. Jordan: Just a moment. I am going to object to what the approved routine method of examination is.

The Court: Overruled.

A May I answer without saying yes or no?

Q Any way you want to answer it.

A In my opinion a correct psychiatric examination is conversation.

Q And that is exactly the examination that you conducted?

A Exactly.

Q Now, Doctor, will you please answer my question then?

A In my judgment Mr. Louis Perroni is not in such a state of idiocy, imbecility, or insanity as to be unable to understand the charges.

Q Or the proceedings?

A Or the proceedings against him.

Q Or to making his defense?

A Or to making his defense.

Q Is there the slightest doubt in your mind, Doctor, about your conclusion?

A No more doubt than about anything else I have in my mind. I always have doubt.

Mr. Gross: I see. That's all.

Cross-examination by Mr. Jordan

Q Now, Doctor, you are a psychiatrist, sir?

A Yes.

Q And will you call yourself—with due respect to modesty, sir—an expert on psychiatry?

A That is for others to judge.

Q All right. Are you also a theologian, would you say?

A No.

Q Now I am referring, Doctor, to *The Myth of Mental Illness,* written by you, sir. In that book I think you went into the realm of religion—part of that book, would you say?

A Yes.

Q And you also made various comments about the historical context of the New Testament and the Old Testament, is that correct?

A I did.

Q Did you quote a person by the name of Bridgman in your book, sir?

A I have.

Q And if I may read from page 199 in the book *The Myth of Mental Illness:* "More recently Bridgman noted that 'Christian ethics is primarily the ethics of partners in misery. A society like a modern democracy would have been unthinkable to St. Paul.' " Do you agree with that, Sir?

A I do.

...

Q Would you say that the more democracy we have the less need for the Bible?

A I don't know about that.

Q What would you say about that, Doctor? Can you expand on that statement a little bit?

A Can you be more specific? Explain what?

Q That statement you made in your book.

A Can you read it again, perhaps two or three sentences before it, because I am not certain of the context.

Q The sentence before it is "Lincoln said, 'As I would not be a slave, so I would not be a master. This expresses my idea of democracy. Whatever differs from this, to the extent of the difference, is not democracy.' "

A I like that.

Q You like that statement?

A I like that statement.

Q Who said that?

A Lincoln.

Q Lincoln said that?

A Yes.

Q And then you differ from Abraham Lincoln's definition of democracy in your book, is that correct?

A That is not correct.

...

Q Now, Doctor, you call it *The Myth of Mental Illness.* In my layman's terms would that mean that mental illness doesn't exist?

A You could put it that way.

Q So you are of the belief, Doctor, that there is no such thing as mental illness, is that correct?

A That is fairly correct. Only fairly.

Q Only fairly? Well, Doctor, I want to be fair. You tell me what it is.

A I will be glad to. It means that the phenomena—the human behaviors which some people call mental illnesses—do indeed exist. But I think that calling them mental illnesses is about as accurate as to call them witchcraft, which they used to be called. Many people behave badly, annoy society—as the defendant has done socially—but to call him mentally ill is to do him a grave harm.

Q Could anybody be mentally ill, Doctor?

A I have just explained my objection to the term. If you define mental illness as social misbehavior, then certainly people can be mentally ill.

. . .

Q Doctor, are you a qualified psychiatrist?

A Qualified by whom?

Q Isn't there a term in the State of New York "a qualified psychiatrist"?

A You mean qualified by the State Department of Mental Hygiene?

Q Yes.

A No.

Q You are not?

A No, I am not.

Q Now, if you would say that there is a myth of mental illness, if you examined Mr. Perroni and, say, one hundred other people, would you ever come to the conclusion that any one of those people are mentally ill?

A I was not hired to examine Mr. Perroni to determine whether he was mentally ill.

Q Will you please answer my question, sir?

A You have asked a hypothetical question. In my professional life I have gone out of my way to be sure I would not be put in the position of having to do what you are asking me to do, namely of having to pronounce somebody mentally ill— because this is like branding him a criminal without a trial in this day and age. I would not do this. I would not accept the position.

Q Doctor, isn't it true that in the development of the law, that one of the great beauties of the law is that a mentally ill person is not responsible for his acts?

A I consider this is one of the most catastrophic things in American law.

Q Would you rather have it this way, that a person who would be called mentally ill at the time he killed somebody should be hung or sent to the electric chair?

A I am also opposed to the death penalty.

Q Given life sentence, Doctor?

A I think that every person accused of crime should stand trial. This is my bias.

. . .

Q Doctor, did you make any notes on your examination of Mr. Perroni?

A No.

Q You made no notes at all?

A No notes at all.

Q And how long were you with Mr. Perroni?

A Approximately one hour and forty-five minutes the first time, one half-hour the second time.

Q What did your examination consist of, Doctor?

A Conversation.

Q Conversation? Would that take the form of a narrative or questions and answers?

A A friendly conversation, questions and answers, but not a stoical "Did you do this?" or "Did you do that?"

Q What questions did you ask him, Doctor?

A I asked him about what happened when he was first apprehended. I told him to tell me only what he wanted to tell me because I may have to reveal in Court whatever he tells me.

The Court: Did he respond to that question?

A He responded just as humanly as we are responding to each other, I would say. I also asked him about his marriage. I asked him about many of the things that were covered in the previous testimony.

Q You have come to the conclusion that this man is not in such a state of idiocy, imbecility, and insanity as to be incapable of understanding the charges against him?

A Yes.

Q How many people have you examined, Doctor, as a psychiatrist?

A Total people?

Q Say, in the last two or three years. Say, in the last two years?

A In the last two years—very few.

Q Fifty?

A Less than that, I am sure.

. . .

Q Can you diagnose schizophrenia as a result of a conversation with an individual?

A This is a loaded question because I don't believe in the diagnosis—

Q (Interrupting) You don't believe in diagnosis, Doctor?

A No, I don't believe in diagnosis. I know how to make one. But I disbelieve in it.

Q You don't believe such a thing as schizophrenia exists?

A Not otherwise than as ink marks on a piece of paper. It is a name. But that the disease exists, no, I don't believe it.

Q You don't believe the disease exists?

A No.

Q What about pneumonia—do you think that disease exists?

A Yes, I think that disease exists.

Q How do you distinguish—how do you know it exists and schizophrenia does not exist?

A I know that by virtue of the fact that pneumonia refers to a physical-chemical alteration in the human body. That exists in the same sense as a table exists. It is an object. But schizophrenia is supposed to be, even according to those who use it—it is like patriotism or democracy. It is a theoretical term. An abstraction. It can exist only as an abstract idea exists.

Q It helps us from one person communicating to another to use a word?

A It helps us. And it does something else even more—it hurts and confuses us.

Q Would you say that for all psychiatry, Doctor?

A I would say that for all psychiatric diagnostic terms. I think psychiatry is a fine enterprise if practiced properly.

Q Would you be of the mind to redefine all psychiatric terms?

A Why should I do that?

Q In other words, if you say all psychiatric terms confuse us?

A I didn't say that. I said diagnostic terms.

Q Diagnostic terms? Would you substitute other terms?

A No.

Q Less confusing?

A No. I would retain them. I would retain the terms we have. I don't believe in adding more words.

Q So even though the terms we now have are confusing you would still retain them?

A Yes. I would do something else, too.

Q What would you do?

A I would make clear the social context—the social situation—in which they originate historically and in which they are used. May I illustrate?

Q Sure, go ahead.

A If you came to me as a private patient—nobody knows about this—and if I say "You have schizophrenia. You should come and see me for interviews and maybe I can help you," this will not affect you directly, socially. If you want to come, you come. If you don't, you don't. You will not lose your job, nothing dire will happen. But if I use the word *schizophrenia* outside of my office or in a courtroom it is a terrible thing. It is not the word—it is the context in which you say it that matters. . . . So these diagnostic terms have a tremendous social impact. To be called mentally ill is like being called a Negro in Alabama or a Jew in Nazi Germany—or to be called a schizophrenic in a courtroom. You are finished, unless somebody defends you. You can't stand trial, you have no rights, you can't get out of the hospital. Everybody is protecting you. Even the District Attorney is protecting you. Once this word gets out, particularly in the courtroom, you are finished. You have no more rights. Everybody all of a sudden wants to help, and you have no more enemies. Someone said "Protect me from my friends, and I will take care of my enemies." The so-called patient has no enemies; everybody wants to help. Has it occurred to his friends that letting him stand trial would be good for him?

Q Doctor, someday when I may have a little more time I would like to answer some of your questions, but right now I want you to do the answering.

A Well, I have answered, I think, your question.

Q Do you think everybody is against Mr. Perroni in this case?

A On the contrary. I have just tried to explain that everybody is for him. You should be against him and then he could stand trial. This is my point. You shouldn't be for him; be against him. Let Mr. Gross be for him and me. Don't let Dr. Lipsky be for him, but let him be his adversary. I believe in the American adversary system of justice. It may be old-fashioned but I believe in it. But I don't believe that people opposed to the defendant should be allowed to retain a psychiatrist. I think this is gross misrepresentation.

Q Didn't you hear the psychiatrists say who examined him as a result of the Court order that they had no disposition whatever, didn't you hear that?

A No disposition? I am sorry.

Q They didn't care one way or the other which way it went.

A I heard it and I do not believe it for a moment. As a human being I believe, I know as surely as I am sitting here, that it is impossible to be impartial in a case like this. How can you be impartial? This case has been in the papers for seven years.

. . .

Q Well, Doctor, you don't like a man being examined by a psychiatrist who you think is against him because they come out prejudiced, is that correct?

A Correct.

Q What about psychiatrists retained by the patient or his agents to examine him—do they come out prejudiced?

A I have been trying to tell you about my prejudice for the last hour. I don't claim to be impartial. But I would say more. Not only do I not claim to be impartial, but it is my opinion that no psychiatrist is impartial in a case like this. I may be wrong. This is my opinion.

Q You are of the opinion that this man was not insane before you even saw him, right?

A No, that is not my opinion. In fact, I would like to tell you how I was retained in this case, if I may, because I think it is relevant at this point.

Q Go ahead, Doctor.

A I told Mr. Perroni's brother when he asked me to see Mr. Louis Perroni that I would not accept the case until I have had a chance to talk at sufficient length with Mr. Louis Perroni to see whether or not he is really out in left field—whether or not he thinks he is Jesus Christ, or that right is left, or day is night—or if he is completely disoriented. . . . So I said to Mr. Perroni's brother that I would like to talk to Mr. Louis Perroni, and if he seems to know what is going on then I would be glad to take his case. Otherwise, I would not—would have nothing to do with it. But you are quite right in one respect. In no circumstances would I be willing to examine him, take his money, then testify that he is mentally ill.

. . .

Q Did you tell the brothers of Mr. Perroni that you will continue to treat him?

A The subject never came up.

Q So you aren't there to treat Mr. Perroni, are you, sir?

A Certainly not.

Q Just to examine him?

A No, not to examine him. To give this testimony. The examination is just a preliminary. This was the point of my intervention, as I understood it. This was what I was hired for.

Q To give testimony?

A To give testimony.

Q Not to examine him?

A The examination was a preliminary, a necessity, in order for me to give rational, relevant, meaningful testimony.

* * *

Approximately six weeks after the hearing, Judge Kirby handed down his decision: he found Mr. Louis Perroni incompetent to stand trial. Mr. Perroni was thereupon transferred from the Cedar Street Jail in Syracuse to the Matteawan State Hospital in Beacon, N.Y. Appeals from the Court's ruling have failed. At the time of this writing (February 1965), Mr. Perroni remains confined at Matteawan. He has now been incarcerated for nearly ten years.

III

It would be superfluous to comment on this tragic story. What could one say?

I should, however, like to call attention to two issues which we encounter in this case and in many others in which the accused is forced to submit to pretrial psychiatric examination. One is the pressure on the defendant to incriminate himself to the psychiatrist, and the dire consequences of his refusal; the other is the prosecution's prerogative to request and obtain not just one pretrial psychiatric examination but several.

The defendant forced to submit to court-ordered psychiatric examination before trial is under strong pressure to "cooperate" with the examining psychiatrists. However, it is a euphemism to speak of "cooperation" here. For the accused is in a bind: he is damned if he cooperates and damned if he does not.

When Mr. Perroni was arrested in 1955 and ordered to undergo pretrial psychiatric examination, he cooperated with the psychiatrists. (He had, incidentally, no counsel until after he was declared unfit to stand trial and committed to Matteawan.) Mr. Perroni trusted the psychiatrists who came to see him. He talked to them. He explained his reasons for acting as he did. The psychiatrists regarded his reasons evidence of mental illness and declared him unfit to stand trial. Thus, by "cooperating" with the court-appointed psychiatrists, Mr. Perroni incriminated himself as "mentally ill."

Seven years later, assisted by defense counsel, Mr. Perroni was less cooperative: he declined to discuss the circumstances of his alleged offense. Yet, despite his assertion that he was doing so in an effort to protect himself, the court-appointed psychiatrists persisted in quizzing him about the details of his crime. It is important to note that information elicited in this type of examination is not protected under the principle of medical confidentiality, and is admissible in court as evidence against the defendant. Nevertheless, the examining psychiatrists maintained that their questions served a purely psychiatric purpose and interpreted Mr. Perroni's refusal to answer, not as an exercise of good judgment, but as "lack of cooperativeness" and "negativism" which added up to "mental illness."

This invitation to self-incrimination, as guilty, mentally sick, or both, is present in all such examinations. . . .

Of equal or perhaps greater significance is the issue of the prosecution's privilege to request, and obtain, not just one but several pretrial psychiatric examinations of the defendant.

This must be contrasted with the single chance of the district attorney to prosecute. At the conclusion of a criminal trial, if the defendant is acquitted, the prosecutor cannot appeal and request a retrial; however, if convicted, the defendant can appeal. This asymmetrical arrangement serves to protect the weak citizen from the strong state.

No such rule constrains the prosecution in its efforts to obtain a psychiatric "conviction." Since a psychiatric finding of unfitness to stand trial (with subsequent incarceration in a hospital for the criminally insane) is not considered a "verdict" like one reached at the conclusion of a criminal trial, the district attorney may request repeated examinations of the defendant. Once the "logic" of the medical view of this situation is accepted, it is reasonable that he should do so; after all, it is always possible that the defendant might have become "sick" again since his most recent examination.

In practice, this means that even if a defendant declared mentally unfit to stand trial manages to reverse this finding in a habeas corpus hearing and succeeds in being returned to court for trial, instead of being tried he may be ordered to submit to a fresh psychiatric examination. This is precisely what happened to Mr. Perroni. In June 1961, after spending approximately six years at the Matteawan State Hospital, Mr. Perroni and his attorney obtained a favorable ruling in one of their numerous habeas corpus hearings. Mr. Perroni was returned to court in Onondaga County (where the alleged crime had been committed). But again, despite the decision of a State Supreme Court Judge in Dutchess County that Perroni was fit to stand trial, the district attorney moved that he was not fit and should be examined by psychiatrists. Again the court concurred, ordered the examination, declared Perroni unfit to stand trial, and recommitted him to Matteawan.

In brief, it is possible—and legally proper—to force a defendant to submit to any number of pretrial psychiatric examinations, thus increasing the likelihood, which is high in any case, that he will be found mentally incompetent to stand trial. . . .

Postscript, 1973

Mr. Perroni was released from Matteawan State Hospital in 1968 and returned to Onondaga County for trial on the original charges, which were then dismissed. He has been a free man since then.

Diagnostic Bias in Community Mental Health

By MAURICE K. TEMERLIN

5

While valiant efforts have been made to develop objective criteria upon which to base diagnostic labels, in point of fact, the labeling procedure is a highly subjective one. Just how subjective and distorted it can be on occasion is illustrated in this study by Dr. Temerlin of the Psychology Department of the University of Oklahoma.

A group of mental health professionals—psychiatrists and clinical psychologists—tended to diagnose a healthy man as mentally ill after they had observed an interview in which a renowned mental health professional, acting as a confederate with the experimenter, characterized him as psychotic. One psychiatrist actually said, "I thought he was psychotic from the moment he said he was a mathematician, since mathematicians are highly abstract and depersonalized people who live in a world of their own." Dr. Temerlin expresses special concern about the damaging effects of labeling when used with the poor and disadvantaged and argues for mental health to be conceived of as social well-being.

THE MENTAL HEALTH PROFESSIONAL working in a community setting interacts daily with many other members of the community: businessmen, judges, legislators, poverty workers, and city officials, as well as other mental health professionals and "indigenous nonprofessionals." In these interpersonal transactions the mental health specialist should be aware of the subtle suggestion effects his diagnostic opinions may have on

From *Community Mental Health Journal*, vol. 6 (1970), no. 2. Reprinted by permission of the author and Behavioral Publications, Inc.

This study was partially supported by the faculty research fund of the University of Oklahoma. For their help, the author wishes to thank Jane Chapman, Helen Klein, Ruth Mansfield, Robert Ragland, and Dr. Duane Roller, chairman, Faculty Research Committee.

both fellow professionals and nonprofessional members of the community. Paradoxically, whereas being a mental patient connotes social stigmata, a mental health professional, as an expert in a mysterious field, frequently occupies high social status. As such, he carries considerable prestige: for members of his own profession, if he is a diplomate, publisher, or distinguished practitioner, and for those members of the general public who accept mental illness as an explanation for maladaptive, deviant, or bizarre behavior. This paper describes an experiment which demonstrates the extreme degree to which the prestige of a mental health professional may bias interpersonal perception: the diagnosis of a healthy man as neurotic or psychotic.

As one part of a research program to study interpersonal influences upon psychiatric diagnosis, a mentally healthy man was introduced into both traditional and community mental health settings as if he were a prospective patient. Since judgments of mental health are often made by judges, attorneys, and juries of laymen, he also was "diagnosed" by several nonprofessional groups. Both professional and nonprofessional groups diagnosed with the expectation, created by the suggestion of a confederate with prestige, that they were observing a clinical interview with a psychotic.

CRITERIA OF COMMUNITY MENTAL HEALTH

Mental illness implies the existence of a psychological state called mental health. However, the criteria for recognizing mental health rarely are explicit. Functioning effectively in the community is inadequate by itself, because many people may perform effectively in a work setting yet experience considerable subjective distress; or they may function effectively on the job while being incapacitated in an intimate setting such as family life. "Social well-being" lacks specificity and denotable criteria. Because theorists disagree—mental health is genitality to Freudians, personality integration to holists, autonomous selfhood to existentialists, self-actualization to humanists, etc. —it was assumed that, for purposes of this research, a man was healthy mentally if he: was happy and effective in his work; typically established warm, cordial, loving, and relaxed relationships with other members of the community; was happily married; enjoyed sexual intercourse free of anxiety, fear, or guilt; was self-confident, without being arrogant or grandiose; and if he was free of depression, psychosomatic symptoms, inappropriate affect, hostility, suspiciousness, delinquency, excessive drinking, and conceptual disorganization.

Recognizing the imperfectibility of men, a professional actor was trained to portray a healthy man, by the above criteria, while talking about himself in a diagnostic interview with a clinician. To give him a reason for being in a clinical setting which would not automatically define him as sick, he said he was a successful, happy, and productive physical scientist and mathematician who had just read a book on psychotherapy, and wanted to talk about it. Since the "patient" thus had high social status, the design was loaded against his being diagnosed as mentally ill, since mental illness varies inversely with socioeconomic status (Hollingshead and Redlich, 1958). He appeared at a university-community clinic and was interviewed as if he were a regular client, the interviewer simply asking him to talk about himself after his initial curiosity about psychotherapy had been expressed. The interview was tape recorded (a transcription is available upon request) and subsequently was diagnosed by the following groups:

SUBJECTS

1. Clinical psychologists and psychiatrists: 25 each, selected from three cities on a stratified random basis from community clinics, state mental hospitals, veterans hospitals, and private practice.
2. Graduate students in clinical psychology: 45, enrolled in advanced courses in clinical psychology at two state universities, each with an APA-approved doctoral program.
3. Law students: 40, enrolled in a class in criminal law; 30 were seniors within a month of graduation; 10 were juniors. Law students were used because they quickly become the judges, legislators, civic officials, and businessmen whose

attitudes towards mental health are so important in the community.

4. Undergraduates: 156, predominately freshmen and sophomores, enrolled in an introductory course in personality.

PROCEDURE

Because Ss were run in the clinics, classrooms, and hospitals of two midwestern university communities, a state mental hospital, and in the offices of private practitioners, some details of the procedure varied slightly, as indicated:

1. Clinical psychologists and graduate students in clinical psychology listened to the interview as part of a diagnostic staff meeting, practicum course meeting, or inservice training program in diagnostic interviewing. In either case, the prestige confederate was a well-known psychologist with many professional honors. Shortly before the interview began he remarked: "I know the man being interviewed today. He's a very interesting man because he looks neurotic but actually is quite psychotic."

2. Psychiatrists were asked to give a diagnostic opinion to be used as a criterial diagnosis against which test scores would be correlated. They were told "two board-certified psychiatrists, one also a psychoanalyst, felt the patient looked neurotic, but actually was quite psychotic," but that "two opinions are not enough for a criterion group in a research project."

3. Law students were asked to participate as jurors in a mock sanity hearing. Their professor of criminal law was the prestige confederate. When the experimenter was out of the room, and ostensibly to encourage their cooperation in the project, he told them they would find participation interesting because they would observe a diagnostic interview with a man who "looked neurotic but actually was quite psychotic."

4. Undergraduates: After giving several lectures on mental health, the instructor agreed (after a rigged student request) to let the class listen to tape-recorded interviews with mental patients. He introduced the interview with the remark that this was an interesting case because "the man looks neurotic but actually is quite psychotic."

All groups listened to the same tape-recorded interview and then indicated their specific diagnosis on a data sheet which listed 30 psychiatric categories: 10 psychoses, 10 neuroses and character disorders, and 10 miscellaneous personality types, including "healthy personality." After indicating the psychiatric category which best fit the patient, Ss wrote a qualitative personality description to report the behavioral observations on which they had based their diagnosis. Ss were debriefed after all data had been collected, and Ss experience of the procedure was recorded either by the experimenter or confederates.

CONTROLS

Three matched groups, stratified for professional identity, diagnosed the same interview with no prior prestige suggestion; with the prestige suggestion reversed; and outside a clinical setting, as follows: Since simply being interviewed in a mental health setting might be interpreted as evidence of mental illness, a third control group "diagnosed" as part of a procedure for selecting scientists to work in industrial research. The clinical interview was changed into a personnel interview by deleting the first 30 seconds, in which curiosity about psychotherapy was expressed, and substituting a director of personnel for a clinician. The personnel director said that his company ". . . liked to know a man as well as possible before hiring him," and then asked the "candidate" to talk about himself in detail, and to include personal information. Otherwise the interview was unchanged. Ss listened to "a new kind of personnel interview designed to elicit the kind of personal information related to scientific productivity" and then evaluated the candidate for employment on 10 scales. The scales were responsibility, creativity, relations with colleagues, probable scientific productivity, etc.—all obviously related to employability. Embedded among these distractor scales was a mental health scale with psychoses and health at the extremes and neurosis in the center.

As a fourth control, a mock sanity hearing was conducted in a county courthouse. With the cooperation of the court, jurors were selected randomly from the regular jury wheel, physicians and teachers being excused, per standard procedure in the selection of jurors. The jury was told that the court was experimenting with a new procedure for use in sanity hearings which involved their listening to the diagnostic interview itself instead of basing their decisions upon expert testimony. After listening to the same interview, jurors voted individually by secret ballot, then discussed the case and voted again.

Control data are presented in Table 1.

TABLE 1 Diagnoses of control subjects

	Mental illness		Mental health
	Psychosis	Neurosis and character disorder	
No prestige suggestion (N = 21*)	0	9	12
Suggestion of mental health (N = 20*)	0	0	20
Employment interview (N = 24*)	0	7	17
Sanity hearing (N = 12)	0	0	12

* N's indicated by asterisk are totals after a replication, grouped together when no differences were found on replication.

In general, control Ss diagnosed mental health correctly; none diagnosed psychosis. However, 16 Ss diagnosed some neurosis or character disorder. These Ss were asked the reasons for their diagnosis, and their answers fell within one or both of these categories: 1. They had implicitly used a personalized definition of neurosis. For example, they had considered him neurotic "because he was an agnostic, and did not attend church," or because he "openly talked about sex." These Ss felt such attitudes were sufficiently rare that they "must" reflect mental illness. 2. They had expanded the concept of mental illness to cover all human imperfection, or the existential conditions of human life. For example, "He looked healthy, but I called him neurotic as he must experience the loneliness and alienation of modern man."

RESULTS

Diagnoses of experimental Ss are presented in Table 2.

TABLE 2 Diagnoses of experimental subjects

| | Mental illness | | Mental health |
	Psychosis	Neurosis and character disorder	
Psychiatrists (N = 25)	15	10	0
Clinical psychologists (N = 25)	7	15	3
Graduate students in clinical psychology (N = 45)	5	35	5
Law students (N = 40)	7	29	4
Undergraduates (N = 156)	47	84	25

$x^2 = 26.65$, df $= 8$, p $< .001$

A X^2 analysis of the differences between experimental and control groups indicates that all differences are significant at the .01 level, whether the differences are between specific experimental and control groups, or combined groups. Clearly, prestige suggestion affected diagnoses; in its absence, no S ever diagnosed psychosis, while when the suggestion was present, 60 percent of the psychiatrists, 28 percent of the clinical psychologists, 11 percent of the graduate students, 17 percent of the law students, and 30 percent of the undergraduates diagnosed psychosis.

Differences between experimental groups also were significant, suggesting a relationship between the effect of the suggestion and professional identity. Psychiatrists thus gave more diagnoses of psychosis, fewer of health, than any other group. Conversely, undergraduates, law students, and graduate students in clinical psychology, having in common the fact of little or no identity as mental health professionals, gave fewer diagnoses of psychosis, and more of health, than did psychiatrists or clinical psychologists. That these results reflect an interaction between the prestige suggestion and professional identity, rather than a result of differences in training, is evidenced by the fact that psychologists, psychiatrists, and laymen did not diagnose differently in the control groups. These results obviously do not mean that professional training reduces the accuracy of diagnosis; rather, they suggest that being a mental health professional may constitute a set to perceive mental illness, and that the effect of this set may be increased by prestige suggestion. Indeed, it is logical to assume that the diagnostic opinion of a renowned psychologist or psychiatrist would carry considerable weight with other mental health professionals, and that laymen would naturally be more reluctant than professionals to diagnose mental illness, particularly psychosis.

QUALITATIVE RESULTS

Subjects who had diagnosed correctly were interviewed at length, to study the process by which they had avoided the pit into which about 90 percent had fallen. Paraphrasing their responses, they seemed to have diagnosed correctly for one or more of these reasons:
1. They had discarded or ignored the prestige suggestion, either because they typically were skeptical people, were negativistic towards authority, or were less "field dependent" than other Ss in arriving at diagnostic conclusions.
2. They had avoided categorization until the last minute, when the data sheets forced them to do so. They had a large capacity to keep an open mind, to take in interpersonal impressions and store them without organizing them into categories. They functioned in a manner diametrically opposed to the psychiatrist who said: "I thought he was psychotic from the moment he said he was a mathematician, since mathematicians are highly abstract and depersonalized people who live in a world of their own," and who then perceived none of the highly socialized and interpersonally effective behavior of the actor.
3. Several Ss had considered diagnosis a problem of understanding a particular person in a unique life situation, and felt that categorization occluded individuality. They had looked for a pattern of attitudes or personality characteristics which defined a unique individual in a particular life situation, lending consistency and predictability to the flux

of words and interpersonal impressions coming to them over the tape. They had categorized only when forced to do so by the data sheets, and by that time they had become aware that no psychiatric category described this particular person.

DISCUSSION

At the level of clinical practice, these results mean that community-oriented diagnosis might be improved if measures are taken to guard against suggestion effects; for example, through the judicious use of professional peers, through independent diagnosis, through creation of a democratic and scientific atmosphere in which skepticism is cherished, and by avoiding the traditional model of basing diagnoses upon "staffings" led by a director, superintendent, or expert consultant.

At a theoretical level, these results suggest that community-oriented diagnoses should avoid all labels and, instead, be a process of personality description, portraying the unique life situation and functioning in the community of each client—his assets, liabilities, joys and pains, and whether or not the agency might be of help, and how.

Szasz (1961) has argued that mental illness is a myth in the sense that psychiatric categories are not classifications of diseases, but are labels applied to disordered social behavior. While this study neither confirms nor rejects Szasz's position, it does demonstrate that a diagnosis may have a profound effect upon interpersonal perception, whether or not the diagnostic label refers to a disease which actually exists. When Ss heard the prestige figure describe the interviewee as psychotic, they also diagnosed him as mentally ill (either neurotic or psychotic) in spite of the fact that he portrayed himself on the tape as successful and productive in the community, happily married, and had a relaxed, warm, and cordial relationship with the interviewer, etc. Considering the socially stigmatizing effect of being mentally ill, it is doubtful that a community-oriented mental health center should diagnose at all. (For example, no one would be surprised to read that "John Jones, a former mental patient, was arrested for the rape of a seventy-five-year-old woman," but who would believe, "John Jones, a former mental patient, was elected president of the Chamber of Commerce.") The community orientation to mental health implies a definition of mental health as socially effective functioning within the community, or social well-being in general. Nonetheless, it is not unusual to find the diagnostic labels of traditional psychiatry applied in community settings with but slight modification; for example, "schizophrenic" may become "ambulatory schizophrenia" or "schizoid." This study illustrates the dangers of this practice.

For community mental health to eschew psychiatric diagnosis does not mean that it should ignore disordered social behavior. Disordered social behavior certainly occurs, and does so with greater than chance frequency in the lives of some people—those now diagnosed as mentally ill. But to label as mentally ill people who exhibit disordered social behavior helps neither to understand nor to change the behavior. Nor does it insure a more humane treatment of the person so labeled, in view of the stigmatizing connotations of the label.

As an example, consider two men, each effective in his work, but unhappily married, who finally decide to obtain a divorce. Although both wives are distraught when informed, one negotiates a settlement to protect herself and her children, and each individual reorganizes his life. This kind of interpersonal reorganization is often painful, but there is nothing about it which inherently is sick. Suppose, however, the second wife raises the question of her husband's mental health, which can always be done sanctimoniously, because the sick need help or treatment. For example: "He says he wants a divorce because he doesn't love me any more, but I think he needs help, because he's never acted this way before." Once this question is raised, subtle changes occur: personal preferences and decisions are not recognized and respected; a hypothesized internal state, which cannot be observed directly, acquires responsibility for the behavior; and divorce, basically a social problem, becomes a medical problem. If, now, a specific psychiatric label is applied (and these results suggest this could happen), socially disastrous consequences could occur; an unnecessary commitment, for example. Yet in this process nothing has been contributed to the social well-being of either party, or to an understanding of the causes of the divorce.

The susceptibility of psychiatric diagnosis to distortion through prestige suggestion, in combination with the stigmatizing connotation of psychiatric diagnosis, suggests that traditional diagnostic labels should not be used; instead, the definition of mental health as social well-being should be refined so that ever more precise criteria may be developed.

REFERENCES

Hollingshead, A. B., and Redlich, F. C. 1958. *Social class and mental illness: A community study.* New York: Wiley.

Szasz, T. 1961. *The myth of mental illness.* New York: Hoeber-Harper.

What Western Psychotherapists Can Learn from Witchdoctors

By E. FULLER TORREY

6

To many, the term *psychotherapist* elicits images of a highly trained professional—one whose years spent studying modern psychology and perhaps medicine afford him a unique and rare understanding of behavior disorders. According to the image, the practitioner possesses the latest scientific information on human behavior and knows how to put this information to work in helping others.

But just how unique is this alleged knowledge, and to what extent is it based on modern science? Dr. E. Fuller Torrey, a psychiatrist with the National Institute of Mental Health, presents some troubling doubts about these issues. According to Dr. Torrey, psychotherapy today is much the same as that practiced by "witchdoctors" in other cultures. Torrey's thesis provides three important messages: (1) Psychotherapists of the western world could learn much from the helping professions of other cultures; (2) our methods of treating behavior disorders have not changed much from the early days of mankind; and (3) numerous variables which influence behavior often go unrecognized. These matters are explored more fully in the author's book, *The Mind Game: Witchdoctors and Psychiatrists,* published by Emerson Hall.

WITCHDOCTORS ARE RELATED to witchcraft in the same way as they are related to witch hazel. It is the same relationship that springtime has to Springfield, Massachusetts,

From *American Journal of Orthopsychiatry,* vol. 43, no. 1 (January, 1972). Copyright © American Orthopsychiatric Association, Inc. Reproduced by permission.

Presented at the 1971 annual meeting of the American Orthopsychiatric Association, Washington, D.C.

Brief portions of this paper are adapted from *The Mind Game: Witchdoctors and Psychiatrists* by E. Fuller Torrey (New York: Emerson Hall, 1972).

or that a nightclub has to a nightingale. The relationship, in short, is not a relationship at all but only a semantic association. Furthermore this semantic association is our association, not theirs. If you go to another culture and ask to see their witchdoctor, they will not understand what you want unless they have been reading *The New Yorker* cartoons. *Witchdoctor* is a term that arose out of the eighteenth- and nineteenth-century exploration of Africa. The world was simpler then, and the newly discovered cultures were quickly assigned their proper status in The Order of Things. We were white, they were black. We were civilized, they were primitive. We were Christian, they were pagan. We used science, they used magic. We had doctors, they had witchdoctors. The term *witchdoctor*, then, is a vestige of imperialism and ethnocentrism—the reflection seen by those who would look out upon the world through their own umbilical cord.

The term *witchdoctor* implies that a doctor is also a witch, a witch being a person who practices black magic. This combination simply does not exist anywhere except in our minds. All cultures have people who play the role of doctors or healers, and most cultures have people who play (or at least are suspected of playing) the role of witch. But the two are never the same. Just as in our culture we distinguish doctor-healers (and such subtypes of doctors as psychiatrists) from witches, so in other cultures they make similar divisions. This is reflected, among other ways, in the names that are used. For instance in Mexico a doctor-healer is a *curandero*, whereas a witch is a *bruja*. And to reinforce the division, doctor-healers in many cultures take an oath that they will not use their knowledge or powers for evil purposes. In our culture this is incorporated in the Hippocratic Oath. In some other cultures, such as Western Nigeria, it is similarly incorporated in an oath the doctor-healer must take before he becomes fully accredited.

The term *witchdoctor*, then, covers the whole spectrum of doctor-healers in other cultures. It is a broad generic term incorporating regional names for doctor-healers (such as *curandero*, medium, medicine man, shaman, or marabout) as well as the specific names used by a given subculture or tribe (such as *babalawo, mganga, miko,* or *baroom xam-xam*).

Since there are functional equivalents in other cultures to our own doctor-healers, it is possible that we can learn something from studying them. It was with this in mind that I undertook a search of the anthropological and psychiatric literature on healers in other cultures. I supplemented this search by personal observations of healers in Ethiopia, Sarawak, Bali, Hong Kong, and within subcultures in our own country.

What I learned from these doctor-healers was that I, as a psychiatrist, was using the same mechanisms for curing my patients as they were. And, not surprisingly, I was getting about the same results. The mechanisms can be classified under four categories that are, I submit, the common components of curing used by doctor-healers all over the world. Witchdoctors and psychiatrists are really one behind their exterior mask and pipe.

THE PRINCIPLE OF RUMPELSTILTSKIN

The first component used by healers everywhere is the Principle of Rumpelstiltskin. Based upon personality studies of the Brothers Grimm in the early nineteenth century, the principle demonstrates the magic of the right word. Let me illustrate:

The psychiatrist looked thoughtfully at his patient. "You looked angry when you were just talking about your father. You often look angry when you talk about him. I wonder if something happened to you once that made you very angry at him." At this point the patient broke down sobbing, blurting out a forgotten history of neglect and deceit by a thoughtless father toward a little girl. Afterwards the patient felt better. After several more sessions in which she was able to explore her feelings of anger she began to get better.

The witchdoctor stared solemnly at the small shells. They had landed in a pattern resembling the shape of a large animal. He picked one shell up and examined it minutely. "You have broken a taboo of your family. It has offended the sacred bear that protects your ancestors. That is why you are sick." The patient and her family breathed a sigh of relief. It was as they had suspected. Now that they knew for certain what was wrong they could proceed with the necessary sacrifices. After these had been made the patient began to get better.

Both of these therapists are able to name what is wrong with their patients. The very act of the naming is therapeutic. The identification of the offending agent (childhood experience, violation of a taboo) may activate a series of associated ideas in the patient's mind producing confession, abreaction, and general catharsis. It also conveys to the patient that someone understands. Since the doctor-healer is usually a man of considerable status, the patient's anxiety is allayed even further. And since his problem can be understood, then, implicitly, it can be cured. There is nothing more frightening to the human animal than the unknown; the worst of the monsters and goblins pale beside this terrifying specter.

Psychotherapists in our culture use the naming process very effectively to get their patients well. The American Psychiatric Association, for instance, provides psychiatrists with an official "diagnostic classification of mental disorders" that achieves lofty heights of empty verbiage. Although terms like *hypochondriacal neurosis* or *neurasthenic neurosis* are almost meaningless, if you attach them to a patient, the patient may feel considerably better.

It works exactly the same way in other cultures. Psychiatrist G. Morris Carstairs (1955) has observed among the healers in rural India:

What was expected from the healer was reassurance. So long as the illness was nameless, patients felt desperately afraid, but once its magic origin had been defined and the appropriate measures taken, they could face the outcome calmly. The parallel with our own clinical experience is obvious.

Underlying the principle of Rumpelstiltskin is an important assumption—that the therapist knows the right name to put on the disease. And in order to know the right name the therapist must share some of the patient's world view, especially that part of the world view concerning the disease itself. A psychiatrist who tells an illiterate African that his phobia is related to a fear of failure, or a witchdoctor who tells an American tourist that his phobia is related to possession by an ancestral spirit will be met by equally blank stares. And as therapists they will be equally irrelevant and ineffective. This is one of the major reasons why most attempts to do cross-cultural psychotherapy fail.

PERSONAL QUALITIES OF THE THERAPIST

The second component used by healers everywhere is the effect of their personal qualities. Psychiatrists, witchdoctors, and therapists of every other name use their qualities to help cure their patients.

In our own culture the best expositions of this aspect of therapy are those by Rogers, Truax, Carkhuff, et al. Stated briefly, the research shows that certain personal qualities of the therapist—accurate empathy, nonpossessive warmth, and genuineness—are of crucial importance in producing effective psychotherapy. The therapists who possess these qualities consistently and convincingly get better results than those who do not possess them.

Now the optimal personal qualities for therapists in our culture would not necessarily be the same for therapists in other cultures. In keeping with the fact that different groups of people do think differently, it would be logical to expect that the optimal personal qualities for therapists might differ. We need much more data on this.

One other aspect of personal qualities of healers should be mentioned here. This is the long-standing axiom among anthropologists that many, if not most, therapists in other cultures are at least deviant individuals if not outright schizophrenics. This axiom has been repeated so often that it has become codified in personality and culture literature as fact. It is, quite simply, false. It arose from the observations of a group of anthropologists earlier in this century—men like A. L. Kroeber, George Devereux, and Ralph Linton—who were very strongly influenced by psychoanalytic theories. Most of these men underwent analysis and, in the case of Devereux, even conducted analysis himself. Because of their psychoanalytic experiences, they were completely unable to see therapists in other cultures with any objectivity. After all, if your analysis is successful, how can you see a witchdoctor as doing the same thing as your analyst (Torrey, 1970)?

The truth of the matter is that healers all over the world probably include a similar spectrum of deviant individuals, schizophrenics, and relatively normal people. The best study done on this to date is one by Dr. Yuji Sasaki, a Japanese psychiatrist who studied 56 Japanese shamans. He found (Sasaki, 1969) that 38 of the shamans were relatively normal,

10 had some degree of neurosis, 6 were psychotic, and 2 had organic brain disease. Although there is no comparable study of Western therapists with which to compare it, this distribution among shamans corresponds with the distribution of pathology among any 56 random psychiatrists whom I know.

PATIENTS' EXPECTATIONS

The third component of the healing process that appears to be universal is the patients' expectations. This aspect of therapy has been studied and recorded most explicitly by Jerome Frank. The great importance of patients' expectations is clearly seen in studies of placebos as well as in studies of the self-fulfilling prophecy in social psychology.

There are many different ways that healers all over the world raise the expectations of their patients. The first way is the trip itself to the healer. Although never documented, it is a common observation that the farther a person goes to be healed, the greater are the chances that he will be healed. This is called the pilgrimage. Thus sick people in Boston may go to the Menninger Clinic in Topeka, while sick people in Topeka go to the Leahy Clinic in Boston. The resulting therapeutic effects of the trip are exactly the same as have operated at Delphi or Lourdes for centuries.

The next way to raise patients' expectations is the building used for the healing. The more impressive it is, the greater will be the patients' expectations. This has been called the edifice complex (Wilmer, 1962). The edifice complex is the light in the patient's eyes when you tell him you are associated with The Medical Center. It is the misty prestige of antibiotics and open-heart surgery seeping down the hall to the Department of Psychiatry.

Therapists do other things as well to raise the expectations of their patients. In most cultures they stand out as different, apart from the great mass of people. In Western culture, psychotherapists even stand apart from their healing brethren in other medical specialties. They dress differently, have beards, and are rarely in danger of being confused with surgeons or pediatricians. American Indian medicine men had distinctive dwellings and diet as well as dress, and the colorful regalia of African witchdoctors is well known. It is interesting to speculate whether there is any relationship between the face paint and mask commonly adopted by therapists in other cultures and the beard and pipe used by psychiatrists in our own culture.

Individuality of the therapist, though usually not consciously affected, tends to increase the patient's expectations of him. The therapist is different. He has high status in the society and is accorded respect and sometimes reverence. Simultaneously he is held in awe and sometimes fear. Most members of the society have a lurking suspicion that he has a special relationship with occult or mystical power. The feelings of a Yoruba tribesman toward a *babalawo* (literally, "father of mysteries") have an exact counterpart in the feelings of a cocktail party guest toward the psychiatrist in the room—attraction, awe, avoidance, fear. In his study of Indian medicine men, Maddox (1923) sums up this aspect of them; his description fits many cultures:

He is readily distinguishable from the laity by his taciturnity, his grave and solemn countenance, his dignified step, and his circumspection. All of these peculiarities tend to heighten his influence, and, by rendering his appearance impressive and suggestive of superiority, serve to increase his control over the people.

Certain paraphernalia are used by therapists in different cultures to increase patient expectations. In Western culture nonpsychiatric healers have their stethoscope, and psychotherapists are supposed to have their couch. With the decline of classical psychoanalysis there has been an accompanying disappearance of the couch, and therapists frequently observe their patients looking furtively around for it on their first visit. Therapists in other cultures have their counterpart trademark, often a special drum, mask, or amulet.

Therapists in some cultures use magical techniques to increase their patients' expectations. Before the patient tells what is wrong, the healer may give the patient a detailed description of his symptoms. This can be combined with various types of divination such as casting nuts or shells, handtrembling, water gazing, or feeling the patient's pulse. Eskimo shamans were known to be especially clever at such things as ventriloquism, and could put on a show that would impress their patients profoundly.

Finally there is the aspect of patients' expectations that rests upon the therapist's training. Some sort of training program is found for healers in almost all cultures. The Blackfoot Indians, for instance, had to complete a seven-year period of training in order to qualify as medicine men. Training courses may include the learning of a body of theory (for instance a body of literature or set of rituals), certain practicum (like water gazing or divining), and finally some self-knowledge and self-control. To become a Ute Indian medicine man, for instance, an individual had to first have his dreams analyzed.

I was pleased to learn that some of the training of witch-doctors is just as irrelevant as was some of mine. For instance, an Eskimo shaman must learn and be able to name ". . . all the parts of his body, every single bone by name in the sacred shaman's language" (Holtved, 1967). Shades of anatomy in the sacred language of Latin! I felt a kinship with my Eskimo brother, and hoped that he was working toward curriculum reform.

A few cultures other than Western cultures have a regular examination at the end of training. The Association of Nigerian Doctors, for example, both holds an examination and grants a certificate to be a witchdoctor (Prince, 1962). The best description of such a system is anthropologist George Murdock's (1965) account of Tenino Indian shamans:

> To practice, it was not sufficient merely to have accumulated the requisite number and variety of spirit helpers. The prospective shaman also had to pass the equivalent of a state medical board examination conducted by the shamans who had already been admitted to practice.

The purposes of this board examination, according to Murdock, were to disqualify false shamans who did not really believe in their own power and ". . . to review carefully the entire life of the candidate." He concludes that

> . . . their decision as to whether or not to admit him to practice seems clearly to have rested on their collective estimate of his personal characteristics, of his fitness to be entrusted with the exercise of great power [Murdock, 1965].

TECHNIQUES OF THERAPY

The final aspect of therapy used by healers all over the world is the techniques of therapy. And it is this aspect of therapy to which we are most wedded as "Western" or "scientific," and, therefore, it is the most difficult to see in cross-cultural perspective.

First a word about the term *scientific*. We would like to believe that the techniques used by Western therapists are "scientific" and those used by therapists elsewhere are "magical." In fact this is erroneous. The techniques used by Western therapists (in the field of psychiatry) are on exactly the same scientific plane as those used by witchdoctors. If one is science, then so is the other. If one is magic, then so is the other. The reasons we have failed to see this in the past are that we have confused our technology with our techniques; in other words, whatever goes on in a modern office must be science, whereas what goes on in a grass hut must be magic. We have also confused education with techniques; we assume that a Ph.D. or M.D. only does scientific things, whereas a person who is illiterate must do magical things. Finally, our insight into the problem is partially obtunded by the amount of magic in our own lives that we do not wish to see—our horoscopes and lucky numbers and superstitions and the charms we wear around our neck. We live in a culture where organized religion changes wine into blood and advises us to pray for protection "from goblins and ghoulies and long-legged ghosties, and things that go bump in the night." How can we really expect to be able to sort out magic from science?

The same techniques of therapy are used by therapists all over the world. It is true, of course, that some cultures favor one technique, and other cultures favor another. But there is no technique used by Western therapists that is not also found in other cultures. Let me provide a few examples.

Drugs are one of the techniques of Western therapy of which we are most proud. Since the introduction of the major tranquilizers in the 1950s, they have become the mainstay in our therapeutic armamentarium. However, drugs are used by healers in other cultures as well.

Rauwolfia root is a good example. This drug was introduced into Western psychiatry as Reserpine in the 1950s as a major tranquilizer. It was pointed out at the time that it had been used in India for centuries as a tranquilizer. Later it was found that it was also in wide use in West Africa and had been for many years. In 1925, in fact, a famous Nigerian witchdoctor was summoned to England to treat an eminent Nigerian who had become psychotic there (Prince, 1960). Armed with his Rauwolfia root, the witchdoctor certainly had better medicine to offer the psychotic patient than did any English psychiatrist of that period. Rauwolfia remains a favorite among West African witchdoctors as an initial treatment for acutely disturbed patients, often to make them more amenable to the psychosocial therapies. This is the same way major tranquilizers are often used in the West. Rauwolfia has also been observed being used to produce prolonged sleep therapy in Nigeria, a type of treatment popular in French psychiatry (Prince and Wittkower, 1964).

Another example is shock therapy. When electric shock was introduced by Cerletti in the 1930s, he was not aware that it had been in use in some cultures up to 4,000 years before. The technique, applying electric eels to the head of the patient, is referred to in the writings of Aristotle, Pliny, and Plutarch, and is suspected of being used by the ancient Egyptians (Kellaway, 1946).

Still another example is the use of dream analysis in psychoanalytic technique. Probably the best study of dream interpretation in another culture was done by Anthony F. C. Wallace, a highly respected anthropologist who studied the seventeenth-century Iroquois Indians. He observed:

The Iroquois looked upon dreams as the windows of the soul, and their theory of dreams was remarkably similar to the psychoanalytic theory of dreams developed by Freud and his associates. In brief, the Iroquois believed that the soul had wishes of which the conscious intelligence was unaware, but which expressed themselves in dreams (Wallace, 1959).

And in another passage:

. . . Intuitively, the Iroquois had achieved a great deal of psychological sophistication. They recognized conscious and unconscious parts of the mind. They knew the great force of unconscious desires, and were aware that the frustration of these desires could cause mental and physical ("psychosomatic") illness. They understood that these desires were expressed in symbolic form by dreams, but that the individual could not always properly interpret these dreams himself. They had noted the distinction between the manifest and latent content of dreams, and employed what sounds like the technique of free association to uncover the latent meaning. And they considered that the best method for the relief of psychic and psychosomatic distress was to give the frustrated desire satisfaction, either directly or symbolically (Wallace, 1958).

Wallace concluded that Iroquoian and Freudian dream theory are not exactly the same, but that the differences are not more marked than the differences between, for instance, Jungian and Freudian theories of dream interpretation.

Finally, let me cite an example of a conditioning technique found in another culture. In Western Nigeria a toad is tied by string to the penis of male children who are wetting their beds. When the child wets, the toad croaks, and the child wakes up (Lambo, 1962). This is almost exactly analogous to a conditioning technique recently introduced in England, in which a bell rings each time the child starts to urinate.

These, then, are some of the things that we as Western psychotherapists can learn from witchdoctors. We can see the components of our therapy system in relief. We can learn why we are effective—or not effective. And we can learn to be less ethnocentric and arrogant about our own therapy and more tolerant of others. If we can learn all this from witchdoctors, then we will have learned much.

REFERENCES

Carstairs, G. 1955. Medicine and faith in rural Rajasthan. In *Health, Culture, and Community*, ed. B. Paul. New York: Russell Sage Foundation.

Holtved, E. 1967. Eskimo shamanism. In *Studies in shamanism*, ed. C. Edsman. Stockholm: Almquist and Weksell.

Kellaway, P. 1946. The part played by electric fish in the early history of bioelectricity and electrotherapy. *Bulletin of the History of Medicine* 20:112–137.

Lambo, T., ed. 1962. *First Pan-African psychiatric conference*. Ibadan, Nigeria: Government Printer.

Maddox, J. 1923. *The medicine man: A sociological study of the character and evolution of shamanism.* New York: Macmillan.

Murdock, G. 1965. Tenino shamanism. *Ethnology* 4:165–171.

Prince, R. 1962. Some notes on Yoruba native doctors and their management of mental illness. In *First Pan-African psychiatric conference*, ed. T. Lambo. Ibadan, Nigeria: Government Printer.

Prince, R. 1960. The use of rauwolfia for the treatment of psychoses by Nigerian native doctors. *American Journal of Psychiatry* 118:147–149.

Prince, R., and Wittkower, E. 1964. The care of the mentally ill in a changing culture (Nigeria). *American Journal of Psychotherapy* 18(4):644–648.

Sasaki, Y. 1969. Psychiatric study of the shaman in Japan. In *Mental health research in Asia and the Pacific*, ed. W. Caudill and T. Lin. Honolulu: East-West Center Press.

Torrey, E. 1970. Spiritualists and shamans as psychotherapists: An account of original anthropological sin. Presented at the meeting of the American Anthropological Association, San Diego.

Wallace, A. 1958. Dreams and the wishes of the soul: A type of psychoanalytic theory among seventeenth century Iroquois. *American Anthropologist* 60:234–248.

Wallace, A. 1959. The institutionalization of cathartic and control strategies in Iroquois religious psychotherapy. In *Culture and mental health*, ed. M. Opler. New York: Macmillan.

Wilmer, H. 1962. Transference to a medical center. *California Medicine* 96(3):173–180.

Clinical Innovation and the Mental Health Power Structure: A Social Case History

7

By ANTHONY M. GRAZIANO

During the early 1960s efforts began to be made to abandon the medical model through the creation of community mental health centers. Reports about the effectiveness of these centers are difficult to obtain; thus it is all but impossible to document just how well the centers have succeeded in being different as they have worked with disordered behavior. The present paper suggests, however, that the medical model continues to flourish and that the power structure it has built over the years actively prevents innovations.

Dr. Graziano of the State University of New York at Buffalo advances two major propositions: (1) that the two aspects of conceiving innovation through science and humanitarianism on the one hand, and implementing innovation through politics on the other, are directly incompatible and mutually inhibiting factors; and (2) that the pursuit of political power has almost totally replaced humanitarian and scientific ideals in the mental health field. These propositions are illustrated by a case history of groups in a community as they sought to promote change. Many of the author's explanatory observations about power and authority apply, more than likely, to other organizations and institutions.

THE 1960s HAVE BEEN A DECADE of increased involvement by social scientists and educators in the problems and welfare of society. Turning their professional acumen to the very old problems of employment, housing, education, poverty, mental health, and others, many have heard the repeated call to "inno-

From *American Psychologist*, vol. 24, no. 3 (January, 1969), pp. 10–18. Copyright 1969 by the American Psychological Association, and reproduced by permission.

Paper presented at the meeting of the Eastern Psychological Association, Washington, D.C., April, 1968.

vate" creative and "bold new approaches" to our vexing social problems. The ensuing increase in new programs, all actively seeking humanitarian goals, has led many of us to suspect that humanitarian aims and scientific methodology have finally come together and melded into a broad new mobilization of the previously unfocused humane and scientific strengths of our culture. In the field of mental health we have seen new developments in the use of subprofessional manpower, the development of behavior-modification approaches to therapy, and plans to develop new comprehensive community mental health centers designed to increase the scope of services.

The common sound in those approaches is "innovation"; it is in the air, and in these conceptually fertile sixties many innovative ideas have been conceived and put forth. However, it should be clearly noted that the *conception* of innovative ideas in mental health depends upon creative humanitarian and scientific forces, while their *implementation* depends, not on science or humanitarianism, but on a broad spectrum of professional and social politics!

The main points of this paper are (a) that these two aspects, conceiving innovation through science and humanitarianism on the one hand, and implementing innovation through politics on the other, are directly incompatible and mutually inhibiting factors; and (b) our pursuit of political power has almost totally replaced humanitarian and scientific ideals in the mental health field. Innovations, by definition, introduce change; political power structures resist change. Thus while the cry for innovation has been heard throughout the 1960s, we must clearly recognize that it has been innovative "talking" which has been encouraged, while innovative *action* has been resisted. It has been the "nature of the sixties," as it were, to simultaneously encourage and dampen innovation in mental health. A major question for the next decade is: following this "reciprocal inhibition" of both innovative and "status quo" responses, which of the two will emerge strongest, and what are we, as psychologists, doing about it?

The following discussion is an attempt to trace the progress of innovative ideas to the level of action, by examining a single case history in which a group of people with new ideas about the treatment of severely disturbed children encountered the resistance of the local mental health power structure. The developments, which cover some 11 years, are briefly described, and, recognizing the danger of generalizing from the single case, we nevertheless do so and attempt to suggest conclusions about our contemporary mental health professions.

THE CASE HISTORY

About 11 years ago a small group of parents sought treatment for autistic children, and found available only expensive psychiatrists or the depressing custodialism of back-ward children's units at the state hospital. Local clinics were of little help since they operated on the familiar assumption that their services were best limited to those who could "profit most" from therapy, and, given a choice between a rampaging psychotic child and one with less severe behavior, the clinics tended to treat the latter and send the others off to the state hospitals. Unwilling to accept either deadly placement (private therapists or state hospitals), parents cast around and were eventually referred to the "experts," that is, the same clinics and private-practice psychiatrists who had previously failed to help those children. They were nevertheless still considered to be the proper agents to carry out a new program, now that a few determined *lay* people had thought of it. This is an important and recurrent point, suggesting that any new mental health service or idea, regardless of its origin, is automatically referred back into the control of the same people who had achieved so little in the past, perhaps insuring that little will be done in the future. The territorial claims of professionals, it seems, are seldom challenged, despite what might be a history of failure, irrelevance, or ignorance.

Following some two years of work, the lay group arranged with a local child clinic to create special services for autistic children. The result, a psychoanalytically oriented group program, operated uneasily for four years, amidst laymen-professional controversy over roles, responsibility, finances, and, finally, the program's therapeutic effectiveness. The lay people, rightly seeing themselves as the "originators" of the program, felt that they were being "displaced" by the professionals. The professionals, on the other hand, saw the laymen as naïve, not recognizing their own limitations and trying to preempt clearly professional territory. Threatened and angered, both sides retreated to positions which were more acrimonious than communicative. "Don't trust the professional!" and "Beware the layman!" were often heard in varied ways.

Hostilities grew, the groups split, and, after four years of their cooperative program, these two groups, the "insider" professional clinic with its continuing program and the "outsider" lay group now determined to have its own program, were directly competing for the same pool of local and state funds.

The clinic, embedded within the professional community, had operated for some 25 years and espoused no new, radical, or untried approaches. It argued that it was an experienced, traditional, cooperating part of the local mental health community; that it was properly medically directed; that its approaches were based on "the tried and true methods of psychoanalysis." The clinic based its arguments on experience, professionalism, and stability as a successful community agency, and offered to continue the accepted psychoanalytic methodology.

The "outsiders," having acquired the services of a young and still idealistic psychologist who was just two years out of graduate school, contended that because psychoanalytic approaches had not resulted in significant improvement for autistic children the community should support many reasonable alternative approaches rather than insisting upon the pseudoefficiency of a single program to avoid "duplication of services." One alternative was proposed, the modification of behavior through the application of psychological learning theory, that is, *teaching* adaptive behavior rather than *treating* internal sickness. Further, because this approach was psychological, it therefore would properly be psychologically and not medically directed.

Thus they criticized the establishment and proposed change, attempting new approaches based on a psychological rather than medical model, and insisting on including poverty children in the program. Naïvely stepping on many toes, they said all the wrong things; one does not successfully seek support from a professionally conservative community by criticizing it and promising to provide new and different services which are grossly at odds with accepted certainties, essentially untried, and, in many respects, ambiguous. Early in 1963, to offer psychological learning concepts as alternatives to psychoanalytic treatment of children and to insist that traditional clinics had failed to help low-income children was not well received. From the beginning, then, this group, henceforth referred to as ASMIC (Association for Mentally Ill Children), were cast as "radicals" and "trouble-makers."

Hoping to avoid competing within the clinical structure, ASMIC proposed to the local university in 1963 a small-scale research and training project to develop child-therapy approaches from learning theory, and to select and train non-degree undergraduate and master's level students as child group workers and behavior therapists. It was hoped that, after a year or two of preliminary investigation, federal support would be available through the university. Approved by the chairman and the dean, the proposal was rejected at the higher administrative levels because (a) the project was too radical and would only create continuing controversy; (b) the local mental health professionals had already clearly indicated their opposition to it; and (c) the university, always cognizant of town-gown problems, could not risk becoming involved.

The message was clear: the project was opposed by the local mental health professionals, it had already caused controversy, would create more, and the university was no place for controversy! (sic)

Thus denied the more cloistered university environment, ASMIC moved to compete within the closed-rank mental health agency structure, where they soon encountered what we shall refer to as the United Agency. That agency's annual fund-raising campaign is carried out with intense publicity, and donating through one's place of employment seems to have become somewhat less than voluntary. Operated primarily by business and industrial men, the United Agency had some million and a half dollars to distribute to agencies of their choice, thus giving a small group of traditionally conservative businessmen considerable power over the city's social action programs.

Having been advised that ASMIC's proposed program could not long survive, the United Agency's apparent tactic was to delay for a few months, until ASMIC demised quietly. That delaying tactic was implemented as follows:

1. The United Agency listened to ASMIC's preliminary ideas but could not act until they had a written proposal.

2. A month later the United Agency rejected the written proposal because it was only a "paper program"!

3. ASMIC's program was started and expanded but after six months of operation was again denied support because it had been too brief a time on which to base a decision. The group was advised to apply again after a longer period of operation.

4. After a year of operation ASMIC's next request was denied on the basis that the program had to be "professionally evaluated" before the United Agency could act. And who would carry out the evaluation? The local mental health professionals, of course. ASMIC objected to being evaluated by their competitors but agreed to an evaluation by the State Department of Mental Health, although they, too, had previously refused to support the program. This was to be the "final" hurdle and, if the evaluation was positive, the United Agency would grant funds for the program.

5. Completing its professional evaluation, the State Department returned a highly positive report, and strongly recommended that ASMIC be supported. Apparently caught off guard, the United Agency was strangely unresponsive, and several months elapsed before the next request for funds was again deferred, on the basis that the question of "duplication of services" had never been resolved.

6. After additional state endorsement and high praise for the program as a nonduplicated service, the United Agency rejected ASMIC's next request, replying that if the state thought so highly of the program, then why did not they support it? "Come back," they said, "when you get state support."

7. Six months later and nearly three years after starting the program, ASMIC had a state grant. The United Agency then allocated $3,000.00, which, they said, would be forwarded as soon as ASMIC provided the United Agency with (a) an official tax-exemption statement, (b) the names and addresses of all children who had received ASMIC's services, and (c) the names of the fathers and their employers.

For three years ASMIC had met all of the United Agency's conditions; they had provided a detailed proposal, launched the program, had successfully operated for three years, had expanded, had received high professional evaluations, had resolved the duplication-of-service issue, had provided the tax-exemption voucher but could not, they explained, provide confidential information such as names, addresses, and fathers' places of employment.

The United Agency, however, blandly refused support because ASMIC was, after all, "uncooperative" in refusing to supply the requested information.

ASMIC's final attempt to gain local mental health support was with an agency we will call "Urban Action," whose function, at least partly, was to help ameliorate poverty conditions through federally supported programs.

Arguing that the city had no mental health services of any scope for poverty-level children, ASMIC proposed to apply and evaluate techniques of behavior modification, environmental manipulation, and selection and training of "indigenous" subprofessionals, mothers, and siblings, to help emotionally disturbed poverty-level children.

The written proposal was met with enthusiasm, but, the agency explained, in keeping with the concept of "total community" focus, more than one agency had to be involved. They therefore suggested inviting the local mental health association to join the project, even if only on a consultant basis. The mental health association, of course, was comprised of the same professionals who had opposed ASMIC's program from the beginning. Skeptical but nevertheless in good faith, ASMIC distributed copies of their proposal to the mental health association, again referring something new back to the old power structure. Five months later a prediction was borne out; the mental health association returned the proposal as "unworkable" and, in its place, submitted their own highly traditional psychiatric version, which was ultimately rejected in Washington. Those poverty-level children who received no mental health services in 1963 still receive no services, and there are no indications that the situation will be any different in the next few years.

The "outside" group, its new ideas clashing with the professional establishment, repeatedly encountered barriers composed of the same people and never did receive support from the local mental health agencies, the United Agency, the university, or the Urban Action Agency. For the first two years it subsisted on small tuition fees and a spate of cake sales organized by a few determined ladies, and eventually did receive significant state support from the Departments of Education and Mental Health. Thus it carried out its programs, in spite of the opposition and lack of support of the local mental health professionals.

This case history of an innovator ends on two quite ironic points. Moving into its fifth year, ASMIC had successfully overcome all major external obstacles and, having been evaluated by both the state Departments of Education and Mental Health, was receiving significant support. The first irony is that having successfully overcome the external opposition, the agency began to disintegrate internally. Having achieved some status, success, and continuing support, it no longer had the cohesive force generated by battling an external foe. Its own internal bickering, previously overshadowed by the "larger battle," now became dominant, and the agency splintered, again along laymen-professional lines. The precipitating factor this time was the professionals' insistence on including poverty-level children, who were nearly all Negro and Puerto Rican. A few lay persons, actively supported in their anger by the professional director of an actively competing agency, objected to the "unfairness" of allowing Negroes into the program "free," that is, supported through a grant, while their "own" children had to pay a small fee. Poverty funds could not be used to support the more affluent white children, as the lay people demanded, and the professional staff was then faced with two main alternatives: (a) abandon the poverty program and work with only middle-class white children or (b) resign from the agency and continue the program under other auspices. The staff decided on the latter alternative.

The second irony is that, while the staff successfully continues its behavior-modification group program, neither the originally sponsoring agency, ASMIC, nor the opposed, traditional, and still well-supported child clinic has been able to maintain its group program for autistic children!

Thus, turning innovation concepts, that is, group behavior therapy and the inclusion of low socio-economic-level children, into actual programs required a good deal more than humanitarian beliefs and scientific objectivity. The eventual reality of the program depended upon its ability to maintain its integrity throughout all of the political buffeting. The program continues today, well supported by the state, but no support was ever obtained from the local mental health area.

LOCAL AGENCIES AS A FIELD OF
PARALLEL BUREAUCRACIES

In spite of the expressed support of the state and of many "outside" professionals, the local traditional agencies, such as the hospital, the clinic, the mental health association, United Agency, city clinics, and Urban Action, all maintained a closed-rank rejection of the program. It seemed apparent that a workable set of relationships among the various mental health agencies had developed over a period of years. In fact "interagency cooperation," ostensibly in the service of clients, seemed to also provide important reciprocal support for the agencies.

Despite overlap, the agencies were differentiated according to major functions: some were referral sources (schools and churches); some provided services (the hospital, the clinic, the center for retarded children); some were financial supporters (United Agency, Community Chest); some acted as community planners (the Mental Health Association); some had dual functions such as the State Department of Mental Health and the anti-poverty agency, both involved in community planning and in funneling federal money to agencies of their choice.

Each agency had its own administrative structure with its own bureaucracy, decision-makers, and line personnel. Thus there existed several autonomous, parallel bureaucratic structures, some larger than others, but all trying to deal with some aspect of human health. Their work was clinical, practical, dealing with issues of immediate reality. On the assertion of too much pressing immediate work, these agencies had no use for research of any kind, and therefore no adequate evaluation of the few available services was ever made. The agencies tended to give support to each other through their mutual referrals, and maintained an uncritical acceptance of the various territorial claims, never openly questioning the value of their own or other agencies' work.

Gradually another level of interagency cooperation became apparent; for example, the director of the leading mental health agency which received funds was also a ranking member of the major mental health planning group, which made recommendations about what agencies would receive funds; some persons were not only important members of agencies which allocated money, but also of agencies which received the money; some sat on boards of several agencies; some positions were held concurrently, while some people "rotated" through the various agencies. In a period of four years, the same relatively few people were repeatedly encountered in various roles associated with one or another of the agencies and making the major decisions regarding local mental health services. In other words, while the parallel bureaucracies which made up the "mental health community" were ostensibly autonomous, each with its own demarcated area of functioning, interagency sharing of upper-level decision-makers occurred, and the situation approached that of the "interlocking directorates" of big business.

There was yet another way in which the parallel bureaucracies cooperated: based on some immediate issue or problem, temporary agency "coalitions" were formed. The composition varied according to the nature of the issue, and the coalition relaxed when the issue was resolved. One such coalition was the original cooperation of ASMIC and the clinic, while the United Agency stood opposed. Later, when conditions had changed, a new set of coalitions formed, this time finding the United Agency and the clinic together.

Thus the active mental health field in this city was made up of parallel bureaucracies, that is, various social agencies which, by virtue of their "expertise," had been granted legitimate social power by the community in the area of mental health. Despite the essential autonomy of the bureaucratic structures, they closely cooperated in several major ways which tended toward mutual support and perpetuation of the existing bureaucratic structures. This cooperation occurred through (a) normal and clearly legitimate professional channels, such as reciprocal referrals of clients; (b) tacit uncritical acceptance of agency "territories" and functions; (c) interagency "sharing" of upper-level decision-making personnel; (d) temporary variable-composition coalitions which briefly intensified agency power in order to deal with specific issues.

MENTAL HEALTH POWER STRUCTURE

We have thus far described the practice of the mental health professions as a legitimized special interest segment of a community. That segment, or field, was composed of parallel bureaucratic agencies which, by virtue of their control over professional and financial resources, cooperated in their own mutual support and tended to maintain decision-making power within that field. There thus existed a definable and relatively stable social structure through which agencies shared leadership, made cooperative decisions, and wielded legitimized social power which tended to support, strengthen, and perpetuate the viability of the structure itself. Schermerhorn (1964) notes, "The power process frequently crystallizes into more or less stable configurations designed as centers or structures of power [p. 18]." Clearly what has been described is a *power structure*, a "temporarily stable organization of power resources permitting an effectual directive control over selective aspects of the social process [p. 24]."

Polsby (1963), who takes issue with the prevalent "stratification" theory of authority power structures, nevertheless notes that

By describing and specifying leadership roles in concrete situations, [we] are in a position to determine the extent to which a power structure exists. High degrees of overlap in decision-making personnel among issue-areas, or high degrees of institutionalization in the bases of power in specified issue areas, or high degrees of regularity in the procedures of decision-making—any one of these situations, if found to exist, could conceivably justify an empirical conclusion that some kind of power structure exists [p. 119].

We have tried to show that such conditions did obtain and therefore conclude that there existed a viable *mental health power structure* which made all major decisions in the "mental health field" of this community. Never static, the mental health power structure continues to react to new pressures, and to maneuver, in a changing world, in order to maintain and further strengthen itself. In so doing, it becomes a defender of its own status quo. It is our contention that local mental health power structures across the country have become so thoroughly concerned with maintaining themselves that the *major portion* of their commitment has been diverted from the original ideals of science and humanitarianism, and invested instead in the everyday politics of survival.

Selznick (1943), writing about bureaucracies, noted:

Running an organization as a specialized and essential activity generates problems which have no necessary (and often opposed) relationships to the professed or "original" goals of the organization . . . [these activities] come to consume an increasing proportion of the time and thoughts of the participants, they are . . . substituted for the professed goals. . . . In that context the professed goals will tend to go down in defeat, usually through the process of being extensively ignored [p. 49].

Thus we maintain that contemporary mental health practice is carried out within power structures which are primarily concerned with justifying and maintaining themselves, while they pay scant attention to the scope of mental health services and even less to the objective evaluation of quality or effectiveness. They maintain their own self-interest which conflicts with humanitarian ideals, science, and social progress. Such conflict is clearly evident in the power structures' relationships to (a) their clientele and (b) any intruding innovator.

RELATIONSHIP TO CLIENTS

Because of the proliferation of agencies with their territorial claims on one community, there must be some means of parceling out the available client pool. Some agencies deal with children, others with adults; some deal with poor children, some with retarded children; some with Catholics and some with Jews; some with immigrants and others with unemployed. None deals with just people, but all deal with "certain kinds" of people who are categorized and parceled out. To whatever category he might be assigned, it is implicit that the client is, in some way, a failure; that he has folded up and dropped out; that he is marginal; that he is not as bright as "we," or as well adjusted as "we," or as well employed as "we," or as nicely colored as "we." There is always an implicit and very real distance which separates the clinician from the client. And at the upper end of this breach is the righteous and very certain knowledge of the professional that he is behaving nobly, in a humanitarian cause. While the clinician focuses on each "client-failure," society is busy producing several more. We too often fail to recognize that our individual internally focused ministrations have little if anything to do with the amelioration of those social conditions which have shaped up the individual's disorder in the first place. To say that the mental health professionals have failed to recognize the crucial importance of external *social conditions* in shaping disturbed behavior is another way of saying that *professionals refuse to recognize that we labor to rebuild those lives which we, in our other social roles, have helped to shatter.* Nowhere is this more obvious than in the area of civil rights, where a clinician might occasionally help some poverty-level minority group member, and later go home to his restrictive suburb, attend his restrictive club, play golf on a restrictive course, and share a restrictive drink in a restrictive bar with businessmen who hire Negroes last, in good times, and fire them first in bad times. By fully accepting the "official" power-structure view of the "sick" individual in an otherwise fine society, we clinicians never admit the validity of such nonscientific analyses as Kozol's (1967) shattering "Death at an Early Age"; and we therefore need not admit that the restrictiveness of our own lives has anything to do with the frustrations of someone else, in another place.

The power-structure clinics tend to limit their services to white middle-class children with mild to moderate disturbances, that is, to those children with the best chances of improving even when left alone; those children whose parents would be most cooperative in keeping appointments, being on time, accepting the structure, and, of course, paying the fees; those children who do not present the vexing and, to the middle-class clinician, *alien* problems of lower-class minority groups. Certainly a clinic is much "safer," much "quieter," more neatly run, when it limits itself to the most cooperative clientele and, we might suggest, when it *selectively creates a pool of cooperative clients.* The waiting list is one of the selective devices used to weed out the impatient and retain the most docile clients. By insisting on the incredibly lengthy and largely irrelevant traditional psychodynamic study, the clinics refuse to deal immediately with a client's problems. Instead they artificially create a waiting list which then serves as an objective validation of the continuing "need" for clinic services over the next year or so. The length of the waiting list is, in fact, often seen as a positive indication of the value of the clinic. Thus, in some perverse manner, the slower and less efficient the clinic and the longer its waiting list, the greater is that clinic's claim to importance and to increased money and power! It would not be surprising to find that a clinic that efficiently handled all new referrals within an hour would be considered of dubious quality because it had no customers waiting at the door.

Thus the structure, responding primarily to its own needs for self-perpetuation, has created a mythical client beset by dramatic internal conflicts, hidden even from himself, but who is apparently little affected by the realities of external social conditions. The professional, with his role clearly delimited by the power structure, continues his myopic psychodynamic dissection of individuals, and never perceives the larger social, moral, or, if you will, *human* realities of that client's existence. The power structure, further insuring its own perpetuation, carefully selects clients who best meet the structure's needs, and rejects the great majority who do not. The "most hopeful" but still doubtful psychiatric services are offered mainly to bright, verbal, adult, neurotic, upper-class whites. In the context of contemporary social reality, the mental health professions now exist as expensive and busy political power structures which have little relevance for anything except their own self-preservation. In this process, we suspect, the client might too often be exploited rather than helped.

RESPONSE TO INTRUDING INNOVATIONS

The mental health power structure, committed primarily to its own preservation, is alertly opposed to any events that might change it. Thus when innovation intrudes, the structure responds with various strategies to deal with the threat; it might incorporate the new event and alter it to fit the preexisting structure so that, in effect, nothing is really changed. It might deal with it also by active rejection, calling upon all of its resources to "starve out" the innovator by insuring a lack of support.

The most subtle defense, however, is to ostensibly accept and encourage the innovator, to publicly proclaim support of innovative goals, and while doing that to build in various controlling safeguards, such as special committees, thereby insuring that the work is always accomplished through power structure channels and thus effecting no real change. This tactic achieves the nullification of the innovator while at the same time giving the power structure the public semblance of progressiveness. The power structure can become so involved in this pose that the lower-line personnel come to honestly believe that they are working for the stated ideals such as humanitarianism, science, and progress, while in reality they labor to maintain the political power of the status quo.

This has occurred in civil rights and antipoverty programs where federal money has been poured into the old local power structures which have loudly proclaimed innovation, improvement, progressiveness, while all the time protecting themselves by actually nullifying those efforts. After several years of public speeches and much money, it becomes clear to the citizens of the deprived area that nothing has changed. Then, frustrated and angry, many submerge themselves into nonprotesting apathy, and others, perhaps the more hopeful ones, erupt into violence, smashing their world, trying, perhaps, to destroy in order to rebuild.

Hence while the power structure continues to proclaim innovation, it expends great energy to insure, through its defensive maneuvers, the maintenance of its status quo. Innovation is thus allowed, and even encouraged, as long as it remains on the level of conceptual abstractions, and provided that it does not, in reality, change anything! The hallmark of this interesting but deadly phenomenon, of spending vast sums of money and effort to bring about no change, all in the name of innovation, might be summed up in what I recently suggested as a motto for one of those agencies, *Innovation without Change!* This motto reflects a central tendency of mental health services in the 1960s: maintaining our primary allegiance to the power structures, rather than to science and humanitarianisms, and continuing our busy employment, creating innovations without changing reality.

Every community has its built-in safeguards which, in the mental health field, guarantee rejection, neutralization, or at least deceleration of any new approaches which do not fit the prevailing power structure. Significant progress in mental health, then, will not be achieved through systematic research or the guidance of humanitarian ideals, since they are neutralized by being filtered through the existing structure. In order for those scientific and humanitarian conceptual innovations to remain intact and reach the level of clinical application, they must avoid that destructive "filtering" process.

Likewise progress will not be initiated by or through the power structure, but will depend upon successfully changing or ignoring that structure. It does not seem possible at this point to join the structure and still maintain the integrity of both areas, that is, the essentially political power structure and the humanitarian and scientific ideals. The two areas are incompatible; science and humanitarianism cannot be achieved through the present self-perpetuating focus of the power structure.

A case in point is the present interest in the development of comprehensive mental health centers. When a community commits itself to the vastly expensive reality of a mental health center, and then *refers control of that center back to the existing power structure,* it has created "innovation without change." The major result might be to enrich and reinforce the old power structure, thus making it vastly more capable of further entrenching itself, and successfully resisting change for many more years.

Our personal experience in contributing to the planning of comprehensive mental health services led us to the conclusion that the comprehensive centers would provide only "more of the same." Instead of trying to determine the needs of the people in the urban area, and then create the appropriate approaches, the planners asked questions such as: "How can we extend psychiatric services to treat more alcoholics?" "How many beds do we need for acute cases?" "How can we increase our services to schizophrenic children?" "How can we pool our resources for more efficient diagnostic workup of cases?" etc. The questions themselves assumed the validity of the existing power structure and were aimed at *extending old services* rather than determining needs and *creating new services.* Only the scope and not the relevance or effectiveness of existing approaches was questioned.

Thus, surrounded by the modish aura of "innovation," the existing structure not only remains intact, but becomes enriched, and continues its existence irrespective of the real and changing needs of its clients. By allocating a great deal of money to the existing power structures, whether through mental health centers, antipoverty programs, special education, or other action, we are playing the game of the "sixties," "Innovation without Change," and, win or lose, we run the risk of insuring our own stagnation.

In summary we have maintained that contemporary United States mental health professions have developed viable community-based professional and lay power structures which are composed of mutually benefiting bureaucracies. Scientific and humanitarian ideals are incompatible with and have been supplanted by the professionals' primary loyalty to the political power structure itself. By virtue of their focus on self-preservation, these power structures (a) maintain a dogmatically restrictive view of human behavior and the roles of the professionals within that structure and (b) prevent the development of true innovations. The basic self-defeating weakness in the variety of current attempts at innovative social action is their unintended strengthening of the existing power structure which is incompatible with innovation. Thus, future advances in the practices of mental health will most readily occur outside of the current mental health power structures.

Contemporary American mental health professions base their major decisions neither on science nor humanitarianism, and certainly not on honest self-appraisal, but on the everyday politics of bureaucratic survival in local communities. As Murray and Adeline Levine (1968) have pointed out, while the professions operate to maintain themselves, society changes, and the two grow farther apart. Eventually the mental health professions become grossly alienated from the human realities of the very clients they purport to help, and the professions soon achieve the status of being irrelevant. Admitting no need for critical evaluation, the professional continues to provide services which are, in fact, of limited scope, questionable value, and extremely high price. As long as we continue to uncritically refer all new developments back into the control of the old power structure, we will continue to insure "innovation without change." Then, as professionals, we can all continue going about our business, keeping our private lives out of phase with our professional pose, and keeping both of them alienated from larger social realities. In this way, we need never allow the restrictiveness of our lives to mar the nobility of our profession.

REFERENCES

Kozol, J. 1967. Death at an early age. New York: Houghton Mifflin.

Levine, M., and Levine, A. 1968. The time for action: A history of social change and helping forms. Unpublished manuscript. Yale University.

Polsby, N. W. 1963. Community power and political theory. New Haven: Yale University Press.

Schermerhorn, R. A. 1964. Society and power. New York: Random House.

Selznick, P. 1943. An approach to a theory of bureaucracy. American Sociological Review 8:47–54.

Part II:
Situational Influences

The Psychological Power and Pathology of Imprisonment

By PHILIP G. ZIMBARDO

8

This study, which was conceived at Stanford University, was not included because it is about guards and prisoners but because it is such a dramatic illustration of the extent to which behavior can be altered by situational influences. Depending upon the roles in which they were placed, some of the subjects became aggressive and cruel, while others were passive and withdrawn. The results of this investigation should be compared with those in Selection 9.

"I WAS RECENTLY RELEASED from 'solitary confinement' after being held therein for 37 months [months!]. A silent system was imposed upon me and to even 'whisper' to the man in the next cell resulted in being beaten by guards, sprayed with chemical mace, black-jacked, stomped, and thrown into a 'strip-cell' naked to sleep on a concrete floor without bedding, covering, wash basin, or even a toilet. The floor served as toilet and bed, and even there the 'silent system' was enforced. To let a 'moan' escape your lips because of the pain and discomfort . . . resulted in another beating. I spent not days, but months there during my 37 months in solitary. . . . I have filed every writ possible against the administrative acts of brutality. The State Courts have all denied the petitions. Because of my refusal to let the 'things die down' and 'forget' all that happened during my 37 months in solitary . . . , I am the most hated prisoner in ————— Penitentiary, and called a 'hard-core incorrigible.'

"Professor Zimbardo, maybe I am an incorrigible, but if true, it's because I would rather die than to accept being

A statement prepared for the United States House of Representatives Committee on the Judiciary (Subcommittee No. 3, Robert Kastenmeir, Chairman, Hearings on Prison Reform). San Francisco, California, October 25, 1971. Reproduced by permission of the author.

treated less than a human being. I have never complained of my prison sentence as being unjustified except through legal means of appeals. I have never put a knife on a guard's throat and demanded my release. I know that thieves must be punished and I don't justify stealing, even though I am a thief myself. But now I don't think I will be a thief when I am released. No, I'm not rehabilitated. It's just that I no longer think of becoming wealthy by stealing. I now only think of 'killing.' Killing those who have beaten me and treated me as if I were a dog. I hope and pray for the sake of my own soul and future life of freedom, that I am able to overcome the bitterness and hatred which eats daily at my soul, but I know to overcome it will not be easy."

This eloquent plea for prison reform, for humane treatment of human beings, for the basic dignity that is the right of every American, came to me this week in a letter from a prisoner, who cannot be identified because he is still part of a state correctional institution. He sent it to me because he read of an experiment I conducted recently at Stanford University. In an attempt to understand just what it means psychologically to be a prisoner or a prison guard, we created our own prison. We carefully screened over 70 volunteers who answered an ad in the Palo Alto City newspaper and ended up with about two dozen young men who were selected to be part of this study. They were mature, emotionally stable, normal, intelligent college students from middle-class homes throughout the United States and Canada. They appeared to represent the "cream of the crop" of this generation. None had any criminal record, and all were relatively homogeneous on many dimensions initially.

Half were arbitrarily designated as "prisoners" by a flip of a coin, the others as "guards." These were the roles they were to play in our simulated prison. The guards were made aware of the potential seriousness and danger of the situation, and their own vulnerability. They made up their own formal rules for maintaining law, order, and respect, and were generally free to improvise new ones during their eight-hour, three-man shifts. The prisoners were unexpectedly picked up at their homes by a city policeman in a squad car, searched, handcuffed, fingerprinted, booked at the station house, and taken blindfolded to our jail. There they were stripped, deloused, put into a uniform, given a number, and put into a cell with two other prisoners, where they expected to live for the next two weeks. The pay was good ($15 a day) and their motivation was to make money.

We observed and recorded on videotape the events that occurred in the prison, and we interviewed and tested the prisoners and guards at various points throughout the study. These data will be available to the committee in a forthcoming report. Some of the videotapes of the actual encounters between the prisoners and guards can be seen on the NBC news feature Chronolog, November 26, 1971.

In the short time available at this hearing, I can only outline the major results of this experiment, and then briefly relate them to the "experiment" which our society is conducting using involuntary subjects. Finally, I wish to suggest some modest proposals to help make "real" prisons become more successful experiments.

At the end of only six days we had to close down our mock prison because what we saw was frightening. It was no longer apparent to us or most of the subjects where they ended and their roles began. The majority had indeed become "prisoners" or "guards," no longer able to clearly differentiate between role-playing and self. There were dramatic changes in virtually every aspect of their behavior, thinking, and feeling. In less than a week, the experience of imprisonment undid (temporarily) a lifetime of learning; human values were suspended; self-concepts were challenged; and the ugliest, most base, pathological side of human nature surfaced. We were horrified because we saw some boys ("guards") treat other boys as if they were despicable animals, taking pleasure in cruelty, while other boys ("prisoners") became servile, dehumanized robots who thought only of escape, of their own individual survival, and of their mounting hatred of the guards.

We had to release three "prisoners" in the first four days because they had such acute situational traumatic reactions as hysterical crying, confusion in thinking, and severe depression. Others begged to be "paroled," and all but three were willing to forfeit all the money they had earned if they could be "paroled." By then, the fifth day, they had been so programmed to think of themselves as "prisoners," that when their request for "parole" was denied, they returned docilely to their cells. Now, had they been thinking as college students acting in an

The Psychological Power and Pathology of Imprisonment   153 oppressive experiment, they would have quit once they no longer wanted the $15 a day we used as our only incentive. However, the reality was not "quitting an experiment," but "being paroled by the parole board from the Stanford County Jail." By the last days, the earlier solidarity among the prisoners (systematically broken by the guards) dissolved into "each man for himself." Finally, when one of their fellows was put in solitary confinement (a small closet) for refusing to eat, the prisoners were given a choice by one of the guards: give up their blankets and the "incorrigible prisoner" would be let out, or keep their blankets and he would be kept in all night. They voted to keep their blankets and to abandon their brother, a suffering prisoner.

About a third of the guards became tyrannical in their arbitrary use of power, in enjoying their control over other people. They were corrupted by the power of their roles and became quite inventive in their techniques of breaking the spirit of the prisoners and making them feel they were worthless. Some of the guards merely did their jobs as "tough but fair" correctional officers. Several were "good guards" from the prisoners' point of view, since they did them small favors and were friendly. However, no "good guard" or any other one ever interfered with a command by any of the "bad guards"; they never intervened on the side of the prisoners; they never told the others to ease off because it was only an experiment; and they never even came to me as prison superintendent or experimenter in charge to complain. In part, they were "good" because the others were "bad"; they needed the others to help establish their own egos in a positive light. In a sense, they perpetuated the prison more than the other guards because their own needs to be liked prevented them from disobeying or violating the implicit guard's code. At the same time, the act of befriending the prisoners created a social reality which made the prisoners less likely to rebel.

By the end of the week, the experiment had become a reality, as if it were a Pirandello play directed by Kafka that just keeps going after the audience has left. The consultant for our prison, Carlo Prescott, an ex-con with 16 years' imprisonment in California's jails, would get so depressed and furious each time he visited our prison, because of its psychological similarity to his experiences, that he would have to leave. A Catholic priest, who was a former prison chaplain in Washington, D.C., talked to our "prisoners" after four days and said they were just like the "first-timers" he had seen.

But in the end, I called off the experiment not because of the horror I saw out there in the prison yard, but because of the horror of realizing that *I* could have easily traded places with the most brutal guard, or become the weakest prisoner full of hate at being so powerless that I could not eat, sleep, or go to the toilet without permission of the authorities. *I* could have become Calley at My Lai, George Jackson at San Quentin, one of the men at Attica, or the prisoner quoted at the beginning of this report. I believe *you* could too.

SIGNIFICANCE OF THESE FINDINGS

1. Individual behavior is largely under the control of social forces and environmental contingencies rather than "personality traits," "character," "will power," or other empirically unvalidated constructs. Thus we create an *illusion of freedom* by attributing more internal control to ourselves, to the individual, than actually exists. We thus underestimate the power and pervasiveness of situational controls over behavior because:

    a. they are often nonobvious and subtle;
    b. we often can avoid entering situations where we might be so controlled;
    c. we label as "weak" or "deviant" people in those situations who do behave differently from how we believe we would.

    Each of us carries around in our heads a favorable self-image in which we are essentially just, fair, humane, understanding, etc. For example, we could not imagine inflicting pain on others without much provocation, or hurting people who had done nothing to us, who in fact were even liked by us. However, there is a growing body of social psychological research which underscores the conclusion derived from this prison study. Many people, perhaps the majority, can be made to do almost anything when put into psychologically compelling situations—regardless of their morals, ethics, values, attitudes, beliefs, or personal convictions. My colleague, Stanley Milgram, has shown that more than

60 percent of the population will deliver what they think is a series of painful electric shocks to another person even after the victim cries for mercy, begs them to stop, and then apparently passes out. The subjects complained that they did not want to hurt him more, but blindly obeyed the command of the authority figure (the experimenter) who said that they must go on. In my research on violence, I have seen mild-mannered co-eds repeatedly give "shocks" (which they thought were causing pain) to another girl, a stranger whom they had rated very favorably, simply by being made to feel anonymous and put in a situation where they were expected to engage in this activity.

Observers of these and similar experimental situations never predict their outcomes and estimate that it is unlikely that they themselves would behave similarly. They can be so confident only when they are outside the situation, but since the majority of people in these studies do act in these "nonrational," "nonobvious" ways, then it follows that the majority of observers would also succumb to the social psychological forces in the situation.

2. With regard to prisons, we can state that the mere act of assigning labels to people, such as "prisoners" and "guards," and putting them into a situation where those labels acquire validity and meaning, is sufficient to elicit pathological behavior. This pathology is not predictable from any available diagnostic indicators we have in the social sciences and is extreme enough to modify in very significant ways fundamental attitudes and behavior. The prison situation, as presently arranged, is guaranteed to generate severe enough pathological reactions in both guards and prisoners as to debase their humanity, lower their feelings of self-worth, and make it difficult for them to be part of a society outside of their prison.

GENERAL CONCLUSIONS AND SPECIFIC RECOMMENDATIONS FOR REFORM

Prison is any situation in which one person's freedom and liberty are denied by virtue of the arbitrary power exercised by another person or group. Thus our prisons of concrete and steel are only metaphors for the social prisons we create and maintain through enforced poverty, racism, sexism, and other forms of social injustice. They are also the physical symbol of the psychological prisons we create for others, by making even our loved ones feel inadequate or self-conscious, and, worst of all, the imprisonment we impose on our own minds and actions through neurotic fears.

The need for "prison reform," then, is a cry not only to change the operating procedures of our penal institutions, but a more basic plea to change the conditions in our society which make us all prisoners, all less happy, less productive, less free to grow, and less concerned about our brothers than about our own survival.

Our national leaders for years have been pointing to the enemies of freedom, to the fascist or communist threat to the American way of life. In so doing, they have overlooked the threat of social anarchy that is building within our own country without any outside agitation. As soon as a person comes to the realization that he is being "imprisoned" by his society or individuals in it, then, in the best American tradition, he demands liberty and rebels, accepting death as an alternative. The third alternative, however, is to allow oneself to become a "good prisoner," docile, cooperative, uncomplaining, conforming in thought and complying in deed.

Our prison authorities now point to the "militant agitators," who are still vaguely part of some communist plot, as the irresponsible, "incorrigible" troublemakers. They imply that there would be no trouble, riots, hostages, or deaths if it weren't for this small band of "bad prisoners." In other words, if they could break these men, then everything would return to "normal" again in the life of our nation's prisons.

The riots in prison are coming from within—from within every man and woman who refuses to let *The System* turn them into an object, a number, a thing, or a no-thing. It is not communist-inspired, but inspired by the spirit of American freedom. No man wants to be enslaved. To be powerless, to be subject to the arbitrary exercise of power, to not be recognized as a human being is to be a slave.

To be a "militant prisoner" is to become aware that the physical jails are but more blatant extensions of the forms of social and psychological oppression experienced daily in the nation's ghettos. They are trying to awaken the conscience of the nation to the ways in which the American ideals are being perverted in the name of "justice," but actually under the banner of apathy, fear, and hatred. If we do not listen to the pleas of the prisoners at Attica to be treated like human beings, then we all have become brutalized by our priorities for property rights over human rights. The consequence will not only be more prison riots, but a loss of all those ideals on which this country was founded.

RECOMMENDATIONS

1. Do not demand simple solutions for the complex problems of crime and law enforcement.
2. Do continue to search for solutions, to question all assumptions regarding the causes of crime, the nature of the criminal, and the function of prisons. Support research which might provide some answers to these issues, and continue to keep the legislature and the public informed about these issues.
3. Put the specific question of prison reform in the broader context of societal reforms and social injustice which may account for why many commit crimes in the first place.
4. Investigate the public's latent attitudes about punishment and retribution, and then initiate programs to reeducate the public as to the rehabilitative purposes and goals of our correctional institutions.
5. Insist that judges have a continuing interest in what happens to people they sentence.
6. Help make the public aware that they own the prisons, and that their business is failing. The 70 percent recidivism rate and the escalation in severity of crimes committed by graduates of our prisons are evidence that current prisons fail to rehabilitate the inmates in any positive way. Rather, they are breeding grounds for hatred of the establishment, a hatred that makes every citizen a target of violent assault. Prisons are a bad investment for us taxpayers. Until now we have not cared; we have turned over to wardens and prison "authorities" the unpleasant job of keeping people who threaten us out of our sight. Now we are shocked to learn that their management practices have failed to improve the product, and instead they are turning petty thieves into murderers. We

must insist upon new management or improved operating procedures.

7. Remove the cloak of secrecy from the prisons. Prisoners claim they are brutalized by the guards; guards say it is a lie. Where is the impartial test of the truth in such a situation? Prison officials have forgotten that they work for us, that they are only public servants whose salaries are paid by our taxes. They act as if it is *their* prison, like a child with a toy he won't share. Neither lawyers, judges, the legislature, nor the public are allowed into prisons to ascertain the truth unless the visit is sanctioned by "authorities" and until all is prepared for their visit. I was shocked to learn that my request to join this committee's tour of San Quentin and Soledad was refused, as was that of the news media. However, after talking with convicts, it is apparent that such a *guided* tour would be the same kind an American general would get in Moscow. Did this committee visit A section of the South Block, the upper floors of the adjustment center, B section, third tier, any floor above the bottom one in the hospital? It is likely they did not, because these are not part of the prison "show rooms" in San Quentin.

8. There should be an ombudsman in every prison, not under the pay or control of the prison authority, responsible only to the courts, state legislature, and the public. Such a person could report on violations of constitutional and human rights.

9. Guards must be given better training than they now receive for the difficult job society imposes upon them. To be a prison guard as now constituted is to be put in a situation of constant threat from within the prison, with no social recognition from the society at large. As was shown graphically at Attica, prison guards are also prisoners of the system who can be sacrificed to the demands of the public to be punitive and the needs of politicians to preserve an image. Social scientists and business training personnel should be called upon to design and help carry out this training.

10. In line with this new human relations training would be changes in the perceived role of the "guards." They would instead be "teachers" or "counselors," and the "prisoners" would be "trainees." The reinforcement (bonus, advance-

ment) for such a "teacher" would be contingent upon the "trainees" learning new social and technical skills which will enable them to leave the "training-rehabilitation" center as early as possible, and not come back.

Positive reinforcement would replace coercion, threats, and isolation as means of behavior management. Most prisoners want to return to their community, to be capable of earning a living, to be socially responsible, and to be needed by others. Many are in prison not because they don't have a manual trade, but because of deficits in social training. Prisons should be reconstituted to provide the opportunity for such people to have positive social experiences, to be responsive to and responsible for others. This could be done by giving them training as psychiatric aides and social workers who must care for other disturbed prisoners. This "peer management" is the best way to build an individual's sense of self-worth and a feeling of community. In addition, these skills are vitally needed in the communities to which the "trainees" will return. College students and professional social scientists could volunteer their services or be part of a Vista campaign to produce such training.

11. The relationship between the individual (who is sentenced by the courts to such a center) and his community must be maintained. How can a "prisoner" return to a dynamically changing society, that most of us cannot cope with, after being out of it for a number of years? There should be more community involvement in these rehabilitation centers, more ties encouraged and promoted between the trainees and family and friends, more educational opportunities to prepare them for returning to their communities as more valuable members of it than they were before they left.

12. Once a trainee has finished the prescribed course and is judged ready to leave the institution, there should be no stigma attached to his training, no need to report to prospective employers that he/she was a "prisoner," no need to be labeled an "ex-con."

13. Finally, the main ingredient necessary to effect any change at all in prison reform, in the rehabilitation of a single prisoner, or even in the optimal development of your own child, is *caring*. That is where all reform must start—with

people caring about the well-being of others, especially people with power, like those on this committee, really caring about the most hardened, allegedly incorrigible prisoner in solitary confinement. Underneath the toughest, society-hating convict, rebel, or anarchist is a human being who wants his existence to be recognized by his fellows, and who wants someone else to care about whether he lives or dies and to be sad if he lives imprisoned rather than lives free.

The Mock Ward: A Study in Simulation

9

By NORMA JEAN ORLANDO

In round numbers, there are one-half million people incarcerated in mental institutions. That statistic is cited so that as you read this selection you will be reminded that the events described are by no means rare. This novel investigation by Norma Jean Orlando of the Elgin State Hospital (Illinois) demonstrates the mental symptoms which "normal" people experience when they are treated only over a weekend in the same manner that actual mental patients are treated routinely.

As you read very carefully that portion of the study which describes admission procedures, wonder how your "identity" would be affected!

HOW IMPORTANT IS THE SET created by the physical setting and by staff attitudes in a mental hospital? What are some of the influences of the hospital milieu on patients? This study explored the set the hospital surroundings per se, including staff attitudes, might produce in mental patients quite apart from their personal forms of disordered behavior.

THE PROBLEM OF SET

The problem of set is a widely recognized one in scientific psychology; moreover, the influence of the environmental milieu in the broad sense has been recognized outside the discipline. For example, Tolstoy in his *War and Peace* suggests that kings themselves sometimes become the slaves of historical forces. Boring (1950), in commenting on Tolstoy's thesis, states that in *War and Peace* the characters suggest "that war transcends the wills and decisions of men who make the war, that they are but agents of greater natural forces." According to

---

This selection was prepared especially for this book.

Boring, Herbert Spencer held a similar view. Woodworth (1948), in his classic text on experimental psychology, deals with the concept of set in a thorough manner; he highlights set as being a definite factor in thinking. Gibson (1941) has pointed to the pervasive influence of set in the experimental realm. Hutt, Gibby, Milton, and Pottharst (1950) demonstrated that varied experimental sets could alter Rorschach test performance; they found that experimental subjects could increase such responses as M and C with comparative ease.

In the field of mental health, studies of institutions, such as those by Belknapp (1956), Caudill (1958), and Stanton and Schwartz (1954) have shown the impact of staff attitudes on the patients themselves. Milieu therapy reflects awareness of the influence the immediate environment may have upon patients. Maxwell Jones's (1953, 1961) notion of the therapeutic community illustrates this point of view. Recently, Zimbardo (1971, 1972) found that college-educated males, when simulating the roles of prisoners and guards, developed attitudes and feelings allegedly experienced by actual guards and prisoners and displayed similar overt behavior. The Zimbardo study suggests that generalizations might be formulated about the influence of the hospital milieu on mental patients.

THE SIMULATION AND METHOD

The present investigation at Elgin State Hospital involved a simulation[1] of a mental hospital ward over a three-day holiday weekend. Ward living conditions were duplicated as much as possible for the subjects, who were all staff members at the hospital. Some staff members acted as observers; others continued in their role as staff members, while the remainder enacted the role of mental patients. Efforts were made to create the kind of environmental milieu such that the patient-subjects would be caused to experience the role of patient. The experiment was conducted in an actual ward that happened to be empty in a building scheduled for demolition.

The subjects were requested prior to the weekend not to bring any valuables, and if they were taking any medication,

---

[1] See J. R. Raser, *Simulation and Society* (Boston: Allyn and Bacon, 1969).

to bring a sufficient supply in a labeled pharmacy bottle. Also, by a written communication, the prospective subjects were warned that the occasion had a high potential for being a very intense, anxiety-arousing experience; they were encouraged to discuss their apprehensions with selected hospital personnel. As a point of fact, the experimental patient-subjects did show a rather high level of anxiety during the admission procedure according to the data recorded by the experimental observers, who used Zeisset's (1972) Checklist for Anxiety-Behavior Observations.

THE SUBJECTS

All subjects had responded to requests for volunteers to participate in a mock ward experiment. The requests were communicated by means of memoranda distributed throughout the hospital and by an advertisement in the hospital newsletter. Every third volunteer was assigned to the role of staff; when a subject made a specific request, however, to serve in a particular role, the request was honored generally.

There were 51 participants with 29 serving as patient-subjects and the remainder as staff. There is some presumptive evidence that a mental set had been established prior to the experiment. In support of this conclusion was the large number of "no shows"; originally, 50 of the volunteers had been scheduled to be admitted as patient-subjects.

The volunteer subject population represented a cross section of the ward personnel; 20 wards (from a total of 47) had staff members included. Educational attainments of the subjects ranged from eight years of schooling to the master's degree; most of the subjects had some college background. The modal age for the patient-subjects was 24; nine of them were over 30 years of age, and some were in their late forties and fifties.

THE ESTABLISHMENT OF THE SET

The admission procedure for patient-subjects involved directing them to appropriate waiting rooms, where a short speech was given by one of the experimental observers. They were then escorted to interviewers, and each one was admitted by an intake worker. Immediately thereafter, the "patient" was directed to the clothing room, where state clothing was issued. The clothing included "scuffies"; these had become one of the earmarks of a mental patient. At this point the patient-subjects were taken in pairs—two of each sex at a time—to appropriate showers. They were stripped of their own clothing; one of the experimental staff members conducted a body check, and another staff member made a record of their personal clothing while placing it in bags with identifying marks. The body check was for the purpose of detecting the possible presence of body lice as well as to record any distinguishing scars and other marks. The record of the body check is also used in connection with any report of injuries by the patient at later dates.

The "patients" were taken from the showers to the locked ward by a runner and were introduced to the staff members *but not vice versa*. Those playing the part of staff members wore mirrored sunglasses; this made it difficult for the "patients" to make eye contact with them. Like many of the wards at Elgin, the mock ward was run on the basis of the token economy. Regular medication periods were observed, and the patient-subjects were given placebos. Among the other steps taken to simulate the actual hospital conditions was the crowded ward—the ward was small, the dormitory was small, and the dayroom was small. Moreover, the patient-subjects were not allowed to go into the dormitory during the day. Recreation was in the same area, the dayroom.

There was a lack of privacy. The toilets were not private, and they were not locked. The dormitories were checked at night as were those of actual mental patients. At times there was open discussion of allegedly private "patient" problems among the staff in the presence of the "patient" but behind his back. To further encourage depersonalization both the staff-subjects and the patient-subjects were assigned new names. When special requests were made by the "patient" that the staff did not want to fulfill, the staff-subject was instructed to reply: "If I let you do it, then everyone else will want to." And, in asking questions of the "patient," the staff member was to ask the question in a manner that let the "patient" know that he (the staff member) was not interested.

The set of low status for the "patients" was established by having the staff always in control; "patients" were made to feel bad if they gained some control. The attitudes encouraged were that once a staff member said something, it was to be carried out so there would be no loss of face. The set of low status was established, in addition, by ill-fitting state clothes, including improperly fit bras, and by the use of shoestrings to hold pants up. The set of dependency was strengthened in the patient-subjects in several ways: (1) they were forced to request the staff to light their cigarettes; (2) the staff unlocked doors for them; (3) they needed staff to get their coffee; (4) the staff threw away coffee in full view of them; and (5) the staff was obviously biased in their affectionate responses for certain patient-subjects. The set of the feeling of helplessness was aided by having too few chairs, with rules that a "patient" could not sit or lie on the floor.

With the exception of meal time, when the subjects of the study dined with actual mental patients in one of the cafeterias, the experimental subjects were not in contact with the residents of the hospital. The study was constantly monitored through videotape; portions of the proceedings were recorded on 16mm. film.

Debriefing took place at the termination of the experiment. After the announcement was made that the experiment was over, the subjects were divided into small groups. All subjects were given the opportunity to ventilate their feelings about the experiences they had undergone. In addition to the immediate sessions, debriefing continued over a period of days at scheduled intervals.

RESULTS AND DISCUSSION

Soon after the patient-subjects began to congregate in the day-room, it became apparent that assuming the roles of mental patients led to behaviors similar to those of actual mental patients. There was incessant back and forth pacing by many, while some sat by the wall, near each other, but without verbal communication. There were instances of extreme behavior, including several escapes; one patient-subject was placed in restraints following his sixth attempt; he remained in restraints four hours. Several of the ward windows were broken, and a carpenter had to be called to install new ones. Several "patients" wept uncontrollably. There was some stealing, not only from the staff but from among the patient-subjects themselves. There was at least one fistfight between a patient-subject and staff member. The altercation occurred following a threat by the staff member to administer a hypodermic injection if the "patient" continued to refuse medication.

There seemed to be a general rise in the level of tension experienced by the "patients." At least one of the patient-subjects expressed a fear of suffering an actual breakdown. Depression was common, and hostility was generally intense. It seems that if a situation is intense enough, most individuals can behave in ways they would like to disown.

There were many complaints by the patient-subjects both during and after the study about what they called "dehumanizing" conditions. They felt they had been reduced to a very low level of existence. The lack of proper facilities for bathing was specifically mentioned. Food, clothing, and noise were also mentioned. The patient-subjects complained that they were treated like children. There were also many comments that the "efficient" manner in which the staff operated made the patient-subjects feel a kind of coldness and distance. Conversely there were several complaints from "patients" that the staff at times was "too nice" and overly solicitous. One patient felt she was not allowed to experience the full intensity of her feelings; she was crying, and the staff tended to stop her from crying. This action on the part of the staff made it difficult for the patient-subject to clarify her patient-status. It tended to make her feel obligated just as a child feels obligated to a comforting mother.

Patient-subjects made many claims about their experiences as participants in the mock ward experiment. They reported following the study:

"Felt like at mercy of personalities. No recourse."

"Patients have no power; can't make decisions."

"Felt labeled as troublemaker because asking for a simple thing. Can't understand rules."

"Anger and hostility when awakened Saturday a.m."

"Everything was patient's fault. No way to let out hostility. Couldn't concentrate. Still upset about clothes on Saturday morning. Staff didn't give a shit how you looked or how you felt."

"Meals—We knew the food was bad; worst was way it was served. Didn't have an appetite. Didn't always have forks; knives and spoons not there."

"No time orientation."

"Paranoid about medication."

"Repression, lack of privacy, feeling like an object, feeling delusional, feeling like of no value because of staff attitudes."

"I don't normally lie or cheat, but I think I would have done all those things just to get what I wanted here, if I had stayed any longer."

"Yesterday I just felt kind of numb. What was reality? Just the same walls."

"Even when you present legitimate arguments, they won't consider them, and then you begin to doubt yourself—and then you get paranoid. You figure they're competent, and you've been told you're not competent just by being here—so you must be wrong."

"Two ways to get through—the passive way or the violent means. When these fail, you just give up—then you feel like a failure."

"When they took my tokens away from me (for a fine), I felt like I had done something really bad—something criminal."

It is apparent that the patient-subjects gave data that would have been more difficult to obtain from some actual mental patients since the subjects in the experiment were persons who were perhaps less afraid to speak freely and critically.

In the following table, the numbers refer to the percentages of "patients" who replied "yes" to each of the statements in a questionnaire administered just prior to the announcement that the experiment was over:

I especially felt a lack of freedom.	100%
I was treated as if my feelings were not important.	96
I felt as if I were incarcerated.	93
At times I felt my identity had been taken away from me.	89
Now I know it must feel terrible to be a patient.	89
I did not feel that the staff really listened to me.	89
There were times when I almost forgot this was an experiment.	79
I really felt like a patient.	75
During the experiment I did not feel that I was treated like a person.	75
At times I felt that nobody cared about me.	75

The results of this study generally parallel those obtained by Zimbardo. Zimbardo's guard and prison subjects developed attitudes strikingly similar to those of actual prisoners and guards, and the patient-subjects at Elgin exhibited behavior and demonstrated attitudes which were indistinguishable at times from those of actual mental patients. The staff subjects demonstrated the usual variability in relating to patients which is found normally in the actual hospital situation.

It is very tempting to speculate that many of the characteristic behaviors of hospital patients which are so often charged to their alleged mental condition may be actually behaviors and mental states engendered by the ward millieu itself. The ward milieu, of course, includes the staff's attitudes and their methods of relating to hospitalized mental patients. The general direction of the data is consistent with the notion that confinement in a mental institution in itself may increase the psychopathology and the deterioration of the behavior of an already disturbed individual. Patients are responsive to the influence in their surroundings and exceedingly vulnerable with respect to the way staff relates to them.

The consequences of assuming certain roles are not really obvious since there are so many confounding variables. Among these confounding variables in the hospital setting, for example, are the willingness of the staff person to be helpful, the personality of the staff person, the specific type of mental illness of the patient, etc. The milieu also includes the power structure, and the power structure exerts a compelling influence over staff-patient interactions. Furthermore, the evidence is accumulating that anyone, if given a situation that is very intense, could act in ways that he would like to disown—that is—contrary to his value system. As Professor Zimbardo has stated: "Many people, perhaps the majority, can be made to do almost anything when put into psychologically compelling situations— regardless of their morals, ethics, values, attitudes, beliefs, or personal convictions."

The conditions of the typical mental hospital ward seem to be debasing to the patient. They tend to reduce his dignity and generally to dehumanize him. It would seem in doing this to mental patients that we hardly prepare them to cope with the many problems they may encounter upon discharge from the hospital. It is not just a matter of providing individual care or a decent physical environment, although both of these may be extremely important. It is also a case of providing a situation which might maximize the patient's chances for real growth and self-determination. This means that we respect the patient's selfhood even if it means a kind of self-assertion on his part that might lead the patient to question some of the instructions given to him by the staff.

And this is where the matter turns; no one relinquishes power without a struggle. We have it; the patients do not. In order for the typical patient, who is usually extremely low in self-esteem, to move toward any kind of self-actualization, we have to be willing to help him to take away our own power over his life. The willingness to give up some of this power would facilitate relating empathetically to the patient. There would be less of a tendency on the part of the staff to put the patient into the child's role.

REFERENCES

Belknapp, I. 1956. *Human problems of a state mental hospital.* New York: McGraw-Hill.

Boring, E. G. 1950. *A history of experimental psychology.* New York: Appleton-Century-Crofts.

Caudill, W. 1958. *The psychiatric hospital as a small society.* Cambridge, Mass.: Harvard University Press.

Gibson, J. J. 1941. A critical review of the concept of set in contemporary experimental psychology. *Psychological Bulletin* **38:** 781–817.

Hutt, M. L.; Gibby, R.; Milton, O.; and Pottharst, K. 1950. The effect of varied experimental "sets" upon Rorschach test performance. *Journal of Projective Techniques* 14:181–187.

Jones, M. 1953. *The therapeutic community.* New York: Basic Books.

Jones, M. 1961. Intra space and extramural community psychiatry. *American Journal of Psychiatry* 117:784–787.

Raser, J. R. 1969. *Simulation and society.* Boston: Allyn and Bacon.

Stanton, A. H., and Schwartz, M. S. 1954. *The mental hospital.* New York: Basic Books.

Woodworth, R. S. 1948. *Experimental psychology.* New York: Henry Holt and Company.

Zeisset, R. M. 1972. Lincoln State Hospital, Lincoln, Nebraska. Personal communication.

Zimbardo, P. G. 1971. *The psychological power and pathology of imprisonment.* Stanford University.

Zimbardo, P. G. 1972. Stanford University. Personal communication.

Emotional Disorder as a Social Problem: Implications for Mental Health Programs

10

By WILLIAM RYAN

This selection is similar in some ways to selections 2 and 7. The author, William Ryan of the Department of Psychology of Boston College, argues that the disease ideology is continuing to interfere with efforts to assist the poor. By maintaining the ideology of "blaming the victim" (also the title of one of the author's books published by Pantheon), we still see the locus of problems within the individual. In selection 1, this was referred to as an in-dwelling property. Ryan also forcefully considers two other variables which are often overlooked as causative factors in behavior disorders—money and power. In the case of money, he illustrates how physical illness is often only a minor irritant to the well-to-do, but how a similar illness for a poor person, because he cannot buy treatment, may continue over a long period of time and thereby add to his troubles (recall the Gallardos, selection 1). As for power, this relates to self-esteem; it is well known that self-esteem is a vital element in mental health.

THE OVERRIDING PROBLEMS in the mental health field are manifold and well documented. The manpower shortages, the maldistribution of care, the deprivation of care suffered by the poor and the black, the fragmentation of services and lack of coordination in programming, and the continuing uncertainty as to how well, in fact, the services we provide meet the needs of those who are in distress.

The community mental health center, to the extent that it is a new kind of institution, is a social invention designed to solve

From American Journal of Orthopsychiatry, vol. 41, no. 4 (July, 1971). Copyright © 1971, the American Orthopsychiatric Association, Inc. Reproduced by permission.

This is a revised version of a paper presented at the 1970 annual meeting of the American Orthopsychiatric Association, San Francisco.

these problems, and, to a substantial and encouraging extent, it is beginning to do so. There is some reason, then, to be optimistic. But there are reasons to be pessimistic that are, at least to me, more compelling and persuasive. For every new center program that is creative and innovative, there are, I fear, a half-dozen that are being assimilated to past practices, that are in fact merely providing more of the same. For every community mental health professional who is approaching these problems in an imaginative and inventive way, there are several who are too bound by their professional identities and ideologies to do much more than spruce up and put a fresh coat of paint on their old-model methods.

In the following pages, I would like to make several points that bear on this issue. First, I would suggest that we are handicapped and blocked in dealing with the basic problems of the mental health field by *ideological* barriers, by distortions and deficiencies in our viewpoint, our way of thinking, our assumptions about the phenomena with which we are supposedly dealing. Second, I will propose that it is more fruitful and effective to think about mental health under the category of social problems than under the category of medical diseases. And, finally, I would like to summarize an ideological analysis of the problem of the mental health of the poor in some detail, as an example of how our thinking about issues is deficient and hampers us in the development of appropriate programs.

Defining a social problem is not so simple as it may seem, as John Seeley (1965) has pointed out. To ask, "What is a social problem?" may seem to be posing an ingenuous question, until one turns to confront its opposite: "What human problem is *not* a social problem?" Since any problem in which people are involved is social, why do we reserve the label for some problems and withhold it from others? The phenomena we look at are bounded by the act of definition. They become a social problem only by being so considered. In Seeley's words, "*naming* it as a problem, after naming it as a *problem*."

In addition to the issue of what is a social problem, there are additional issues of what *causes* social problems and, then, perhaps most important, what do we do about them. C. Wright Mills (1943) has analyzed the ideology of those who write about social problems and demonstrated its relationship to class interest and the preservation of the existent social order. By sifting the material in thirty-one widely used textbooks in social problems, Mills was able to demonstrate a pervasive, coherent ideology with a number of common characteristics. First, the textbooks present material about these problems in simple, descriptive terms, each problem unrelated to the others, and none related in any meaningful way to other aspects of the social environment. Second, the problems are selected and described largely in relation to predetermined norms. The norms themselves are taken as givens, and no effort is made to examine them. Nor is there any thought given to the manner in which norms might themselves contribute to the development of the problems. Within such a framework, then, deviation from norms and standards comes to be defined as failed or incomplete socialization—persons haven't learned the standards and rules or haven't learned how to keep them. A final, variant theme is that of adjustment or adaptation. Those with social problems are viewed as unable or unwilling to adjust to society's standards.

By defining social problems in this way, the social pathologists are, of course, ignoring a whole set of factors that might ordinarily be considered as relevant, such as unequal distribution of income, social stratification, political struggle, ethnic and racial group conflict, and inequality of power. This ideology concentrates almost exclusively on the failure of the deviant. To the extent that society plays any part in social problems, it is said somehow to have failed to socialize the individual, to teach him how to adjust to circumstances, which, though far from perfect, are gradually changing for the better.

This ideology, identified by Mills as the predominant tool used in *analyzing* social problems, also saturates the majority of programs that have been developed to *solve* social problems in America. These programs are based on the assumption that *individuals* "have" social problems as a result of some kind of unusual circumstances—accident, illness, personal defect or handicap, character flaw, or maladjustment—that exclude them from the ordinary mechanisms for maintaining and advancing themselves.

Health care in America, for example, has been predominantly a matter of particular remedial attention provided individually to the more or less random group of persons who have become ill, whose bodily functioning has become deviant and abnormal. In the field of mental health, the same approach has been, and continues to be, dominant. The social problem of mental disease has been viewed as a collection of individual cases of deviance, persons who—through unusual hereditary taint or exceptional distortion of character—have become unfitted for the normal activities of ordinary life.

This has been the dominant style in American social welfare and health activities, then: to treat what we call social problems, such as poverty, disease, and mental illness, in terms of the individual deviance of the special, unusual groups of persons who had those problems. There has also been a competing style, however, much less common, not at all congruent with the prevalent ideology, subordinate, but continually developing parallel to the dominant style. Adherents of this approach tended to search for causes in the community and the environment, rather than individual defect, to emphasize predictability and usualness rather than random deviance, to think about preventing rather than merely repairing or treating, to see social problems, in a word, as social.

In the field of disease, we have the public health approach, whose practitioners sought the cause of disease in environmental factors such as the water supply, the sewage system, and the quality of housing conditions. In the field of income maintenance, this secondary style of solving social problems focused on poverty as a predictable event, on the regularities of income deficiency, and on the development of usual, generalized programs affecting total groups.

These two approaches to the solution of social problems have existed side by side, the former always dominant but the latter gradually expanding, slowly becoming more and more prevalent.

Elsewhere (Ryan, 1969a, 1969b, 1971) I have proposed the dimension of *exceptionalism-universalism* as the ideological underpinning for these two contrasting approaches to the analysis and solution of social problems. The *exceptionalist* viewpoint is reflected in arrangements that are private, voluntary, remedial, special, local, and exclusive. Such arrangements imply that problems occur to specially defined categories of persons in an unpredictable manner. The problems are unusual, even unique; they are exceptions to the rule; they occur as a result of individual defect, accident, or unfortunate circumstance; and they must be remedied by means that are particular and, as it were, tailored to the individual case.

The universalistic viewpoint, on the other hand, is reflected in arrangements that are public, legislated, promotive or preventive, general, national, and inclusive. Inherent in such a viewpoint is the idea that social problems are a function of the social arrangements of the community or the society and that, since these social arrangements are quite imperfect and inequitable, such problems are both predictable and, more important, preventable through public action. They are not unique to the individual, and their encompassing of individual persons does not imply that those persons are themselves defective or abnormal.

Generally speaking, mental health services have, in the past, been organized and arranged in an exceptionalistic fashion. This would be perfectly appropriate if we considered mental illness an illness—a genuine disease—and decided that it was a disease of mysterious and unpredictable proportions. Given the tremendous quantities of evidence amassed in recent years that suggest the conclusion that emotional disorder is, rather, a social problem, with a relatively predictable pattern of incidence, one would argue that mental health services should be organized in a universalistic fashion. What would that mean?

First, it would mean less and less reliance on the private, voluntary sector and much heavier emphasis on public programs based on clear legislative sanctions. Second, it would require an expansion of scope so that mental health programs would concern themselves not merely with remedial treatment activities directed toward a special, unusual, deviant population, but rather with preventive efforts directed toward an entire population. It would also mean that the group taking responsibility for planning and decision-making with respect to the organization of services would be expanded in a parallel fashion so that the community as a whole, through some type of representative mechanism, would have the responsibility and the power to decide the form and structure and priorities of mental health programs.

We find the greatest degree of readiness to view emotional disorder as a social problem among those who have concerned themselves with the mental health of the poor.

In observing the growing interest in the relationship between poverty and mental health, my own mood has ranged from exhilarated gratification through puzzlement to a growing sense of concern and dismay. I see signs that the mental health approach to the problems of the poor is being gradually fitted into the same mold that contains and cripples most other approaches to the poor. The central event in this constraining and crippling process is conceptual or, rather, ideological, what I have called elsewhere "blaming the victim" (Ryan, 1971).

Briefly, "blaming the victim" is an intellectual process whereby a social problem is analyzed in such a way that the causation is found to be in the qualities and characteristics of the victim rather than in any deficiencies or structural defects in his environment. In addition, it is usually found that these characteristics are not inherent or genetic but are, rather, socially determined. They are stigmas of social origin and are therefore no fault of the victim himself. He is to be pitied, not censured, but nevertheless his problems are to be defined as rooted basically in his own characteristics. Some of the common stigmas of social origin that are used to blame the victim are the concept of cultural deprivation as an explanation for the failures of ghetto schools to educate poor and black children and the concept of the crumbling Negro family as a basic explanation of the persistence of inequality between blacks and whites in America today. "Blaming the victim" is differentiated from old-fashioned conservative ideological formulations, such as social Darwinism, racial inferiority, and quasi-Calvinist notions of the prospering elect. It is a liberal ideology.

The theoretical—or, more properly, ideological—formulations that are beginning to attain dominance in considerations of the mental health of the poor show unmistakable family resemblances to the culture of poverty cult and the other victim-blaming ideologies.

An important element in this ideology is the assumption that it is the early experiences of the poor, the failures of mothering, the inconsistent patterns of discipline, the exposure to deviant values and behavior patterns that account for their apparent excessive vulnerability to emotional disorder.

These assumptions, this ideology, boil down to a process of relating mental disorder to social class by relating psychosexual development to presumed cultural features of a subgroup of the population. It derives from the extreme and continuing influence of W. Lloyd Warner in American thinking about social class, in which social class is defined largely in terms of prestige, life-style, social honor.

There are other views about social stratification that have been far less influential but that might in the long run prove more fruitful for understanding the complexities of relationship between class and distress. Max Weber's conception of stratification, for example, which is followed rather closely by C. Wright Mills and others, maintains that there is not one but three dimensions of social ordering. These are *class,* the extent to which one controls property and financial resources and maintains a favorable position in the marketplace; *status,* the manner in which one consumes resources and the extent to which one is accorded social honor (this is the predominant element in Warner's view of social class); and *power,* the extent to which one (or, more commonly, a group of persons, a "party") is able to control and influence the community's decisions.

Now, if one limits one's thinking about relationships between social stratification and emotional disorder to *status* questions (largely disregarding *class* and *power* issues), one starts seeking explanations in terms of status elements, such as child-rearing practices, values, life-style, etc. One is inclined to conclude that the poor are more subject to emotional disorder than the affluent because their patterns of parenting are deficient; their values are different; their time orientation is different, and they cannot defer need-gratification; their life-styles emphasize violence and sexual promiscuity; they have ego deficiencies as a result of their childhood experiences in the culture of poverty, etc.

One hears and sees these kinds of formulations more and more frequently in mental health settings. I fear that an ideology is developing in which the mental health problems of the poor (which one might reasonably have expected would be related to poverty) are being analyzed through status-oriented formulations of class differences, with the result that these problems are being conceptually transformed into one more category of intrapsychic disorder. The consequences of such transformations are predictable. The evidence that appears to relate disorder to environmental circumstances is being rapidly assimilated to preexisting patterns of intrapsychic theorizing, and the status quo is being maintained—which, after all, is the purpose of ideology.

When one focuses on status and life-style as explanatory variables, one omits at the same time the other elements that determine social stratification—power and money. Lack of money as a cause of emotional disorder can be conceptualized through the mediating concept of stress. Stresses relating to lack of money—poor and crowded housing, nutritional deficiencies, medical neglect, unemployment, etc.—have been found as correlates of disorder rather regularly. Moreover, there is evidence that certain kinds of stressful events, such as illness, which can be merely inconvenient for the well-to-do, are often disastrous for the poor. Some of Dohrenwend's (1967) recent work contains some intriguing ideas on the possible relationship between poverty, stress, and emotional disorder. He sets forth the hypothesis that reaction to stress is ordinarily cyclical and time-limited and that most emotional symptomatology evidenced in such reactions is temporary. A prevalence study at a given point in time, then, would tend to include substantial numbers of such temporary stress reactions. If one assumes that stresses in the lives of the poor are both more prevalent and more severe than those in the lives of the more prosperous, one would expect that, at a given point in time, the poor as a group would exhibit more stress reactions and would therefore demonstrate a higher prevalence of emotional disorder. This is one example of the way in which the class-oriented, which is to say the money-oriented, method of dealing with stratification can be introduced into the process of theorizing about the relationship between poverty and mental health.

The third leg of the stratification stool—power—can be dealt with principally through the mediating concept of self-esteem. There is an overwhelming array of theoretical and empirical literature suggesting that self-esteem is a vital element in mental health and, further, that self-esteem is based on a sense of competence, an ability to influence one's environment, a sense of mastery and control over events and circumstances that affect one's life. These are psychological terms that are readily translatable into the sociological concept of power as used by Weber. To the extent that a person is powerful, then, he is more likely to be what we call mentally healthy; to the extent that he is powerless, he is likely to be lacking in this characteristic.

The functional relationship between the exercise of power, feelings of self-esteem, and mental health has been empirically observed in a number of settings—civil rights demonstrations, block organization projects, and even, according to some, in ghetto disorders.

There are, then, relationships to be found between mental health phenomena and issues of money and power that are direct, more direct than the secondary kinds of relationships hypothesized between mental health and social status and life-style. The major difference, however, is in program implications. If one makes the assumption that the relevant variable is status, one tends to work on changing the characteristics of the individual—his life-style, his values, his child-rearing practices, or the effects of the child-rearing practices of his parents. If, on the other hand, one makes the assumption that the relevant variables are money and power, one tends to work toward changing the environment, toward developing programs of social change rather than individual change.

I am dismayed and concerned that we in the mental health field are moving more and more toward a narrow view of status issues, which will permit us to conduct business as usual—focusing on changing the person—and avoid the broader view of class and power issues that would oblige us to alter our methods and start putting our resources into the business of social change.

If we did make such a shift, such a change in our ideology and our assumptions about what is wrong, what alterations would there be in our style of doing business? How might we translate the problems we confront into different kinds of needs? And what kinds of services would we develop to meet those needs?

We would, first of all, turn our attention to the patterns of social inequity and injustice that play such a major role in producing the casualties and victims who come to us for attention. Just as, in years gone by, the pioneers of public health spoke up and cried out for change in housing and sanitation and factory conditions, so would we be required to cry out about our society's basic inequalities in the distribution of money and power. In the councils of professional activity, in the councils of social welfare, and in the councils of government, ours would be a voice agitating for equality as a fundamental prerequisite for mental health.

Second, as we encounter and evaluate—or, as we used to say in the good old days, "diagnose"—our clients, we would necessarily find ourselves including in our thoughts and our repertoire of labels and categories, redevelopment as well as repression, superhighways as well as superegos, police training as well as toilet training, discrimination as well as displacement, and racism as well as autism.

It would also follow that in our interactions with clients drawn from low-income and black neighborhoods, our services would have to be at least partially geared toward the fundamental issues of money and power. We would have to act to increase our clients' resources—through training and referral services to help them get a job, or a better job, through encouragement of the development of unions in unorganized settings to help them get more money, through advocating more public funds for such matters as income maintenance and public assistance, public housing, subsidized medical care, better education, increased day care facilities, etc.

And we would have to act to increase our client's power in the community—primarily through community organization efforts in the low-income neighborhoods of our specific catchment areas, but also through our own political, lobbying, and public educational activities.

An indispensable element in, and touchstone of, our commitment to increase the power of our constituency is the way we deal with the issue of decision-making in our own centers. Power-sharing—like charity—begins at home, which means citizen involvement and participation in shaping the programs and priorities of the mental health center. In a word, community control. If powerlessness gives rise to pathology, and the only cure for powerlessness is power, and we have the occasion to relinquish power to the citizens we profess to serve, the consequences are obvious. We must put our money where our mouth is.

An unexpected by-product of such a shift in orientation, that is, a reconceptualization of the great majority of mental health problems as *social* problems, flowing from structural and environmental distortions on the axis of money and the axis of power, would be the possibility of some easing of the acute shortage of manpower in the psychiatric professions. On the one hand, the mental health center would become one agency among several in an alliance of equals that could attack these problems jointly. (I say alliance of equals deliberately, to distinguish this hypothetical situation from the present case in which a psychiatric facility is seen as a dominant agency collaborating condescendingly with a group of ancillary or paramedical agencies.) And the appropriate manpower to engage in such a preventive, social, universalistic program would not have to include any substantial number of trained mental health professionals.

The latter, the psychiatrists and clinical psychologists and nurses and social workers, could then turn their attention more vigorously to the minority of mental health problems that may be considered more accurately as *medical* or *quasi-medical* in nature—the psychosomatic disorders, the metabolic disorders, the major and minor brain dysfunctions, and the most acute and refractory of the disorders that are characterized by disorientation or thought and mood disruption for which there is some evidence for genetic or other physical causation.

In summary, I am suggesting that the mental health center can fulfill its promise only if those of us in the field consciously undertake to revamp and expand our ideological framework to include the disorder of the community as well as the dysfunction of the individual. We must learn that the emotionally disturbed individual is not an unusual, abnormal, unexpectable "case," but is rather a usual, highly predictable index of the distortion and injustice that pervades our society. Only after such ideological transformation can the community mental health center become what it must become—a committed instrument for social change and social justice.

REFERENCES

Dohrenwend, B. 1967. Social status, stress, and psychological symptoms. *American Journal of Public Health* 57(4):625–632.

Mills, C. W. 1943. The professional ideology of social pathologists. *American Journal of Sociology* 49(2):165–180.

Ryan, W. 1969a. Community care in historical perspective: Implications for mental health services and professionals. *Canada's Mental Health*, supplement no. 60, March-April.

Ryan, W. 1969b. *Distress in the city*. Cleveland: Case Western Reserve Press.

Ryan, W. 1971. *Blaming the victim*. New York: Pantheon.

Seeley, J. 1965. The problem of social problems. *Indian Sociological Bulletin* 2 (3). Also in Seeley, J. 1967. *The Americanization of the unconscious*, pp. 142–148. New York: Science House.

Weber, M. Class, status, and party. In *Essays in sociology*, ed. M. Weber. Translated by H. Gerth and C. W. Mills.

Schizophrenic Patients in the Psychiatric Interview: An Experimental Study of Their Effectiveness at Manipulation

11

By BENJAMIN M. BRAGINSKY
and DOROTHEA D. BRAGINSKY

The "sickness" notion has been partially responsible for schizophrenic (one of the *major* mental illnesses) patients being viewed as helpless, inert, and ineffective people who are at the complete mercy of their environment. These views, in turn, may have accounted to some degree for their legal rights being ignored, as indicated in selections 3 and 4. Several recent studies have indicated that those people labeled "schizophrenic" are not passive pawns. The present study, as one example, suggests that these people do indeed exert control over their surroundings. Moreover, it raises questions about the validity of the "psychiatric interview," as did selection 3. The ideas of these authors about the inadequacies of the "medical model" are elaborated in their book *Methods of Madness*, published by Holt, Rinehart, and Winston.

The senior author is now at Yale University, while the junior author is at Fairfield University.

THE PRESENT INVESTIGATION is concerned with the manipulative behavior of hospitalized schizophrenics in evaluative interview situations. More specifically, the study attempts to answer the question: Can schizophrenic patients effectively control the impressions (impression management, Goffman, 1959) they make on the professional hospital staff?

From *Journal of Consulting Psychology*, vol. 31 (1967), no. 6, pp. 543–547. Reprinted by permission of the authors and the American Psychological Association.

The authors would like to express their appreciation to Doris Seiler and Dennis Ridley for assisting with the data collection.

Typically, the mental patient has been viewed as an extremely ineffectual and helpless individual (e.g., Arieti, 1959; Becker, 1964; Bellak, 1958; Joint Commission on Mental Illness and Health, 1961; Redlich and Freedman, 1966; Schooler and Parkel, 1966; Searles, 1965). For example, Redlich and Freedman (1966) described the mental patient and his pathological status in the following manner: "There is a concomitant loss of focus and coherence and a profound shift in the meaning and value of social relationships and goal-directed behavior. This is evident in the inability realistically to implement future goals and present satisfactions; they are achieved magically or through fantasy and delusion . . . [p. 463]." Schooler and Parkel (1966) similarly underline the mental patients' ineffectual status in this description: "The chronic schizophrenic is not Seneca's 'reasoning animal,' or Spinoza's 'social animal,' or even a reasonably efficient version of Cassirer's 'symbol-using animal.' . . . Since he violates so many functional definitions of man, there is heuristic value in studying him with an approach like that which would be used to study an alien creature [p. 67]."

Thus, the most commonly held assumptions concerning the nature of the schizophrenic patient stress their ineffectuality and impotency. In this context one would expect schizophrenics to perform less than adequately in interpersonal situations, to be unable to initiate manipulative tactics, and, certainly, to be incapable of successful manipulation of other people.[1]

In contrast to the above view of the schizophrenic, a less popular orientation has been expressed by Artiss (1959), Braginsky, Grosse, and Ring (1966), Goffman (1961), Levinson and Gallagher (1964), Rakusin and Fierman (1963), Szasz (1961, 1965), and Towbin (1966). Here schizophrenics are portrayed in terms usually reserved for neurotics and normal persons. Simply, the above authors subscribe to the beliefs that: (a) the typical schizophrenic patient, as compared to normals, is not deficient, defective, or dissimilar in intrapsychic functioning; (b) the typical schizophrenic patient is not a victim of his illness; that is, it is assumed that he is not helpless and unable to control his

---

[1] This statement is explicitly derived from formal theories of schizophrenia and not from clinical observations. It is obvious to some observers, however, that schizophrenics do attempt to manipulate others. The discrepancy between these observations and traditional theoretical assumptions about the nature of schizophrenics is rarely, if ever, reconciled.

behavior or significantly determine life outcomes; (c) the differences that some schizophrenic patients manifest (as compared to normals) are assumed to be more accurately understood in terms of differences in belief systems, goals, hierarchy of needs, and interpersonal strategies, rather than in terms of illness, helplessness, and deficient intrapsychic functioning. This orientation leads to the expectation that schizophrenic patients do try to achieve particular goals and, in the process, effectively manipulate other people.

There is some evidence in support of this viewpoint (e.g., Artiss, 1959; Braginsky, Holzberg, Finison, and Ring, 1967; Levinson and Gallagher, 1964). Furthermore, a recent study (Braginsky et al., 1966) demonstrated that schizophrenic patients responded, on a paper-and-pencil "mental status" test, in a manner that would protect their self-interests. Those who wanted to remain in the hospital (chronic patients) presented themselves as "sick," whereas those who desired to be discharged (first admissions) presented themselves as "healthy." That is, they effectively controlled the impressions they wished to make on others. Their manipulative performance, however, was mediated by an impersonal test.

Therefore, the following question is asked: Can schizophrenics engage in similar manipulative behaviors in a "face-to-face" interview with a psychologist? That is, will chronic schizophrenics who desire to remain in the hospital and live on open wards present themselves in an interview situation when they perceive that their open-ward status is being questioned as (a) "healthy" and, therefore, eligible for open-ward living, and in another interview situation when their residential status is being questioned as (b) "sick" and, therefore, ineligible for discharge? If so, are their performances convincing to a professional audience (i.e., psychiatrists)?

METHOD

A sample of 30 long-term (more than two continuous years of hospitalization) male schizophrenics living on open wards was randomly selected from ward rosters. Two days prior to the experiment the patients were told that they were scheduled for an interview with a staff psychologist. Although each patient was to be interviewed individually, all 30 were brought simultaneously to a waiting room. Each patient interviewed was not allowed to return to this room, to insure that patients who had participated would not communicate with those who had not.

Each patient was escorted to the interview room by an assistant, who casually informed the patient in a tone of confidentiality about the purpose of the interview (preinterview induction). Patients were randomly assigned by the assistant to one of three induction conditions (10 to each condition). The interviewer was unaware of the induction to which the patients were assigned, thereby eliminating interviewer bias.

INDUCTION CONDITIONS

Discharge induction. Patients were told: "I think the person you are going to see is interested in examining patients to see whether they might be ready for discharge."

Open-ward induction.[2] Patients were told: "I think that the person you are going to see is interested in examining patients to see whether they should be on open or closed wards."

Mental status induction.[3] Patients were told: "I think the person you are going to see is interested in how you are feeling and getting along in the hospital."

After greeting each patient the interviewer asked: "How are you feeling?" Patients who responded only with physical descriptions were also asked: "How do you feel mentally?" whereas those who only gave descriptions of their mental state were asked: "How are you feeling physically?" The patients' responses were tape-recorded. The interview was terminated after two minutes,[4] whereupon the purpose of the experiment was disclosed.

---

[2] It may be suggested that the open-ward induction was meaningless, since no patient enjoying open-ward status would believe that he could be put on a closed ward on the basis of an interview. At the time this experiment was being conducted, however, this hospital was in the process of reorganization, and open and closed ward status was a salient and relevant issue.
[3] Mental status evaluation interviews are typically conducted yearly. Thus, patients who have been in the hospital for more than a year expect to be interviewed for the purposes of determining their residency status.
[4] Although, admittedly, psychiatrists would never base decisions concerning mental status and discharge on a two-minute interview, it was adequate for the purposes of this study (namely, to determine if mental patients effectively engage in impression management). The two-minute response to the single question provided sufficient information for psychiatrists to form reliable impressions of the patients. Interestingly, the typical mental status interview conducted by these psychiatrists is rarely longer than 30 minutes.

Three staff psychiatrists from the same hospital separately rated each of the 30 tape-recorded interviews during two 40-minute sessions. The psychiatrists had no knowledge of the experiment, and they were unfamiliar with the patients; they were told by the experimenter that these were mental patients residing in the hospital and that as a group they represented a wide range of diagnostic categories.

The psychiatrists rated the patients on the following dimensions: (a) the patient's degree of psychopathology, using a five-point scale ranging from "not at all ill" to "extremely ill"; (b) the amount of hospital control a patient needed, ranging on an eight-point scale from complete freedom ("discharge") to maximum control ("closed ward, continual observation"); and (c) the structural or qualitative aspects of the patient's speech, such as pressure of speech, affect, volume, etc. The score for each patient's speech characteristic was based on the sum of the psychiatrist's rating of 14 Lorr scale items (Lorr, 1953). Each item was rated on an eight-point scale ranging from not at all atypical to extremely atypical verbal behavior.

PREDICTIONS

If long-term patients are both motivated to live on open wards and to remain in the hospital and if, in addition, they effectively engage in impression management in order to realize these desires, then the following would be expected:

1. Psychiatrists will rate patients in the discharge and the mental status conditions as being similar with respect to psychopathology and need for hospital control. Mental status interviews are generally used by the hospital to evaluate patients for discharge; therefore, the mental status and discharge conditions offer the same potential consequences for patients. Thus, patients in both conditions will give the impression of being "sick" and in need of hospital control in order to decrease the probability of discharge. The purpose of including the discharge induction was to present the consequences of the interview as explicitly as in the open-ward induction.

2. Psychiatrists will rate the patients in the open-ward condition significantly less mentally ill and less in need of hospital control than patients in the discharge and mental status conditions. That is, patients in the open-ward condition will

give the impression of being "healthy" in order to maximize their chances of remaining on an open ward.

SUBJECTS

The mean age of the patients was 47.4 years (SD = 8.36). The mean educational level of the group was 8.05 years of schooling (SD = 3.44). The median length of hospitalization was 10 years. In terms of diagnostic categories, 43 percent of the sample was diagnosed as chronic undifferentiated schizophrenic, 37 percent as paranoid schizophrenic, 10 percent as catatonic, and the remaining 10 percent as simple schizophrenic. There were no differences between the three experimental groups on any of the above variables.

RESULTS AND DISCUSSION

The reliability coefficients of the three psychiatrists' combined ratings of the patient interviews were as follows: (a) ratings of psychopathology—r = .89, $p < .01$; (b) need for hospital control—r = .74, $p < .01$; (c) normality of speech characteristics —r = .65, $p < .01$. Thus, it was concluded that there was significant agreement between the three psychiatrists.

The means of the psychopathology ratings by experimental condition are presented in Table 1. The ratings ranged 1–5. The analysis of variance of the data yielded a significant condition effect (F = 9.38, $p < .01$). The difference between the open-ward and discharge conditions was statistically significant ($p < .01$; Tukey multiple-range test). In addition, the difference between the open-ward and the mental status condition was significant ($p < .01$). As predicted, there was no significant difference between the discharge and mental status conditions.

TABLE 1 Mean Psychopathology and Need-for-Hospital-Control Ratings by Experimental Condition

Rating	Open ward		Mental status		Discharge	
	M	SD	M	SD	M	SD
Psychopathology	2.63	.58	3.66	.65	3.70	.67
Need for hospital control	2.83	1.15	4.10	1.31	4.20	1.42

The means of the ratings of need for hospital control are presented in Table 1. These ratings ranged 1–8. The analysis of these data indicated a significant difference between the means ($F = 3.85$, $p < .05$). Again, significant differences (beyond the .05 level) were obtained between the open-ward and the discharge conditions, as well as between the open-ward and mental status conditions. No difference was found between the discharge and mental status conditions.

On the basis of these analyses it is clear that patients in the open-ward condition appear significantly less mentally ill and in less need of hospital control than patients in either the discharge or mental status conditions. Obviously the patients in these conditions convey different impressions in the interview situation. In order to ascertain the manner by which the patients conveyed these different impressions, the following three manipulative tactics were examined: (a) number of positive statements patients made about themselves, (b) number of negative statements made about themselves (these include both physical and mental referents), and (c) normality of speech characteristics (i.e., how "sick" they sounded, independent of the content of speech). The first two indexes were obtained by counting the number of positive or negative self-referent statements a patient made during the interview. These counts were done by three judges independently, and the reliability coefficient was .95. The third index was based on the psychiatrists' ratings on 14 Lorr scale items of the speech characteristics of patients. A score was obtained for each patient by summing the ratings for the 14 scales.

Ratings of psychopathology and need for hospital control were, in part, determined by the frequency of positive and negative self-referent statements. The greater the frequency of positive statements made by a patient, the less ill he was perceived ($r = -.58$, $p < .01$) and the less in need of hospital control ($r = -.41$, $p < .05$). Conversely, the greater the frequency of negative statements, the more ill a patient was perceived ($r = .53$, $p < .01$) and the more in need of hospital control ($r = .37$, $p < .05$). It is noteworthy that patients were consistent in their performances; that is, those who tended to say positive things about themselves tended not to say negative things ($r = -.55$, $p < .01$).

When self-referent statements were compared by condition, it was found that patients in the open-ward condition presented

Benjamin M. Braginsky and Dorothea D. Braginsky

themselves in a significantly more positive fashion than patients in the discharge and mental status conditions. Only two patients in the open-ward condition reported having physical or mental problems, whereas 13 patients in the mental status and discharge conditions presented such complaints ($\chi^2 = 5.40$, $p < .05$).

The frequency of positive and negative self-referent statements, however, cannot account for important qualitative components of the impressions the patients attempted to convey. For example, a patient may give only one complaint, but it may be serious (e.g., he reports hallucinations), whereas another patient may state five complaints, all of which are relatively benign. In order to examine the severity of symptoms or complaints reported by patients, the number of "psychotic" complaints, namely, reports of hallucinations or bizarre delusions, was tallied. None of the patients in the open-ward condition made reference to having had hallucinations or delusions, while nine patients in the discharge and mental status conditions spontaneously made such reference ($\chi^2 = 4.46$, $p < .05$).

In comparing the structural or qualitative aspects of patient speech no significant differences were obtained between experimental conditions. Patients "sounded" about the same in all three conditions. The majority of patients (80 percent) were rated as having relatively normal speech characteristics. Although there were no differences by condition, there was a significant inverse relationship ($r = -.35$, $p < .05$) between quality of speech and the number of positive statements made. That is, patients were consistent to the extent that those who sounded ill tended not to make positive self-referent statements.

In summary then, the hypotheses were confirmed. It is clear that patients responded to the inductions in a manner which maximized the chances of fulfilling their needs and goals. When their self-interests were at stake, patients could present themselves in a face-to-face interaction as either "sick" or "healthy," whichever was more appropriate to the situation. In the context of this experiment "sick" impressions were conveyed when the patients were faced with the possibility of discharge. On the other hand, impressions of "health" were conveyed when the patients' open-ward status was questioned. Moreover, the impressions they conveyed were convincing to an audience of experienced psychiatrists.

One may argue, however, that the differences between the groups were a function of differential anxiety generated by the inductions rather than a function of the patients' needs, goals, and manipulative strategies. More specifically, the discharge and the mental status conditions would generate more anxiety and, therefore, more pathological behavior than the open-ward condition. As a result, the psychiatrist rated the patients in the discharge and mental status conditions as "sicker" than patients in the open-ward condition. According to this argument, then, the patients who were rated as sick were, in fact, more disturbed, and those rated healthy were, in fact, less disturbed.

No differences, however, were found between conditions in terms of the amount of disturbed behavior during the interview. As was previously mentioned, the psychiatrists did not perceive any differences by condition in atypicality of verbal behavior. On the contrary, the patients were judged as sounding relatively normal. Thus, the psychiatrists' judgments of psychopathology were based primarily on the symptoms patients reported rather than on symptoms manifested. Patients did not behave in a disturbed manner; rather, they told the interviewer how disturbed they were.

The traditional set of assumptions concerning schizophrenics, which stresses their irrationality and interpersonal ineffectuality, would not only preclude the predictions made in this study, but would fail to explain parsimoniously the present observations. It is quite plausible and simple to view these findings in terms of the assumptions held about people in general; that is, schizophrenics, like normal persons, are goal-oriented and are able to control the outcomes of their social encounters in a manner which satisfies their goals.

REFERENCES

Arieti, S. 1959. *American handbook of psychiatry.* New York: Basic Books.

Artiss, K. L. 1959. *The symptom as communication in schizophrenia.* New York: Grune and Stratton.

Becker, E. 1964. *The revolution in psychiatry.* London: Collier-Macmillan.

Bellak, C. 1958. *Schizophrenia: A review of the syndrome.* New York: Logos Press.

Braginsky, B.; Grosse, M.; and Ring, K. 1966. Controlling outcomes through impression-management: An experimental study of the manipulative tactics of mental patients. *Journal of Consulting Psychology* 30:295–300.

Braginsky, B.; Holzberg, J.; Finison, L.; and Ring, K. 1967. Correlates of the mental patient's acquisition of hospital information. *Journal of Personality* 35:323–342.

Goffman, E. 1959. *The presentation of self in everyday life.* New York: Doubleday.

Goffman, E. 1961. *Asylums.* New York: Doubleday.

Joint Commission on Mental Illness and Health. 1961. *Action for mental health.* New York: Basic Books.

Levinson, D. S., and Gallagher, E. B. 1964. *Patienthood in the mental hospital.* Boston: Houghton Mifflin.

Lorr, M. 1953. Multidimensional scale for rating psychiatric patients. *Veterans Administration Technical Bulletin* 51:119–127.

Rakusin, J. M., and Fierman, L. B. 1963. Five assumptions for treating chronic psychotics. *Mental Hospitals* 14:140–148.

Redlich, F. C., and Freedman, D. X. 1966. *The theory and practice of psychiatry.* New York: Basic Books.

Schooler, C., and Parkel, D. 1966. The overt behavior of chronic schizophrenics and its relationship to their internal state and personal history. *Psychiatry* 29:67–77.

Searles, H. F. 1965. *Collected papers on schizophrenia and related subjects.* New York: International Universities Press.

Szasz, T. S. 1961. *The myth of mental illness.* New York: Hoeber-Harper.

Szasz, T. S. 1965. *Psychiatric justice.* New York: Macmillan.

Towbin, A. P. 1966. Understanding the mentally deranged. *Journal of Existentialism* 7:63–83.

Drug Abuse: The Elevator That Went to Hell

12

By ROGER WILCOX

This selection, which was prepared especially for the present volume, was designed deliberately as a mosaic "think" piece about a national, and therefore social, and yet at the same time an individual problem. The author, Dr. Roger Wilcox of Ohio University (Zanesville Campus), in providing a set of fragments—a glimpse of drug abuse—does not draw any distinct lines between "drug abuse" and "drug use." Rather, he sees both activities as a reflection of the "medical model" and of other forces as well. A wealth of information is provided in his exhibits.

THE CYNICAL HALF of this essay's title was lifted from E. B. White's delightful short story concerning the plight of a man and his mistress who board their penthouse elevator to go to dinner only to step off in hell, because it fairly characterizes my own attempt to understand drug abuse. I began fully expecting to arrive at one set of conclusions only to arrive at a far more terrifying sort of understanding after considering the function that drugs may serve for the culture rather than whatever function they may serve for any particular user-abuser. This is not to demean the stringent plight of the heavy user, for whom psychology expresses a justified, sympathetic concern, but rather to suggest that the urgent meaning of drug abuse may lie elsewhere than in the understanding or curing of individuals.

DRUG ABUSE AS A CONSEQUENCE

In order to link our understanding of the personal and social systems that function to propagate and maintain drug abuse to

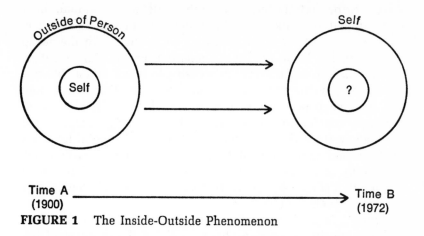

The Inside-Outside Phenomenon

Outside of Person

Self

Self

?

Time A (1900) ⟶ Time B (1972)

FIGURE 1　The Inside-Outside Phenomenon

the area of behavior disorders, perhaps it would help to consider certain insights from personality theory. Also, since the "medical model" is of major concern in this volume, an allied issue is to consider the role that it may play in drug abuse.

Nearly all theories of personality give central importance to the notion of self or personhood. Pervin (1970) sees two basic approaches to self, *self-as-object*, where the self is defined as the person's attitudes and feelings toward himself, and *self-as-process*, where self is defined as a group of psychological processes that govern one's behavior. Theorists such as Carl Rogers consider the self to be a largely innate capacity that may or may not be actualized, while others, such as M. M. Helper, see the self as something essentially acquired or learned in social interaction. Basically this relates to the type and level of awareness that one has of himself, the way he or she feels about his or her self—essentially who we are. A related question of considerable significance concerns the locus of self. For theorists such as Abraham Maslow, the self is best construed as being within an internal, psychological space and only reflected in observable behavior and social interaction. On the other hand, Norman O. Brown suggests that selfhood lies not within the person but outside in the quality and nature of one's interactions with other human beings. A basic model capable of depicting the locus of self has been proposed by Wilcox (1971) and is shown as Figure 1. From Figure 1 you can see that the self could be located completely within psychological space, or, for that matter, at the outside of the individual. Bear in mind that we talk here about the way in which a person tends to visualize or conceptualize "where he is" in the sense of locating his basic self as an existing, psychological entity. In this sense, it is somewhat depressing to recall that a Harvard University psychiatrist now specializes in treating young men who have such personal and even sexual "relationships" with their motorcycles that they are unable to study, sleep, or eat while away from their "thing." At some fundamental level we must assume that many of them do not in fact feel "whole" when they are separated from their machines, and we must imagine that some segment or feature of their psychological self lies within their "cycles."

Figure 1 is also instructive in considering cross-cultural as well as historical trends in conceptualizing the problem of the locus of self. With respect to America, being steeped as we have been in twentieth-century materialism and the continuing technological revolution, it is tempting to say that as a function of time since the nineteenth century the culturally accepted locus of self has migrated from somewhere within people to the outside boundary of their bodies—namely their skin and clothing. This suggests that as a function of historical trends the average person may now literally equate what he sees in the mirror with what he considers to be his basic personhood and may relate to others in much the same way. If this be so, then we may have available a partial answer to the question: Is there a relationship between our historical development as a culture and not only the viability of the medical model within psychology but also the considerable extent to which America currently exhibits social, legal, and illegal drug abuse? The answer is "yes" because it happened that the medical model provided to our various mass media the compelling yet deadly lesson that underlying psychological states and belief systems were comparable to physical states and therefore amenable to manipulation via outside agents. Here, of course, we refer to the whole galaxy of medicines, preparations, cosmetics, drugs, etc., since their advertising develops the belief that one's basic psychology can be changed through the incorporation of simple, physical, outside agents such as deodorants, larger automobiles, body padding, breath sweeteners, and so forth. Though this may seem a hackneyed observation, its implications are not when you consider that it is precisely this point of view that undergirds the basic rationale for both legal and illegal drug abuse. Both media conditioning and drug abuse are complex but straightforward extrapolations of the medical model in that they accept the basic postulate of a real, palpable, manipulable entity within people. Recalling that between 1 and 2 million dollars a day are spent by the tobacco and alcoholic beverage industries to foster the idea that such drugs can make a significant change in the individual psychology of the user, it would be foolish to imagine that such an advertising campaign has no effect upon people, and is, in fact, exemplary of the basic social learning so necessary as a support for drug abuse. It may be interesting to note that many Americans characterize marijuana, hashish, and LSD as "mind-expanding" or "consciousness raising." While Malayans or Brazilians may naïvely be using drugs as escape mechanisms, many of our young Americans caricature them as products which may save our civilization via purported increased levels of sensitivity and awareness. It is not critical to this argument whether or not they are right or wrong so much as we should be aware that they are using the same basic logic inherent in deodorant and brassiere advertisements—take "this" and you will experience "this change." Given this, the rest follows; careful medical diagnosis will provide types of subjects or patients, each of whom will be best served by a particular therapeutic pharmaceutical program. Furthermore, the link between the growth of materialism as a philosophy and the medical model as a therapeutic program is reflected in the steady progression of the locus of self toward the observable, outside layer of the person. It is this accepted, marketed, operational view of mankind that provides the necessary supports for our existing abundance of both legal and illegal drug abuse.

"THERE IS NO DRUG PROBLEM IN THIS COUNTRY!"

Available statistics suggest that the following numbers of Americans participate in either social, legal, or illegal drug abuse and are summarized in Table 1.

TABLE 1   A Sampler of Who Is Taking What

Who	What	What For
200,000 children	Amphetamines, stimulants	Learning disabilities
100,000 children	Tranquilizers, anti-depressants	Learning disabilities
250,000 children	Ritalin	Social-educational control
80,000,000 adults	Alcohol	Pleasure, therapy, etc.
80,000,000 adults	Over-the-counter drugs	Personal therapy, need, etc.
400,000 people	Marijuana	Personal awareness, therapy, etc.
560,000 people*	Heroin	Personal oblivion, etc.
25,000 people	Sniffing: gasoline, glue, plants, etc.	Personal experimentation, etc.
128,000,000 people	Nicotine	Social support, pleasure, etc.

Basic reference sources for data: *Statistical Abstract of the United States,* 1971; Lennard, 1971; and Ray, 1972.

* *Time* magazine, August 28, 1972.

Together with the data in Table 1, the following statements should provide a perspective on drug abuse in terms of the number of American dollars involved. If we are not, in fact, a "drug culture," we have certainly been active in the area. Americans spent $6 billion on prescription drugs in 1970, and roughly 25 percent of these act on the brain and central nervous system. Americans spend about $3 billion a year for over-the-counter drugs. Of the 13,000 children who *annually* suffer from aspirin poisoning, 100 actually die. Each year Americans spend $18 billion on alcohol, $9 billion on tobacco, and $1.5 billion on coffee, tea, and cocoa. It is impossible to estimate the amount of money spent on marijuana, LSD, heroin, and other illegal drugs. However, a fair guess would seem to be $10 billion—roughly the figure spent on tobacco products. These amounts total $47,500,000,000.

To highlight only the basic dollar figures, and in the process ignore a considerable human suffering, consider that this total represents $6 billion more than the *entire* world's gold reserve and more than four times the gold reserve of the United States of America. Looked at another way, the combined 1971 budgets for the states of Ohio and Tennessee of $5.1 billion would buy only slightly more than one-half of the country's tobacco products! This suggests another facet of the drug abuse problem, namely, that it is no small thing, and, in fact, that it occupies a rather sizable portion of the overall American social scene.

Exhibit A: A Gut Level Look at Drug Abuse

What follows is an excerpt from a story concerning a lady called Stark Naked who has been using LSD for an extended period while riding in a van-style bus with fellow drug addicts. They are pulling into Houston, Texas, the last leg of the trip.

Stark Naked waxing weirder and weirder, huddled in the black blanket shivering, then out, bobbing wraith, her little deep red aureolae bobbing in the crazed vibrations—finally they pull into Houston and head for Larry McMurtry's house. They pull up to McMurtry's house, in the suburbs, and the door of the house opens and out comes McMurtry, a slight, slightly wan, kindly-looking shy-looking guy, ambling out, with his little boy, his son, and Cassady opens the door of the bus so everybody can get off, and suddenly Stark Naked shrieks out: "Frankie! Frankie! Frankie! Frankie!"—this being the name of her own divorced-off little boy—and she whips off the blanket and leaps off the bus and out into the suburbs of Houston, Texas, stark naked, and rushes up to McMurtry's little boy and scoops him up and presses him to her skinny breast, crying and shrieking, "Frankie! oh Frankie! my little Frankie! oh! oh! oh!"—while McMurtry doesn't know what in the name of hell to do, reaching tentatively toward her stark-naked shoulder and saying, "Ma'am! Ma'am! Just a minute, ma'am!"—while the Pranksters, spilling out of the bus—stop. The bus is stopped. No roar, no crazed bounce or vibrations, no crazed car beams, no tapes, no microphones. Only Stark Naked, with somebody else's little boy in her arms, is bouncing and vibrating.

And there, amid the peaceful Houston elms on Quenby Road, it dawned on them all that this woman —which one of us even knows her?—had completed her trip. She had gone with the flow. She had gone stark raving mad [Wolfe, 1968, pp. 86–87].*

---

* From *The Electric Kool-Aid Acid Test* by Tom Wolfe. Copyright © 1968. By permission of Farrar, Straus, and Giroux, Inc.

Exhibit B: Survey of Drugs Currently Abused

Adapted from U.S. Department of Health, Education, and Welfare, *Resource Book for Drug Abuse Education* (Chevy Chase, Md.: National Institutes of Mental Health, 1969).

Name	Slang name	Chemical or trade name	Source	Classification	Medical use	How taken
Heroin	H., horse, scat, junk, smack, scag, stuff, harry	Diacetyl-morphine	Semisynthetic (from morphine)	Narcotic	Pain relief	Injected or sniffed
Morphine	White stuff, M.	Morphine sulphate	Natural (from opium)	Narcotic	Pain relief	Swallowed or injected
Codeine	Schoolboy	Methylmorphine	Natural (from opium), Semisynthetic (from morphine)	Narcotic	Ease pain and coughing	Swallowed
Methadone	Dolly	Dolophine amidone	Synthetic	Narcotic	Pain relief	Swallowed or injected
Cocaine	Corrine, gold dust, Coke, Bernice, flake, star dust, snow	Methylester of benzoylecgonine	Natural (from coca, not cacao)	Stimulant, local anesthesia	Local anesthesia	Sniffed, injected, or swallowed
Marijuana	Pot, grass, hashish, tea, gage, reefers	Cannabis sativa	Natural	Relaxant, euphoriant, in high doses hallucinogen	None in U.S.	Smoked, swallowed, or sniffed
Barbiturates	Barbs, blue devils, candy, yellow jackets, phennies, peanuts, blue heavens	Phenobarbital, Nembutal, Seconal, Amytal	Synthetic	Sedative, hypnotic	Sedation, relieve high blood pressure, epilepsy, hyperthyroidism	Swallowed or injected
Amphetamines	Bennies, dexies, speed, wake-ups, lid proppers, hearts, pep pills	Benzedrine, Dexedrine, Desoxyn, meth-amphetamine, Methedrine	Synthetic	Sympatho-mimetic	Relieve mild depression, control appetite and narcolepsy	Swallowed or injected
LSD	Acid, sugar, big D, cubes, trips	d-lysergic acid diethylamide	Semisynthetic (from ergot alkaloids)	Hallucinogen	Experimental study of mental function, alcoholism	Swallowed
DMT	AMT, businessman's high	Dimethyl-triptamine	Synthetic	Hallucinogen	None	Injected
Mescaline	Mesc.	3,4,5-trimeth-oxyphenethyl-amine	Natural (from peyote)	Hallucinogen	None	Swallowed
Psilocybin		3 (2-dimethyl-amino) ethylin-dol-4-oldi hydrogen phosphate	Natural (from Psilocybe)	Hallucinogen	None	Swallowed
Alcohol	Booze, juice, etc.	Ethanol ethyl alcohol	Natural (from grapes, grains, etc., via fermentation)	Sedative, hypnotic	Solvent, antiseptic	Swallowed
Tobacco	Fag, coffin nail, etc.	Nicotinia tabacum	Natural	Stimulant, sedative	Sedative, emetic (nicotine)	Smoked, sniffed, chewed

Chart Listing Drugs, Medical Uses, Symptoms Produced and Their Dependence Potentials

(Question marks indicate conflict of opinion)

Usual dose	Duration of effect	Effects sought	Long-term symptoms	Physical dependence potential	Mental dependence potential	Organic damage potential
Varies	4 hours	Euphoria, prevent withdrawal discomfort	Addiction, constipation, loss of appetite	Yes	Yes	No
15 milligrams	6 hours	Euphoria, prevent withdrawal discomfort	Addiction, constipation, loss of appetite	Yes	Yes	No
30 milligrams	4 hours	Euphoria, prevent withdrawal discomfort	Addiction, constipation, loss of appetite	Yes	Yes	No
10 milligrams	4–6 hours	Prevent withdrawal discomfort	Addiction, constipation, loss of appetite	Yes	Yes	No
Varies	Varies, short	Excitation, talkativeness	Depression, convulsions	No	Yes	Yes?
1–2 cigarettes	4 hours	Relaxation, increased euphoria, perceptions, sociability	Usually none	No	Yes?	No
50–100 milligrams	4 hours	Anxiety reduction, euphoria	Addiction with severe withdrawal symptoms, possible convulsions, toxic psychosis	Yes	Yes	Yes
2.5–5 milligrams	4 hours	Alertness, activeness	Loss of appetite, delusions, hallucinations, toxic psychosis	No?	Yes	Yes?
100–500 micrograms	10 hours	Insightful experiences, exhilaration, distortion of senses	May intensify existing psychosis, panic reactions	No	No?	No?
1–3 milligrams	Less than 1 hour	Insightful experiences, exhilaration, distortion of senses	?	No	No?	No?
350 micrograms	12 hours	Insightful experiences, exhilaration, distortion of senses	?	No	No?	No?
25 milligrams	6–8 hours	Insightful experiences, exhilaration, distortion of senses	?	No	No?	No?
Varies	1–4 hours	Sense alteration, anxiety reduction, sociability	Cirrhosis, toxic psychosis, neurologic damage, addiction	Yes	Yes	Yes
Varies	Varies	Calmness, sociability	Emphysema, lung cancer, mouth and throat cancer, cardiovascular damage, loss of appetite	Yes?	Yes	Yes

Exhibit C: A Glossary of Some Terms

Addiction: A physical and psychic dependence upon drugs produced through a state of chronic, repeated intoxication.

Anti-depressants: Psychomotor drugs which elevate mood level in normal persons but do not increase activity level.

Drugs: Any physical agent capable of, or assumed to be capable of, altering physical-mental states.

Drug abuse: Excessive use of drugs or reliance upon them for psychological, physical, personal, or social support.

Hallucinogenic drugs: Those that "cloud" the consciousness or are mind-"altering." See Exhibit B, LSD, marijuana, etc.

Hard drugs: Typically refers to morphine, heroin, etc. Those drugs with high individual and social lethality. See Exhibit B.

Heroin: A white crystalline powder; an acetyl derivative of morphine. A powerful habit-forming narcotic whose manufacture and importation are now prohibited in the United States.

Illegal drug abuse: Generally seen as part of the "pot" or youth culture, the use of drugs for personal and/or social facilitation or interaction.

Legal drug abuse: The prescription of mood-altering drugs by physicians and psychiatrists for an endless variety of emotional, motivational, learning, and mild psychological disorders or discomforts.

Morphine: Major therapeutic indications are for relief of pain, dysentery, and diarrhea. Raw opium from poppies is the substance from which morphine is extracted and then heroin derived.

Over-the-counter drugs: Psychoactive compounds available in drugstores which range from aspirin to sleeping compounds.

Psychic dependence: Frequent desire for and use of a drug lacking direct organic consequences if withheld or otherwise unattainable.

Psychoactive drugs: Those chemicals that affect the mind. Lennard (1971) feels that the next 10 years could see a hundredfold increase in types available.

Sedatives: Drugs which raise the threshold of central nervous system irritability without directly inducing sleep.

Side effects: Unwanted, often unexpected, irrelevant drug actions.

Social drugs: These include alcohol, nicotine, and caffeine. Related are compounds not originally intended for human consumption such as airplane glue, nutmeg, and morning glory plants.

Stimulants: Psychomotor drugs which tend to increase physical and psychological activity.

Tolerance: Process of decreasing cellular response associated with repeated administration of drugs. Implies increasing dosage levels in order to maintain initial effectiveness or high.

Tranquilizers: A group of drugs developed in the early 1950s that are intended to impart a sense of relaxation or tranquillity.

TREATMENT

A variety of programs are available for the treatment of drug abuse and addiction. Among the more widely known are Addicts Anonymous, Alcoholics Anonymous, National Council for Synanon, and Daytop Lodge. For your convenience and possible use as sources of information, Exhibit D contains the names and addresses of the major organizations and foundations concerned with the understanding and rehabilitation of drug abuse. Daytop Lodge (Shelly and Bassin, 1969), one of the more interesting of the treatment programs, was founded in New York City in the early 1960s. It tended to de-emphasize the medical model view of drug abuse and developed its program around the thinking and techniques of the National Council for Synanon. The program was originally viewed as having great promise, and will be reviewed later. Other programs of interest are the contextual engineering program of Robert O'Briant in San Joaquin County, California, which attempts to treat drug abuse as representative of culturally available support systems; Dr. Mitchell Rosenthal's Phoenix House in New York City; and the continuing programs at the Lexington, Kentucky, United States Public Health Service Hospital and the Juvenile Drug Addiction Program of New York City's Riverside Hospital.

A rational emphasis for treatment programs now seems to be to consider the entire life-style and environment of the person as significant factors in drug abuse. Thus, a more comprehensive model of treatment is emerging which suggests that effective treatment is contingent upon our ability to make significant changes in the drug abuser's total life scheme.

Somewhat on the grim side, the Joint Information Service of the American Psychiatric Association has published a study indicating that the majority of the country's drug rehabilitation programs are actually not very effective. For instance, in their survey of Daytop Lodge they reported that the highly publicized 90 percent cure rates were significantly related to the factor of selective admissions, and that when this was controlled for, the actual cure rate dropped to 1 to 2 percent! The programs surveyed varied from the use of simple methadone therapy to very complex, multi-technique programs, with the typical finding being that few were cured, a few more helped, and the vast majority not much changed by the experience. Interestingly enough, this finding resembles the conclusions advanced by Fiedler and also Eysenck that psychotherapy made little difference in facilitating a cure for behavior disorders. Though neither of these issues is solved—in fact the debate rages on—they do suggest the necessity for a candid appraisal of the effectiveness of various treatment programs.

Lennard (1971) seriously questions the use of methadone therapy for drug addicts, feeling that we are simply trading one addiction for another. Even more critical is his observation that such a therapeutic program also works to perpetuate the outdated medical model of treatment.

Milton and Wahler's thoughtful development of a psychosocial model approach to the problems of behavior disorders in this text underscores the relevance of such an approach in attempting to visualize effective treatment programs for drug abusers or addicts. Specifically, the psychosocial model suggests that the important characteristics of the user, his family setting, the social milieu in which he lives, his occupation, and the various social supports available for his addiction need to be considered as integral features of a functional treatment program. Indeed, some of the basic meaning of the psychosocial model can be derived from Figure 1 by considering the locus of the "problem" in much the same sense as the locus of self. Note that the explanations for the causes of disordered behavior have shifted from the existence of an internal agent or "devil" responsible for mental "illness" to the types of social environments and human interactions that account for the occurrence and maintenance of disordered behavior. Viewed in this way, it is imperative to consider a wider, more comprehensive social environment when designing treatment programs (cf. Lennard, 1971, regarding such treatment programs).

Exhibit D: Names and Addresses of National Organizations Involved with Drug Abuse or Addiction

Addicts Anonymous (AA) (Narcotics)
P.O. Box 2000
Lexington, Kentucky 40501

Al-Anon Family Group Headquarters (Alcohol)
125 East Twenty-third Street
New York, New York 10010

American Business Men's Research Foundation
(ABMRF) (Alcohol)
431 South Dearborn Street
Chicago, Illinois 60605

American Congress of Physical Medicine and Rehabilitation
(ACPMR) (Rehabilitation)
30 North Michigan Avenue
Chicago, Illinois 60602

American Council on Alcohol Problems (ACAP) (Alcohol)
119 Constitution Avenue, N.E.
Washington, D.C. 20002

American Temperance Society (ATS) (Alcohol)
6830 Laurel Street, N.W.
Washington, D.C. 20012

Association of Medical Rehabilitation Directors and Coordinators
(AMRDC) (Rehabilitation)
P.O. Box 22
South Schodack, New York 12162

Calix Society (Alcohol)
2211 Clinton Avenue South
Minneapolis, Minnesota 55404

Castalia Foundation (Narcotics)
Millbrook, New York 12545

Catholic Total Abstinence Union of America (Alcohol)
c/o St. Mary's Seminary
Roland Park
Baltimore, Maryland 21210

Comeback, Inc. (Rehabilitation)
16 West Forty-sixth Street
New York, New York 10036

Friendly Hand Foundation   (*Alcohol*)
347 South Normandie Avenue
Los Angeles, California 90020

General Service Board of Alcoholics Anonymous   (AA)   (*Alcohol*)
P.O. Box 459
Grand Central Station
New York, New York 10017

Intercollegiate Association for Study of the Alcohol Problem
(*Alcohol*)
717 Neil Avenue
Columbus, Ohio 43215

International Commission for the Prevention of Alcoholism
(ICPA)   (*Alcohol*)
6830 Laurel Street, N.W.
Washington, D.C. 20012

International Federation for Narcotic Education   (IFNE)   (*Narcotics*)
918 F Street, N.W.
Washington, D.C. 20004

International Temperance Association   (ITA)   (*Alcohol*)
6830 Laurel Street, N.W.
Washington, D.C. 20012

Lemar   (*Narcotics*)
c/o Randole Wicker
209 Mulberry Street
New York, New York 10012

Narcotics Education   (*Narcotics*)
6830 Laurel Street, N.W.
Washington, D.C. 20012

National Association for the Prevention of Addiction to Narcotics
(NAPAN)   (*Narcotics*)
c/o Arthur Konvitz Associates
Hotel Astor
New York, New York 10036

National Clergy Conference on Alcoholism   (*Alcohol*)
P.O. Box 1194
Indianapolis, Indiana 46206

National Committee for the Prevention of Alcoholism   (*Alcohol*)
6830 Laurel Street, N.W.
Washington, D.C. 20012

National Council on Alcoholism   (NCA)   (*Alcohol*)
New York Academy of Medicine Building
2 East 103rd Street
New York, New York 10029

National Council for Synanon   (*Narcotics*)
35 Riverside Drive
New York, New York 10023

National Family Council on Drug Addiction   (*Narcotics*)
403 West End Avenue
New York, New York 10024

National Temperance and Prohibition Council   (NTPC)   (*Alcohol*)
1730 Chicago Avenue
Evanston, Illinois 60201

National Woman's Christian Temperance Union   (WCTU)   (*Alcohol*)
1730 Chicago Avenue
Evanston, Illinois 60201

New York Temperance Civic League   (*Alcohol*)
1690½ Western Avenue
Albany, New York 12203

North American Association of Alcoholism Programs
(NAAAP)   (*Alcohol*)
323 Dupont Circle Building
Washington, D.C. 20036

Sons of Temperance of North America   (*Alcohol*)
8 Retreat Avenue
Armdale, Nova Scotia, Canada

Anyanon Foundation   (*Narcotics*)
1351 Pacific Coast Highway
Santa Monica, California 90401

Temperance Education Foundation   (*Alcohol*)
110 South State Street
Westerville, Ohio 43081

REGRET AS A CONCLUSION

Since our culture develops and therefore evolves we need to
carefully consider where it is we are headed and what we shall
be when we arrive. In large measure our cultural heritage has

been marked with strength, diversity, humor, and incredible beauty. However, there is now emerging the specter of a growing drug culture, and its eventual impact upon society can only be imagined. It is probably not all good. The social value of individual human beings is receding somehow toward a mass-produced, mass-oriented society in which too many have become precisely what they appear to be.

With respect to the causes of drug abuse, I am suggesting here that America is nearly the perfect climate for a widespread drug culture because of the course of our development since the industrial revolution with its accompanying philosophy of "materialism." Both of these in concert with the pervasive medical model of psychological phenomena provide a setting in which people are being covertly "trained" to see themselves as potential drug users who will benefit from the experience. Today's overwhelming cultural message is that there is something to be gained from drug use.

In addition, many drug abusers cite misunderstandings with parents or loved ones, interpersonal stresses, and environmental-social pressures among the causes or reasons for excessive use. For young people this may be inevitable, since there are very probably no adult–young person relationships devoid of considerable tension and equally probably few if any young people immune to the natural stress associated with becoming an adult member of a social community. This means that certain of the frequently cited reasons for drug abuse are actually the cultural imperative of twentieth-century society and provide the riddle that all young people must solve. Consequently, many could be expected to decide that one or the other of the available drugs could ameliorate their anxieties and strains while perhaps increasing the level of their self-and-other awareness.

We come now full circle: from a particular type of materialistic society, to the existence of such universal problems as maturity and self-awareness, to the problem-solving techniques provided by a particular society, to the individual utilization of such techniques as coping strategies. Since all humans are compelled to make some response, irrespective of whether it be adaptive or lethal, we are uncertain as to how widespread will be the growth of a drug culture as a problem-solving strategy. Certainly the groundwork has been laid to prepare the way for such a movement.

As if all of this were not sufficient, consider the highly likely effects of population density upon meaningful human relationships: less need for others as "individuals," less need for others as pivotal social forces, and all this coupled with a diminishing awareness of the self as a viable, significant, human unit. It is into a relentlessly impending boredom and loss of love such as this that the "hope of" and "faith in" drugs could conceivably insinuate themselves. As a result of widening dependence upon a drug culture as a social form, each of us could be doomed to become not only less human and loving but also less capable of being approached as humankind. For reasons such as these, the understanding of the role that drugs may have come to play in our culture as well as the available social supports for this role become matters of critical import. Equally urgent is the observation that far more research and study need to be done to increase our ability to meaningfully cure those now burdened with drug abuse or addiction—for there are so many.

REFERENCES

Allegro, J. M. 1970. *The sacred mushroom and the cross*. New York: Doubleday.

Allentuck, S., and Bowman, K. M. 1942. The psychiatric aspects of marihuana intoxication. *American Journal of Psychiatry* 99:249.

Ardrey, R. 1966. *The territorial imperative*. New York: Atheneum.

Barker, R. 1960. Ecological psychology. *Nebraska symposium on motivation*. Lincoln: University of Nebraska Press.

Bloomquist, E. R. 1970. The use and abuse of stimulants. In *Principles of psychopharmacology*, ed. W. G. Clark and J. del Giudice, pp. 477–488. New York: Academic Press.

Blum, R. H., et al. 1970. *Society and drugs: Drugs I*. San Francisco: Jossey-Bass.

Blum, R. H., et al. 1970. *Students and drugs: Drugs II*. San Francisco: Jossey-Bass.

Bogen, E. 1932. The human toxicology of alcohol. In *Alcohol and man*, ed. H. Emerson, pp. 126–152. New York: Macmillan.

Brehm, M. L., and Back, K. W. 1968. Self image and attitudes toward drugs. *Journal of Personality* 36:299–314.

Brown, N. O. 1966. *Love's body.* New York: Random House.

Calhoun, J. B. 1962. Population density and social pathology. *Scientific American* 206:139–148.

Clark, W. H. 1969. *Chemical ecstasy: Psychedelic drugs and religion.* New York: Sheed and Ward.

Competitive problems in the drug industry. 1969. Hearings before the Subcommittee on Small Business, United States Senate, Ninety-first Congress, First Session (July 16, 29, 30 and October 27, 1969), part 13, Psychotropic Drugs, p. 5460. Washington, D.C.: U.S. Government Printing Office.

Crime in America—why eight billion amphetamines? 1970. Hearings before the Select Committee on Crime, House of Representatives, Ninety-first Congress, First Session, p. 44. Washington, D.C.: U.S. Government Printing Office.

Editorial Board CIBA. 1971. *The hyperactive child.* Summit, N.J.: CIBA Pharmaceutical Company.

Eibl-Eibesfeldt, I. 1970. *Ethology: The biology of behavior.* New York: Holt, Rinehart, and Winston.

Eiseley, L. 1957. *The immense journey.* New York: Random House.

Eiseley, L. 1970. *The invisible pyramid.* New York: Scribner.

Ellinwood, E. H. 1971. Amphetamine abuse. *Science* 171:420–421.

Evans, W., and Kline, N., eds. 1971. *Psychotropic drugs in the year 2000.* New York: McGraw-Hill.

Facts and fancies about marihuana. 1936. *Literary Digest* 122:7–8.

Fort, J. 1969. *The pleasure seekers.* New York: Bobbs-Merrill. Pp. 212–213.

Goldstein, A., and Kaizer, S. 1969. Psychotropic effects of caffeine in man. *Clinical Pharmacology and Therapeutics* 10 (4):477–488.

Haddon, J., et al. 1969. Acute barbiturate poisoning. *Journal of the American Medical Association* 209 (6):893–900.

Hall, E. T. 1966. *The hidden dimension.* Garden City, N.Y.: Doubleday.

Hallucinogens. 1968. *Columbia Law Review* 68 (3):521.

Harris, R. T.; McIsaac, W. M.; and Schuster, C. R., eds. 1970. *Drug dependence.* Austin: University of Texas Press.

The health consequences of smoking. 1967. Public Health Service Publication no. 1696. Washington, D.C.: U.S. Government Printing Office.

Hoffman, A. 1968. *Drugs affecting the central nervous system: vol. 2, Psychotomimetic Agents*, pp. 169–235. New York: Marcel Decker.

Houston, J. 1969. Phenomenology of the psychedelic experience. In *Psychedelic drugs*, ed. R. E. Hicks and P. J. Fink, pp. 1–7. New York: Grune and Stratton.

Kaplan, J. 1970. *Marihuana—the new prohibition*. New York: World Publishing Company.

Keeler, M. H.; Reifler, C. B.; and Liptzin, M. B. 1968. Spontaneous recurrence of marihuana effect. *American Journal of Psychiatry* 125:384–386.

Klein, D. F., and Davis, J. M. 1969. *Diagnosis and drug treatment of psychiatric disorders*. Baltimore: Williams and Wilkins.

LaBarre, W. 1960. Twenty years of peyote studies. *Current Anthropology* 1 (1):45.

Lawton, M. P., and Phillips, R. W. 1956. The relationship between excessive cigarette smoking and psychological tension. *American Journal of the Medical Sciences* 232:397–402.

Lennard, H. L., et al. 1971. *Mystification and drug misuse: Hazards in using psychoactive drugs*. San Francisco: Jossey-Bass.

Lindesmith, A. R. 1965. *The addict and the law*. Bloomington: Indiana University Press.

McGlothlin, W. H., and West, L. J. 1968. The marihuana problem: An overview. *American Journal of Psychiatry* 99:249.

Marihuana and health. 1971. Department of Health, Education, and Welfare. Washington, D.C.: U.S. Government Printing Office.

Matarazzo, J. D., and Saslow, G. 1960. Psychological and related characteristics of smokers and nonsmokers. *Psychological Bulletin* 57 (6):493–513.

Meyers, F. H.; Rose, A. J.; and Smith, D. E. 1967–1968. Incidents involving the Haight-Ashbury population and some uncommonly used drugs. *Journal of Psychedelic Drugs* 1 (2):140–146.

Morgan, M. 1970. *Drug abuse: Various collected papers*. Santa Clara Drug Abuse Center, California.

Mosher, L. R., et al. 1970. *Special report on schizophrenia.* U.S. Department of Health, Education, and Welfare, National Institute of Mental Health.

National Clearinghouse for Mental Health Information. 1970. Publication no. 5027.

Nowlis, H. H. 1969. *Drugs on the college campus.* New York: Doubleday.

Parry, H. J. 1968. Use of psychotropic drugs by U.S. adults. *Public Health Reports* 83 (10):799–810.

Percy, W. 1960. *The moviegoer.* New York: Knopf.

President's Commission on Law Enforcement and Administration of Justice. 1967. *Task force report: Narcotics and drug abuse.* Washington, D.C.: U.S. Government Printing Office.

Ray, O. S., ed. 1972. *Drugs, society, and human behavior.* Saint Louis: Mosby.

Richards, L. G., and Carroll, E. E. 1970. Illicit drug use and addiction in the United States. *U.S. Public Health Reports* 85 (12): 1035–1041.

Rickels, K., and Cattell, R. B. 1969. Drug and placebo response as a function of doctor and patient type. In *Psychotropic drug response,* ed. P. R. A. May and J. R. Wittenborn, pp. 126–140. Springfield, Ill.: Thomas.

Rubin, E., and Lieber, C. S. 1971. Alcoholism, alcohol, and drugs. *Science* 172:1097–1102.

Ruesch, J. 1967. Technological civilization and human affairs. *Journal of Nervous and Mental Disease* 145:193–205.

Schultes, R. E. 1970. The plant kingdom and hallucinogens, part 3. *Bulletin on Narcotics* 22 (1):43–46.

Scott, J. M. 1969. *The white poppy: A history of opium.* New York: Funk and Wagnalls.

Sharpless, S. K. 1970. Hypnotics and sedatives. In *The pharmacological basis of therapeutics,* ed. L. Goodman and A. Gilman, pp. 98, 100, 103. New York: Macmillan.

Shelly, J. A., and Bassin, A. 1969. Daytop Lodge: A new treatment approach for drug addicts. In *Behavior disorders: Perspectives and trends,* ed. O. Milton and R. G. Wahler. Philadelphia: Lippincott.

Smythies, J. R. 1970. The mode of action of psychotomimetic drugs. *Neuro-Sciences Research Program Bulletin* 8 (1):63.

Stimulants calm overactive kids. 1970. *American Druggist*, vol. 162, August 24, p. 37.

Task Force on Prescription Drugs. 1969. Final report, pp. 10, 31. Washington, D.C.: U.S. Department of Health, Education, and Welfare.

Taylor, N. 1965. *Plant drugs that changed the world*, p. 12. New York: Dodd, Mead.

Tourney, G. 1967. A history of therapeutic fashions in psychiatry, 1800–1966. *American Journal of Psychiatry* 124 (6):784–796.

Wheatley, D. 1968. Effects of doctors' and patients' attitudes and other factors on response to drugs. In *Non-specific factors in drug therapy*, ed. K. Rickels, pp. 73–79. Springfield, Ill.: Thomas.

White House Conference on Narcotics and Drug Abuse. 1963. Washington, D.C.: U.S. Government Printing Office. P. 288.

Wilcox, R. 1971. The special characteristics of technical learning: 2000 AD. Unpublished manuscript, Ohio University, Zanesville.

Witter, C. 1971. Drugging and schooling. *Trans-action* 8 (9–10): 31–34.

Wolfe, T. 1968. *The electric kool-aid acid test*. New York: Farrar, Straus, and Giroux.

Part III:
Alteration of behavior

The Quest for Identity

By ALLEN WHEELIS

13

As Milton and Wahler (selection 1) suggested, a basic tenet of humanism is the necessity for freedom of choice by the individual; in turn, this can occur only if the individual is aware. Dr. Wheelis, in this article, argues lucidly about some of the social forces which tend to interfere with awareness. His discussion is especially pertinent for understanding the concept of identity—the frequent anguished expressions of "Who am I?" and "What is the meaning of life?"

In former years, apparently there was much less floundering than there is at the present time, and Dr. Wheelis parades many of the most important reasons for the difference—a difference which helps to explain "alienation" and "dropping-out." In some instances and by some authorities, such vague and amorphous complaints as "I'm just not happy" are labeled as *neurosis*.

THE EVOLUTION OF SOCIAL CHARACTER

THE OLD AND THE NEW

WITH INCREASING FREQUENCY in recent years a change in the character of the American people has been reported and described.[1] The change is within the lifetime of most persons

---

Chapter 1, The Evolution of Social Character, pages 17–25 and 38–44. Reprinted from *The Quest for Identity* by Allen Wheelis by permission of W. W. Norton and Company, Inc. Copyright © 1958 by W. W. Norton and Company, Inc. Also permission for British Commonwealth and Empire, except Canada from Laurence Pollinger, Ltd.

Dr. Wheelis is a psychiatrist staff member of the Mt. Zion Psychiatric Clinic and an instructor in the San Francisco Psychoanalytic Institute.

[1] David Riesman, Nathan Glazer, and Reuel Denney, *The Lonely Crowd* (New Haven: Yale University Press, 1950); Henry Steele Commager, *The American Mind* (New Haven: Yale University Press, 1950); Erik Erikson, *Childhood and Society* (New York: W. W. Norton and Company, 1950); Margaret Mead, *Male and Female* (New York: William Morrow and Company, 1949); Walter Lippmann, *The Public Philosophy* (Boston: Little Brown and Company, 1955).

of middle or advanced years, and the process of change is still under way. The social character[2] of ourselves and our children is unmistakably different from what we remember of the character of our grandparents.

Our grandparents had less trouble than we do in finding themselves. There were lost souls, to be sure, but no lost generation. More commonly then than now a young man followed his father, in character as in vocation, and often so naturally as to be unaware of having made a choice. Though the frontier was gone, there was still, for those who needed it, the open West. Sooner rather than later one found his calling, and, having found it, failure did not readily cause one to reconsider, but often was a goad to greater effort. The goal was achievement, not adjustment; the young were taught to work, not to socialize. Popularity was not important, but strength of character was essential. Nobody worried about rigidity of character; it was supposed to be rigid. If it were flexible, you couldn't count on it. Change of character was desirable only for the wicked.

Many of us still remember the bearded old men: the country doctor, the circuit rider, the blacksmith, the farmer. They were old when we were young, and they are dead now. We remember the high shoes, the heavy watch chain, the chewing tobacco, the shiny black suit on Sunday. The costume and make-up may still be seen, as they turn up in plays now and then. The character that went with them is disappearing, and soon even its memory will be lost.

Nowadays the sense of self is deficient. The questions of adolescence—"Who am I?" "Where am I going?" "What is the meaning of life?"—receive no final answers. Nor can they be laid aside. The uncertainty persists. The period of being uncommitted is longer, the choices with which it terminates more tentative. Personal identity does not become fixed, does not, therefore, provide an unchanging vantage point from which to view experience. Man is still the measure of all things, but it is no longer the inner man that measures; it is the other man.

---

2 The concept of social character refers not to the character of society, but, somewhat paradoxically, to the character of individuals. It is that nucleus of individual character which is shared by a significantly large social group. Since it is what we have in common with others, we take it for granted and most of the time are unaware of its existence.

Specifically, it is the plurality of men, the group. And what the group provides is shifting patterns; what it measures is conformity. It does not provide the hard inner core by which the value of patterns and conformity is determined. The hard inner core has in our time become diffuse, elusive, often fluid. More than ever before one is aware of the identity he appears to have, and more than ever before is dissatisfied with it. It doesn't fit, it seems alien, as though the unique course of one's life had been determined by untoward accident. Commitments of all kinds—social, vocational, marital, moral—are made more tentatively. Long-term goals seem to become progressively less feasible.

Identity[3] is a coherent sense of self. It depends upon the awareness that one's endeavors and one's life make sense, that they are meaningful in the context in which life is lived. It depends also upon stable values, and upon the conviction that one's actions and values are harmoniously related. It is a sense of wholeness, of integration, of knowing what is right and what is wrong and of being able to choose.

During the past fifty years there has been a change in the experienced quality of life, with the result that identity is now harder to achieve and harder to maintain. The formerly dedicated Marxist who now is unsure of everything; the Christian who loses his faith; the workman who comes to feel that his work is piecemeal and meaningless; the scientist who decides that science is futile, that the fate of the world will be determined by power politics—such persons are of our time, and they suffer the loss or impairment of identity.

Identity can survive major conflict provided the supporting framework of life is stable, but not when that framework is lost. One cannot exert leverage except from a fixed point. Putting one's shoulder to the wheel presupposes a patch of solid ground to stand on. Many persons these days find no firm footing; and if everything is open to question, no question can be answered. The past half-century has encompassed

---

[3] *Identity* is used throughout this work in its ordinary lay meaning. In psychoanalytic literature it bears a larger and more precise meaning, indicating a psychic organization which develops in successive phases throughout life, and which is partly unconscious. Cf. Erik Erikson, "The Problem of Ego Identity," *Journal of the American Psychoanalytic Association*, vol. 4, no. 1 (January, 1956), pp. 56–121.

enormous gains in understanding and in mastery, but many of the old fixed points of reference have been lost and have not been replaced.

The change in social character is often described as a decline of individualism, but individualism means many things, and not all of them have declined. Individualism means self-reliance, productive self-sufficiency, following one's chosen course despite social criticism, and bearing personally the risks of one's undertakings, and all of these are on the wane. Ours is an age of reliance on experts, of specialized production, of deference to public opinion, and of collective security. But individualism means, also, the awareness of individuality, and this has increased. For accompanying the other changes there has occurred an extension of awareness.

Modern man has become more perceptive of covert motivations, in both himself and others. Areas of experience formerly dissociated from consciousness have become commonplace knowledge. Passivity, anxiety, disguised hostility, masochism, latent homosexuality—these are not new with the present generation; what is new is the greater awareness of them. We deride the affectations which this heightened awareness so facilely serves—the "parlor psychiatry," the "curbstone interpretation"—but overlook the emergent fact of extended awareness of which the affectation is symptomatic. As man has lost his sense of identity, he has, paradoxically, discovered more of those elements of his nature out of which identity may be formed, the raw materials with which to build. In losing the whole he has found some of the previously lost parts.

This extended awareness is both cause and effect of the loss of identity. It is a cause for the reason that identity is harder to achieve if renegade motivations have free access to consciousness. If one is able to deny with finality those lurking tendencies that run counter to the dominant trends of personality, then it is easier to know who one is and where one stands. This is of relevance in comparing the unsure man of today with his very sure grandfather. His sense of identity is less firm, but the elements he is called upon to integrate are more numerous and less homogeneous. The identity of his grandfather was like the log cabin of the frontier; it was small and dark, but it was put up with dispatch and was sturdy and snug. The grandson is fumbling as a builder, and keeps hankering to turn the whole job over to a professional architect, but it is to be noted that his job is harder. The materials with which he must work are more variegated. Their proper integration would achieve not a log cabin, but a more complicated and interesting structure, admitting more light and air and providing more room for living.

The extended awareness is also an effect of the loss of identity for the reason that, being unsure of who one is and where one stands, it behooves one to be more alert and perceptive. A firm sense of identity provides both a compass to determine one's course in life and ballast to keep one steady. So equipped and provisioned, one can safely ignore much of the buffeting. Without such protection more vigilance is needed; each vicissitude, inner and outer, must be defined and watched.

A change has occurred, also, in the dimensions of our existence. During this century, it is said, our lives have been both lengthened and narrowed. This makes reference to our longer life expectancy and to the increasing industrialization that is thought to diminish the meaning of life by the kind of work it imposes. The increased life-span is indisputable, and doubtless much clerical and assembly-line work is monotonous. Yet in a somewhat different sense the dimensional change is just the opposite of that proposed: our lives have been enriched cross-sectionally and diminished longitudinally.

In our time the range and variety of experience has been enormously extended. It is less integrated and less stable, but it is far wider in scope. Fifty years ago the great orchestras could be heard in only a few cities; now they are heard, by radio and recording, in every village across the continent. Comparable changes have occurred in the availability of all the arts. Better means of communication enable us to experience meanings that occur at great distances, better methods of travel to experience persons and areas heretofore inaccessible. Though these experiences are more easily had by the rich, they are to a notable degree available, also, to the assembly-line worker whose life is thought to be so impoverished. A war in Korea, a play on Broadway, a new philosophy in France—all are experienced more quickly and more widely than ever before.

Nor has the depth or meaningfulness of this experience been diminished. When radios became common, it was sometimes predicted that the musical taste of the nation would be depraved by the constant din of jazz. In fact, the relatively small amount of serious music that was broadcast along with the jazz developed the musical appreciation of millions. Serious music is now understood and valued by a far higher proportion of the people than would have been possible without the advent of radio. "Twenty years ago you couldn't sell Beethoven out of New York," reports a record salesman. "Today we sell Palestrina, Monteverdi, Gabrielli, and renaissance and baroque music in large quantities."[4] Parallel developments could be cited for countless other areas of experience. The gain in breadth of experience has generally been accompanied by a gain, also, in depth. Not only is the man of today constantly informed of a larger number of world events than was his grandfather; he understands them better. And within his own home he understands his children better. In all of these ways our lives have been cross-sectionally enriched.

But as our span of years has increased, our span of significant time has diminished. In some measure we have lost the sense of continuity with past and future. More and more quickly the past becomes outdated, and if we look back two or three generations, the character and values of our forebears become as strange to us as their beards and high collars. Family portraits no longer hang in homes; there is no place for them in modern houses. And as we have lost touch with the past, so we have lost touch with the future. We know that we are in motion but do not know where we are going, and hence cannot predict the values of our children. Our grandfathers are likely to have dreamt of leaving as legacy a tract of land which would stay in the family and be maintained by their descendants; of building a house that would endure and be lived in after they were gone; of a profession that would become a tradition and be carried on by sons; of a name that would be wrought in iron over the carriage gate, the prestige of which would be shared and furthered by all who bore it. Seeing how these dreams have come to naught in us, we no longer try to direct or even to foresee the values of our descendants. We cannot now, with loving foresight, further their ends, for we do not know what ends they will pursue, nor where. We feel lucky if we can give our children an education. The founders of this country had a lively sense of the future, knew that posterity would vindicate their revolution, their moving west, their capitalism, their com-

---

[4] Quoted by Daniel Bell, "The Theory of Mass Society," Commentary, vol. 22, no. 1 (July, 1956), pp. 75–83.

petition, their church. We—who have no idea of what posterity will honor—live more largely in the present.

Becker has pointed out that this is an age in which we cannot feel that we understand anything until we know its history.[5] As we become more aware of how things change, it becomes more important to know how they developed, how they got to be the way they are. But this does not mean that we feel more related to the past and future. It is rather the other way round: our feeling of estrangement in time and of the transience of the present prompts the historical approach. The historical approach is a symptom of our trouble. We are trying to recapture the sense of continuity, to find again the durable patterns of life—hoping we shall not lose altogether our connections with those who have lived before and those who will live after.

THE CHANGE IN NEUROTIC PATTERNS

Doctor Thurston was a kind man and often was sympathetic with emotional disorders. He would prescribe tonics, advise work, and would give generously of encouragement and reassurance. When these measures did not help, however—as often they did not—and when the patient became more demanding, his patience would be short. Of a neurotic woman he would say, "She's not sick, she's got hysterics." If her complaints were only in her mind, then obviously they were not real. "She just *thinks* she's sick." If he had made his call under difficult conditions, he would be cross, would feel that his time was being wasted. If she should prove hard to handle, his sense of moral indignation would be indicated by his readiness to shift the diagnosis from hysteria to malingering. This was the attitude, also, of the patient's family and of society. She would receive little indulgence, but would be regarded with humor or derision. It was a disgrace, and if she did not snap out of it the disgrace would deepen.

This intolerance amounted to a pressure against the emergence or admission of neurosis, and it had varying effects. It forced the suppression of symptoms or the ability to live with them

---

[5] "Historical-mindedness is so much a preconception of modern thought that we can identify a particular thing only by pointing to the various things it successively was before it became that particular thing that it will presently cease to be." Carl L. Becker, *The Heavenly City of the Eighteenth-Century Philosophers* (New Haven: Yale University Press, 1932), p. 19.

and despite them and to keep going. It forced, also, some curable neurotics into suicide, and it locked up and made custodial cases of some who, in a different setting, might have recovered.

This pressure has, in large measure, been replaced by tolerance. Now there is no difference in degree of reality between mental and physical illness; one is as genuine as the other. They differ in origin, development, and recovery, but are alike in that in neither case is one expected simply to "snap out of it." By this change in attitude neurosis has been admitted into the realm of medicine, becoming entitled thereby to the designation of illness, with all the rights and privileges pertaining thereunto. Among these are the right to professional attention and the privilege of delivering responsibility for the care and cure of one's illness into the hands of a physician. From the untoward consequences of this latter development psychiatrists are still trying, somewhat awkwardly, to extricate themselves.

The new orientation is regarded as a great social gain. Not only does it banish the old bigotry; it will also—we are assured —diminish the prevalence and severity of neurosis. For with the elimination of the stigma, the need for secrecy is gone. Since our culture does not enforce the suppression of neurosis, one is more free to acknowledge the difficulty and to seek help. And since psychiatric treatment is regarded as the royal—and, usually, the only—road to recovery, it is assumed that more people will get well.

Such optimism overreaches itself. Get well from what? Most often nowadays it is from loneliness, insecurity, doubt, boredom, restlessness, and marital discord. The hysteria of the last century has mysteriously disappeared—as completely as the intolerance with which it was viewed. The tolerant psychoanalyst of today deals rather with vague conditions of maladjustment and discontent. For it has come about that, as the social attitude toward neurosis has changed, the patterns of neuroses have themselves undergone a change of equal magnitude.[6] This is within the personal experience of older psycho-

---

[6] ". . . the patient of today suffers most under the problem of what he should believe in and who he should—or, indeed, might—be or become; while the patient of early psychoanalysis suffered most under inhibitions which prevented him from being what and who he thought he knew he was." Erik Erikson, *Childhood and Society* (New York: W. W. Norton and Company, 1950), p. 239.

analysts. Younger analysts become aware of it from the discrepancy between the older descriptions of neuroses and the problems presented by the patients who come daily to their offices. The change is from symptom neuroses to character disorders.

A symptom neurosis was understood as a breakthrough in distorted form of a previously repressed impulse. The neurosis appeared as a phobia, an obsession, a compulsion, or as a physical symptom without a physical cause; was characterized by a definite, and often sudden, onset; and occurred in the setting of a relatively well-integrated and adequately functioning personality. It had the quality of a syndrome or illness. Diagnosis was relatively easy. It was the classical indication for psychoanalysis, and with such conditions analysis has had its greatest success. Insight was often quickly effective. Analyses were short, a matter of months rather than years. Such a case has always been considered ideal for teaching purposes, and its current rarity can be attested by almost any analyst in training.

In contrast, the more frequently encountered character disorder of today cannot be adequately understood as the eruption of a previously repressed impulse, for the defensive warping of character is apt to loom larger and prove more troublesome than the erupting impulse. The conflict is less likely to manifest itself in the form of specific symptoms or to have the quality of a syndrome, but is vague and amorphous, pervading the entire personality. Complaints of a general nature become more common, such as, "difficulties in relations with people," "I'm just not very happy, feel I ought to be getting more out of life," or "I'm too rigid." Normality has largely replaced morality as a standard of operational adequacy.[7] The significance of inner conflict to all manner of difficulties in living has been so incontrovertibly established that, for many people, any condition of unhappiness is prima facie evidence of neurosis and hence reason enough to consult a psychoanalyst. Diagnosis becomes increasingly difficult; no one term covers the many things that are wrong; and case reports conclude with formulations of remarkable length and complexity—for example, "reactive depression in a decompensating narcissistic-compulsive charac-

---

[7] Norman Reider, "The Concept of Normality," Psychoanalytic Quarterly, vol. 19 (1950), pp. 43–51.

ter with paranoid, hysterical, and some psychopathic tendencies." With such conditions psychoanalysis is less successful, insight less curative. The analyst speaks less often of "cure" and more frequently of "progress." Analyses become longer, three years and more being quite common, and the time is long past when a second analysis was claim to distinction. The goals of analysis are not fully achieved; both patient and therapist must settle for less than had been hoped for.

THE DECLINE OF WILL

Toward the end of the long analyses that now have become so common, the therapist may find himself wishing that the patient were capable of more push, more determination, a greater willingness to make the best of it. Often this wish eventuates in remarks to the patient: "People must help themselves"; "Nothing worthwhile is achieved without effort"; "You have to try." Such interventions are seldom included in case reports, for it is assumed that they possess neither the dignity nor effectiveness of interpretation. Often an analyst feels uncomfortable about such appeals to volition, as though he were using something he didn't believe in, and as though this would have been unnecessary had only he analyzed more skillfully. The deficiency of will in the patient is mirrored by the loss, in the analyst, of a belief in the efficacy of will. The same culture produces both patient and analyst, and it is a culture in which the strength of individuals is no longer thought to be located in the strength of will.

When human affairs appear to be inexorably determined by forces over which man has no control, the concept of will has little significance. When human affairs are characterized by a sense of freedom, when society concerns itself with the rights and dignity of the individual, the concept of will is of great significance. Since the Renaissance, man's sense of freedom has increased to a point probably unequalled in any prior civilization, achieving such expressions as "I am the master of my fate; I am the captain of my soul." At the same time the material universe was more and more being found to be rigorously determined, more precisely and measurably conforming to natural law. Newtonian mechanics captured the physical sciences for determinism. But, paradoxically, the technological advantages of viewing the universe as "determined" enhanced man's sense of being "free." One cannot build an aeroplane, for example, without allegiance to determinism; yet the creation of an aeroplane tends to support man's sense of standing outside the causal network, of being the master and manipulator of determined events. And so for centuries the inner life of man, the realm of free will, lay outside causality. Even after Darwin captured the biological sciences for determinism, there still seemed to be a place for will in human affairs, and as late as 1892 William James maintained that a sense of integrity depends primarily on the ability to will effectively.[8]

More recently the concept of will has passed into partial eclipse. It is still central to those popular books on self-improvement which crowd the best-seller lists, but in psychology it has lost its position as a primary mental function and has become an epiphenomenon. Among the sophisticated the use of the term *will power* has become perhaps the most unambiguous badge of naïveté. It has become unfashionable to try, by one's unaided efforts, to force one's way out of a condition of neurotic misery, for the stronger the will, the more likely it is to be labeled a "counterphobic maneuver." The unconscious is heir to the prestige of will. As one's fate formerly was determined by will, now it is determined by the repressed in mental life. Knowledgeable moderns put their backs to the couch, and in so doing they fail occasionally to put their shoulders to the wheel. As will has been devalued, so has courage, for courage can exist only in the service of will, and can hardly be valued higher than that which it serves. In our understanding of human nature we have gained determinism and lost determination—though these two things are neither coordinate nor incompatible.

---

[8] ". . . we measure ourselves by many standards. Our strength and our intelligence, our wealth and even our good luck, are things which warm our heart and make us feel ourselves a match for life. But deeper than all such things, and able to suffice unto itself without them, is the sense of the amount of effort which we can put forth. . . . He who can make none is but a shadow; he who can make much is a hero." William James, *Psychology* (New York: Henry Holt and Company, 1892), p. 458.

Healthy Personality and
Self-Disclosure

By SIDNEY M. JOURARD

14

Dr. Sidney Jourard of the University of Florida emphasizes cne aspect of the humanistic focus on personal freedom. Freedom of choice presumes that one is aware of options available in the present environment. As Milton and Wahler pointed out (selection 1), disturbed people seem to have fewer choices or options—either because they are unaware that other options exist or because they are afraid to sample new events. In a very real sense, such people are "locked" into narrow behavior patterns.

Jourard's emphasis on self-disclosure refers to man's ability to describe his own behavior, feelings, and thoughts—particularly in the presence of other people. Self-disclosure requires that one first be aware of his own behavior, feelings, and thoughts and, second, that he be willing to disclose these events to someone else. If his awareness is limited, or if he masks his self-description to other people, he has reduced his freedom of choice and therefore must act in a circumscribed manner. While his hidden feelings and thoughts offer other ways of behaving, he has no access to them. Jourard's thesis is that such access can be obtained by disclosing these events to another person within a context of love. These ideas are explored further in the author's book, The Transparent Self, published by Van Nostrand Reinhold.

FOR A LONG TIME, health and well-being have been taken for granted as "givens," and disease has been viewed as the problem for man to solve. Today, however, increasing numbers of scientists have begun to adopt a reverse point of view: disease and trouble are coming to be viewed as the givens, and specification of positive health and its conditions as the important goal. Physical, mental, and social health are values representing restrictions on the total variance of being. The scien-

From Mental Hygiene, vol. 6 (1959). Reprinted by permission of the author and the National Association for Mental Health.

tific problem here consists in arriving at a definition of health, determining its relevant dimensions, and then identifying the independent variables of which these are a function.

Scientists, however, are supposed to be hard-boiled, and they insist that phenomena, in order to be counted "real," must be public. Hence, many behavioral scientists ignore man's self, or soul, since it is essentially a private phenomenon. Others, however, are not so quick to allocate man's self to the limbo of the unimportant, and they insist that we cannot understand man and his lot until we take his self into account.

I probably fall into the camp of these investigators who want to explore health as a positive problem in its own right and who, further, take man's self seriously—as a reality to be explained and as a variable which produces consequences for weal or woe. In this chapter, I would like more fully to explore the connection between positive health and the disclosure of self. Let me commence with some sociological truisms.

Social systems require their members to play certain roles. Unless the roles are adequately played, the social systems will not produce the results for which they have been organized. This flat statement applies to social systems as simple as one developed by an engaged couple and to those as complex as a total nation among nations.

Societies have socialization "factories" and "mills"—families and schools—which serve the function of training people to play the age, sex, and occupational roles which they shall be obliged to play throughout their life in the social system. Broadly speaking, if a person plays his roles suitably, he can be regarded as a more or less normal personality. *Normal personalities, however, are not necessarily healthy personalities* (Jourard, 1958, pp. 16–18).

Healthy personalities are people who play their roles satisfactorily and at the same time derive personal satisfaction from role enactment; more, they keep growing, and they maintain a high-level physical wellness (Dunn, 1958). It is probably enough, speaking from the standpoint of a stable social system, for people to be normal personalities. But it is possible to be a normal personality and be absolutely miserable. We would count such a normal personality unhealthy. In fact, normality in some social systems—successful acculturation to them—reliably produces ulcers, piles, paranoia, or compulsiveness. We also have to regard as unhealthy those people who have never been able to enact the roles that legitimately can be expected from them.

Counselors, guidance workers, and psychotherapists are obliged to treat with both patterns of unhealthy personality—those people who have been unable to learn their roles and those who play their roles quite well, but suffer the agonies of boredom, frustration, anxiety, or stultification. If our clients are to be helped, they must change, and change in *valued* directions. A change in a valued direction may arbitrarily be called growth. We have yet to give explicit statement to these valued directions for growth, though a beginning has been made (Fromm, 1947; Jahoda, 1958; Jourard, 1958; Maslow, 1954; Rogers, 1954). We who are professionally concerned with the happiness, growth, and well-being of our clients may be regarded as professional lovers, not unlike the Cyprian sisterhood. It would be fascinating to pursue this parallel further, but for the moment let us ask instead what this has to do with self-disclosure.

To answer this question, let's tune in on an imaginary interview between a client and his counselor. The client says, "I have never told this to a soul, doctor, but I can't stand my wife, my mother is a nag, my father is a bore, and my boss is an absolutely hateful and despicable tyrant. I have been carrying on an affair for the past ten years with the lady next door, and at the same time I am a deacon in the church." The counselor says, showing great understanding and empathy, "Mm-humm!"

If we listened for a long enough period of time, we would find that the client talks and talks about himself to this highly sympathetic and empathic listener. At some later time, the client may eventually say, "Gosh, you have helped me a lot. I see what I must do, and I will go ahead and do it."

Now this talking about oneself to another person is what I call self-disclosure. It would appear, without assuming anything, that self-disclosure is a factor in the process of effective counseling or psychotherapy. Would it be too arbitrary an assumption to propose that people become clients *because they have not disclosed themselves in some optimum degree to the people in their life?*

An historical digression: Toward the end of the nineteenth century, Joseph Breuer, a Viennese physician, discovered (probably accidentally) that when his hysterical patients talked about themselves, disclosing not only the verbal content of their memories, but also the feelings that they had suppressed at the time of assorted "traumatic" experiences, their hysterical symptoms disappeared. Somewhere along the line, Breuer withdrew from a situation which would have made him Freud's peer in history's hall of fame. When Breuer permitted his patients "to be," it scared him, one gathers, because some of his female patients disclosed themselves to be quite sexy, and what was probably worse, they felt quite sexy toward him. Freud, however, did not flinch. He made the momentous discovery that the neurotic people of his time were struggling like mad to avoid "being," to avoid being known, and in Allport's (1955) terms, to avoid "becoming." He learned that his patients, when they were given the opportunity to "be"—which free association on a couch is nicely designed to do—would disclose that they had all manner of horrendous thoughts and feelings which they did not even dare disclose to themselves, much less express in the presence of another person. Freud learned to permit his patients to be, through permitting them to disclose themselves utterly to another human. He evidently did not trust anyone enough to be willing to disclose himself vis a vis, so he disclosed himself to himself on paper (Freud, 1955) and learned the extent to which he was himself self-alienated. Roles for people in Victorian days were even more restrictive than today, and Freud discovered that when people struggled to avoid being and knowing themselves, they got sick. They could only become well and stay relatively well when they came to know themselves through self-disclosure to another person. This makes me think of Georg Groddeck's magnificent Book of the It (Id), in which, in the guise of letters to a naïve young woman, Groddeck shows the contrast between the public self—pretentious, role-playing—and the warded off but highly dynamic id—which I here very loosely translate as "real self."

Let me at this point draw a distinction between role relationships and interpersonal relationships—a distinction which is often overlooked in the current spate of literature that has to do with human relations. Roles are inescapable. They must be played or else the social system will not work. A role by definition is a repertoire of behavior patterns which must be rattled off in appropriate contexts, and all behavior which is irrelevant to the role must be suppressed. But what we often forget is the fact that it is a person who is playing the role. This person has a self, or I should say he is a self. All too often the roles that a person plays do not do justice to all of his self. In fact, there may be nowhere that he may just be himself. Even more, the person may not know his self. He may, in Horney's (1950) terms, be self-alienated. This fascinating term self-alienation means that an individual is estranged from his real self. His real self becomes a stranger, a feared and distrusted stranger. Estrangement, alienation from one's real self, is at the root of the "neurotic personality of our time" so eloquently described by Horney (1936). Fromm (1957) referred to the same phenomenon as a socially patterned defect. Self-alienation is a sickness which is so widely shared that no one recognizes it. We may take it for granted that all the clients whom we encounter are self-alienated to a greater or lesser extent. If you ask anyone to answer the question, "Who are you?" the answer will generally be "I am a psychologist," "a businessman," a "teacher," or what have you. The respondent will probably tell you the name of the role with which he feels most closely identified. As a matter of fact, the respondent spends a great part of his life trying to discover who he is, and once he has made some such discovery, he spends the rest of his life trying to play the part. Of course, some of the roles—age, sex, family, or occupational roles—may be so restrictive that they fit a person in a manner not too different from the girdle of a 200-pound lady who is struggling to look like Brigitte Bardot. There is Faustian drama all about us in this world of role playing. Everywhere we see people who have sold their soul, or their real self, if you wish, in order to be a psychologist, a businessman, a nurse, a physician, a this or a that.

Now, I have suggested that no social system can exist unless the members play their roles and play them with precision and elegance. But here is an odd observation, and yet one which you can all corroborate just by thinking back over your own experience. It is possible to be involved in a social group such as a family or a work setting for years and years, playing one's roles nicely with the other members—and never getting to know the persons who are playing the other roles. Roles can be played personally and impersonally, as we are beginning to discover. A husband can be married to his wife for fifteen years and never come to know her. He knows her as "the wife." This is the paradox of the "lonely crowd" (Riesman, 1950). It is the loneliness which people try to counter with "togetherness." But much of today's "togetherness" is like the "parallel play" of two-year-old children, or like the professors in Stringfellow Barr's (1958) novel who, when together socially, lecture *past* one another alternately and sometimes simultaneously. There is no real self-to-self or person-to-person meeting in such transactions. Now what does it mean to know a person, or, more accurately, a person's self? I don't mean anything mysterious by "self." All I mean is the person's subjective side—what he thinks, feels, believes, wants, worries about—the kind of thing which one could never know unless one were told. *We get to know the other person's self when he discloses it to us.*

Self-disclosure, letting another person know what you think, feel, or want is the most direct means (though not the only means) by which an individual can make himself known to another person. Personality hygienists place great emphasis upon the importance for mental health of what they call "real-self being," "self-realization," "discovering oneself," and so on. An operational analysis of what goes on in counseling and therapy shows that the patients and clients discover themselves through self-disclosure to the counselor. They talk and, to their shock and amazement, the counselor listens.

I venture to say that there is probably no experience more horrifying and terrifying than that of self-disclosure to "significant others" whose probable reactions are assumed, but not known. Hence the phenomenon of "resistance." This is what makes psychotherapy so difficult to take, and so difficult to administer. If there is any skill to be learned in the art of counseling and psychotherapy, it is the art of coping with the terrors which attend self-disclosure, and the art of decoding the language, verbal and nonverbal, in which a person speaks about his inner experience.

Now what is the connection between self-disclosure and healthy personality? Self-disclosure, or should I say "real"-self-disclosure, is both a symptom of personality health (Jourard, 1958, pp. 218–221) and at the same time a means of ultimately achieving healthy personality. The discloser of self is an animated "real-self be-er." This, of course, takes courage—the "courage to be." I have known people who would rather die than become known. In fact, some did die when it appeared that the chances were great that they would become known. When I say that self-disclosure is a symptom of personality health, what I mean really is that a person who displays many of the other characteristics that betoken healthy personality (Jourard, 1958; Maslow, 1954) *will also display the ability to make himself fully* known *to at least one other significant human being.* When I say that self-disclosure is a means by which one achieves personality health, I mean something like the following: it is not until I *am* my real self and I act my real self that my real self is in a position to grow. One's self grows from the *consequence of being.* People's selves stop growing when they repress them. This growth-arrest in the self is what helps to account for the surprising paradox of finding an infant inside the skin of someone who is playing the role of an adult. In a fascinating analysis of mental disease, Jurgen Ruesch (1957) describes assorted neurotics, psychotics, and psychosomatic patients as persons with selective atrophy and overspecialization in various aspects of the process of communication. This culminates in a foul-up of the processes of knowing others and of becoming known to others. Neurotic and psychotic symptoms might be viewed as smoke screens interposed between the patient's real self and the gaze of the onlooker. We might call the symptoms "devices to avoid becoming known." A new theory of schizophrenia has been proposed by a former patient (Anonymous, 1958) who "was there," and he makes such a point.

Alienation from one's real self not only arrests one's growth as a person; it also tends to make a farce out of one's relationships with people. As the ex-patient mentioned above observed, the crucial "break" in schizophrenia is with *sincerity,* not reality (Anonymous, 1958). A self-alienated person—one who does not disclose himself truthfully and fully—can never love another person, nor can he be loved by the other person. Effective loving calls for knowledge of the object (Fromm, 1956; Jourard, 1958). How can I love a person whom I do not know? How can the other person love me if he does not know me?

Hans Selye (1946) proposed and documented the hypothesis that illness as we know it arises in consequence of stress applied to the organism. Now I rather think that unhealthy *personality* has a similar root cause, and one which is related to Selye's concept of stress. It is this. Every maladjusted person is a person who has not made himself known to another human being and in consequence does not know himself. Nor can he be himself. More than that, *he struggles actively to avoid becoming known by another human being.* He *works* at it ceaselessly, 24 hours daily, and it is work! The fact that resisting becoming known is *work* offers us a research opening, incidentally (cf. Dittes, 1948; Davis and Malmo, 1951). I believe that in the effort to avoid becoming known, a person provides for himself a cancerous kind of stress which is subtle and unrecognized but nonetheless effective in producing, not only the assorted patterns of unhealthy personality which psychiatry talks about, but also the wide array of physical ills that have come to be recognized as the stock-in-trade of psychosomatic medicine. Stated another way, I believe that *other people come to be stressors to an individual in direct proportion to his degree of self-alienation.*

If I am struggling to avoid becoming known by other persons, then, of course, I must construct a false public self (Jourard, 1958, pp. 301–302). The greater the discrepancy between my unexpurgated real self and the version of myself that I present to others, the more dangerous will other people be for me. If becoming known by another person is threatening, then the very presence of another person can serve as a stimulus to evoke anxiety, heightened muscle tension, and all the assorted visceral changes which occur when a person is under stress. A beginning already has been made, demonstrating the tension-evoking powers of the other person, through the use of such instruments as are employed in the lie detector, through the measurement of muscle tensions with electromyographic apparatus, and so on (Davis and Malmo, 1958; Dittes, 1958).

Students of psychosomatic medicine have been intimating something of what I have just finished saying explicitly. They say (cf. Alexander, 1950) the ulcer patients, asthmatic patients, patients suffering from colitis, migraine, and the like, are chronic *repressors* of certain needs and emotions, especially hostility and dependency. Now when you repress something, you are not only withholding awareness of this something from yourself, you are also withholding it from the scrutiny of the other person. In fact, the means by which repressions are overcome in the therapeutic situation is through relentless disclosure of self to the therapist. When a patient is finally able to follow the fundamental rule in psychoanalysis and disclose everything which passes through his mind, he is generally shocked and dismayed to observe the breadth, depth, range, and diversity of thoughts, memories, and emotions which pass out of his "unconscious" into overt disclosure. Incidentally, by the time a person is that free to disclose in the presence of another human being, he has doubtless completed much of his therapeutic sequence.

Self-disclosure, then, appears to be one of the means by which a person engages in that elegant activity which we call real-self-being. But is real-self-being synonymous with healthy personality? Not in and of itself. I would say that real-self-being is a necessary but not a sufficient condition for healthy personality. Indeed, an authentic person may not be very "nice." In fact, he may seem much "nicer" socially and appear more mature and healthy when he is *not* being his real self than when he is his real self. But an individual's "obnoxious" but authentic self can never grow in the direction of greater maturity until the person has become acquainted with it and begins to *be* it. Real-self-being produces consequences which, in accordance with well-known principles of behavior (cf. Skinner, 1953), produce changes in the real self. Thus, there can be no real growth of the self without real-self-being. Full disclosure of the self to at least one other significant human being appears to be the means by which a person discovers not only the breadth and depth of his needs and feelings, but also the nature of his own self-affirmed values. There is no necessary conflict, incidentally, between real-self-being and being an ethical or nice person, because for the average member of our society, self-owned ethics are generally acquired during the process of growing up. All too often, however, the self-owned ethics are buried under the authoritarian morals (Fromm, 1947).

If self-disclosure is one of the means by which healthy personality is both achieved and maintained, we can also note that such activities as loving, psychotherapy, counseling, teaching, and nursing, all are impossible of achievement without the disclosure of the client. It is through self-disclosure that an individual reveals to himself and to the other party just exactly who, what, and where he is. Just as thermometers and sphygmomanometers disclose information about the real state of the body, self-disclosure reveals the real nature of the soul, or self. Such information is vital in order to conduct intelligent evaluations. All I mean by evaluation is comparing how a person is with some concept of optimum. You never really discover how truly sick your psychotherapy patient is until he discloses himself utterly to you. You cannot help your client in vocational guidance until he has disclosed to you something of the impasse in which he finds himself. You cannot love your spouse or your child or your friend unless those persons have permitted you to know them and to know what they need in order to move toward greater health and well-being. Nurses cannot nurse patients in any meaningful way unless they have permitted the patients to disclose their needs, wants, worries, anxieties and doubts, and so forth. Teachers cannot be very helpful to their students until they have permitted the students to disclose how utterly ignorant and misinformed they presently are. Teachers cannot even provide helpful information to the students until they have permitted the students to disclose exactly what they are interested in.

I believe we should reserve the term interpersonal relationships to refer to transactions between "I and thou" (Buber, 1937), between person and person, not between role and role. A truly personal relationship between two people involves disclosure of self one to the other in full and spontaneous honesty. The data that we have collected up to the present time have shown us some rather interesting phenomena. We found (Jourard and Lasakow, 1958), for example, that the women we tested in universities in the Southeast were consistently higher self-disclosers than men; they seem to have a greater capacity for establishing person-to-person relationships, interpersonal relationships, than men. This characteristic of women seems to be a socially patterned phenomenon which sociologists (Parsons and Bales, 1955) refer to as the expressive role of women in contradistinction to the instrumental role which men universally are obliged to adopt. Men seem to be much more skilled at impersonal, instrumental role-playing. But public health officials, very concerned about the sex differential in mortality rates, have been wondering what it is about being a man which makes males die younger than females. Do you suppose that there is any connection whatsoever between the disclosure patterns of men and women and their differential death rates? I have already intimated that withholding self-disclosure seems to impose a certain stress on people. Maybe "being manly," whatever that means, is slow suicide!

I think there is a very general way of stating the relationship between self-disclosure and assorted values such as healthy personality, physical health, group effectiveness, successful marriage, effective teaching, and effective nursing. It is this. A person's self is known to be the immediate determiner of his overt behavior. This is a paraphrase of the phenomenological point of view in psychology (Combs and Snygg, 1959). Now if we want to understand anything, explain it, control it, or predict it, it is helpful if we have available as much pertinent information as we possibly can. Self-disclosure provides a source of information which is relevant. This information has often been overlooked. Where it has not been overlooked, it has often been misinterpreted by observers and practitioners through such devices as projection or attribution. *It seems to be difficult for people to accept the fact that they do not know the very person whom they are confronting at any given moment.* We all seem to assume that we are expert psychologists and that we know the other person, when in fact we have only constructed a more or less autistic concept of him in our mind. If we are to learn more about man's self, we must learn more about self-disclosure—its conditions, dimensions, and consequences. Beginning evidence (cf. Rogers, 1958) shows that actively accepting, empathic, loving, nonpunitive response —in short, love—provides the optimum conditions under which man will disclose, or expose, his naked, quivering self to our gaze. It follows that if we would be helpful (or should I say *human*), we must grow to loving stature and learn, in Buber's terms, to confirm our fellowman in his very being. Probably, this presumes that we must *first* confirm our *own* being.

REFERENCES

Alexander, F. 1950. *Psychosomatic medicine.* New York: Norton.

Allport, G. 1955. *Becoming: Basic considerations of a psychology of personality.* New Haven: Yale University Press.

Anonymous. 1958. A new theory of schizophrenia. *Journal of Abnormal and Social Psychology* 57:226–236.

Barr, S. 1958. *Purely academic.* New York.

Buber, M. 1937. *I and thou.* New York: Scribner.

Davis, F. H., and Malmo, R. B. 1951. Electromyographic recording during interview. *American Journal of Psychiatry* 107:908–916.

Dittes, J. E. 1957. Extinction during psychotherapy of GSR accompanying "embarrassing" statements. *Journal of Abnormal and Social Psychology* 54:187–191.

Dunn, H. L. 1959. Higher-level wellness for man and society. *American Journal of Public Health.*

Freud, S. 1955. *The interpretation of dreams.* New York: Basic Books.

Fromm, E. 1947. *Man for himself.* New York: Rinehart.

Fromm, E. 1957. *The sane society.* New York: Rinehart.

Groddeck, G. 1928. *The book of it.* New York and Washington: Nervous and Mental Disease Publishing Co.

Horney, K. 1950. *Neurosis and human growth.* New York: Norton.

Horney, K. 1936. *The neurotic personality of our time.* New York: Norton.

Jahoda, M. 1958. *Current concepts of positive mental health.* New York: Basic Books.

Jourard, S. M. 1958. *Health personality: An approach through the study of healthy personality.* New York: Macmillan.

Jourard, S. M., and Lasakow, P. 1958. Some factors in self-disclosure. *Journal of Abnormal and Social Psychology* 56:91–98.

Maslow, A. H. 1954. *Motivation and personality.* New York: Harper.

Parsons, T., and Bales, R. F. 1955. *Family, socialization and interaction process.* Glencoe, Ill.: Free Press.

Riesman, D. 1950. *The lonely crowd.* New Haven: Yale University Press.

Rogers, C. R. 1954. The concept of the fully-functioning person. Mimeographed manuscript, privately circulated.

Ruesch, J. 1957. *Disturbed communication.* New York: Norton.

Selye, H. 1946. General adaptation syndrome and diseases of adaptation. *Journal of Clinical Endocrinology* 6:117–128.

Skinner, B. F. 1953. *Science and human behavior.* New York: Macmillan.

Snygg, D., and Combs, A. W. 1949. *Individual behavior.* New York: Harper.

Helping Disturbed Children: Psychological and Ecological Strategies

15

By NICHOLAS HOBBS

"Project Re-ED," described in this selection by its founder, Dr. Nicholas Hobbs of Vanderbilt University and a former president of the American Psychological Association, is a most exciting and significant innovative program for assisting disturbed children.

As you read, note the rationale for rejecting the medical model and especially the altered thinking when the concept of "cure" was abandoned. Twelve very basic concepts about children are important in "Project Re-ED": (1) Life is to be lived, now; (2) time is an ally; (3) trust is essential; (4) competence makes a difference; (5) symptoms can and should be controlled; (6) cognitive control can be taught; (7) feelings should be nurtured; (8) the group is important; (9) ceremony and ritual give order, stability, and confidence; (10) the body is the armature of the self; (11) communities are important; and (12) a child should know joy.

Is "Project Re-ED" humanistic or behavioristic, and is that an important question to decide?

From *American Psychologist*, vol. 21, no. 12 (December, 1966), pp. 1105–1115. Copyright 1966 by the American Psychological Association, and reproduced by permission.

Address of the president to the Seventy-Fourth Annual Convention of the American Psychological Association, New York, September 3, 1966.

The work here reported was made possible by Grant No. MH 929 of the United States Public Health Service, and by funds provided by Peabody College, the state of Tennessee, and the state of North Carolina. We are grateful for the support and wise counsel of Commissioner Joseph J. Baker and Commissioner Nat T. Winston, Jr., of Tennessee, Commissioner Eugene A. Hargrove and Sam O. Cornwell of North Carolina, Leonard J. Duhl and Raymond J. Balester of NIMH, and Paul W. Penningroth and Harold L. McPheeters of the Southern Regional Education Board.

HONORING A LONG TRADITION, I have the privilege tonight to present to you, my colleagues in psychology, an account of my own work in recent years.

I wish to present a case study in institution building, an account of a planful effort at social invention to meet an acute national problem, the problem of emotional disturbance in children.

I should like to cast this account in large context as an example of the kind of responsibility psychologists must assume in order to respond to a major challenge of our time: to help increase the goodness of fit between social institutions and the people they serve. This commitment demands that we invent new social arrangements designed to improve the quality of human life, and, in doing so, to adhere to the exacting traditions of psychological science: that is, to be explicit about what we are doing, to assess outcomes as meticulously as possible, to relate practice and theory to the benefit of both, and to lay our work open to public and professional scrutiny.

Let me acknowledge here that the work I report is the product of a cooperative effort to which a number of psychologists have contributed, notably Lloyd M. Dunn, Wilbert W. Lewis, William C. Rhodes, Matthew J. Trippe, and Laura Weinstein. National Institute of Mental Health officials, mental health commissioners, consultants, and especially the teacher-counselors, have invented the social institution I shall describe. If on occasion I seem unduly enthusiastic, it springs from an admiration of the work of others.

THE PROBLEM

"Project Re-ED" stands for "a project for the reeducation of emotionally disturbed children." Re-ED was developed explicitly as a new way to meet a social need for which current institutional arrangements are conspicuously inadequate. It is estimated that there are some 1½ million emotionally disturbed children in the United States today, children of average or superior intelligence whose behavior is such that they cannot be sustained with normal family, school, and community arrangements. There is one generally endorsed institutional plan for the care of such children: the psychiatric treatment unit of a hospital. But this is not a feasible solution to the problem; the costs are too great, averaging $60 a day, and there are not enough psychiatrists, psychologists, social workers, and psychiatric nurses to staff needed facilities, even if the solution were a good one, an assumption open to question. There is a real possibility that hospitals make children sick. The antiseptic atmosphere, the crepe sole and white coat, the tension, the expectancy of illness may confirm a child's worst fears about himself, firmly setting his aberrant behavior.

But worse things can happen to children, and do. They may be sent to a state hospital to be confined on wards with psychotic adults. They may be put in a jail, euphemistically called a detention home, or committed to an institution for delinquents or for the mentally retarded; or they may be kept at home, hidden away, receiving no help at all, aggravating and being aggravated by what can become an impossible situation.

The problem is further complicated by the professional advocacy of psychotherapy as the only means of effecting changes in behavior and by the pervasive and seldom questioned assumption that it takes at least two years to give any substantial help to a disturbed child. Finally, the availability of locks and drugs makes children containable, and the lack of evaluative research effectively denies feedback on the adequacy of approved methods. We became convinced eight years ago that the problem of the emotionally disturbed child cannot be solved by existing institutional arrangements. The Re-ED program was developed as one alternative, surely not the only one or even the most satisfactory one, but as a feasible alternative that deserved a test.

THE RE-ED SCHOOLS

The National Institute of Mental Health made a test possible by a demonstration grant in 1961 to Peabody College to develop residential schools for disturbed children in which concepts of reeducation could be formulated and tried out. The states of Tennessee and North Carolina, represented by their departments of mental health, joined with Peabody College to translate a general idea into an operational reality. The grant further provided for a training program to prepare a new kind of mental health worker, called a teacher-counselor, and for a research program to evaluate the effectiveness of the schools to be established.

Cumberland House Elementary School in Nashville received its first students in November of 1962, and Wright School of Durham in January of 1963. The schools are located in residential areas not far from the universities (Vanderbilt and Peabody, Duke and North Carolina) that provide personnel and consultation. They are pleasant places, open, friendly, homelike, where children can climb trees and play dodge ball, go to school, and, at night, have a good meal, and a relaxed, amiable evening.

Both schools have nearby camps that are used in the summer and on occasion throughout the year. The camps are simple, even primitive, with children erecting their own shelters, preparing their own meals, making their own schedules. For staff and children alike there is a contagious serenity about the experience. Cooking is a marvelously instructive enterprise; motivation is high, cooperation is necessary, and rewards are immediate. Children for whom failure has become an established expectation, at school and at home, can learn to do things successfully. Nature study is a source of unthreatening instruction. And there is nothing quite like a campfire, or a dark trail and a single flashlight, to promote a sense of community. In this simpler setting, where avoidant responses are few or weakly established, the child can take the first risky steps toward being a more adequate person.

At capacity each school will have 40 children, ages 6 to 12, grouped in five groups of eight children each. Each group is the responsibility of a team of two teacher-counselors, carefully selected young people, most of whom are graduates of a nine-month training program at Peabody. The two teacher-counselors, assisted by college students and by instructors in arts and crafts and physical education, are responsible for the children around the clock. Each school has a principal and an assistant principal, both educators, a liaison department staffed by social workers and liaison teachers, and a secretarial and housekeeping staff, who are full partners in the reeducation effort. The principal of a Re-ED school has an exacting job of management, training, interpretation, and public relations. The two schools have developed under the leaderships of four able men: John R. Ball and Neal C. Buchanan at Wright School and

James W. Cleary and Charles W. McDonald at Cumberland House.[1]

Of course, the teacher-counselors are the heart of Re-ED. They are young people, representing a large manpower pool, who have had experience in elementary school teaching, camping, or other work that demonstrates a long-standing commitment to children. After careful screening, in which self-selection plays an important part, they are given nine months of training in a graduate program leading to the Master of Arts degree. The program includes instruction in the characteristics of disturbed children, in specialized methods of teaching, including evaluation and remediation of deficits in reading, arithmetic, and other school subjects, in the use of consultants from mental health and educational fields, and in arts and crafts and games and other skills useful on the playing field, on a canoe trip, in the living units after dinner at night. They get a thorough introduction to child-serving agencies in the community and to the operation of a Re-ED school through an extensive practicum. Finally they are challenged with the task of helping invent what Re-ED will become.

But most of all a teacher-counselor is a decent adult; educated, well trained; able to give and receive affection, to live relaxed, and to be firm; a person with private resources for the nourishment and refreshment of his own life; not an itinerant worker but a professional through and through; a person with a sense of the significance of time, of the usefulness of today and the promise of tomorrow; a person of hope, quiet confidence, and joy; one who has committed himself to children and to the proposition that children who are emotionally disturbed can be helped by the process of reeducation.

The total school staff, and especially the teacher-counselors who work directly with the children, are backed by a group of consultants from psychiatry, pediatrics, social work, psychology, and education, an arrangement that makes available to the schools the best professional talent in the community and that has the further attractive feature of multiplying the effective-

---

[1] So many people have worked to make Re-ED a reality it is impossible even to record their names. They will have received recompense from seeing children flourish in their care. Yet Alma B. McLain and Letha B. Rowley deserve special recognition for long service and uncommon skill and grace in managing many problems.

ness of scarce and expensive mental health and educational personnel.[2]

THE CHILDREN

What kind of children do the teacher-counselors work with? It can be said, in general, that diagnostic classification has not been differentially related to a successful outcome; that the children are normal or superior in intelligence but are in serious trouble in school, often retarded two or three years in academic development; that they do not need continuing medical or nursing care, and that they can be managed in small groups in an open setting. Re-ED is not a substitute for a hospital. There are children too disturbed, too out of touch, too aggressive, too self-destructive to be worked with successfully in small groups in an open setting. However, Re-ED schools do take many children who would otherwise have to be hospitalized.

Susan was 11, with a diagnosis of childhood schizophrenia. She had attended school one day, the first day of the first grade, and had been in play therapy for four years. She was a pupil at Cumberland House for a year, staying longer than most children. She has been in a regular classroom for three years now, an odd child still but no longer a prospect for lifelong institutionalization. Ron was a cruelly aggressive child, partly an expression of inner turmoil and partly an expression of class values and habits; he is much less destructive now, and is back in school. Danny was simply very immature, so that school was too much for him; his problem could be called school phobia if that would help. Dick was extremely effeminate, wearing mascara and painting his nails. Both boys responded to masculine activities guided by a trusted male counselor. Billy was a gasoline sniffer and an ingenious hypochondriac; he returned to a reunion recently much more mature though still

---

[2] The consultants have meant much more to Project Re-ED than can be recorded in this brief account. We here inadequately recognize the invaluable contribution of our colleagues: Jenny L. Adams, M.S.W., Gus K. Bell, Ph.D., Lloyd J. Borstelmann, Ph.D., Eric M. Chazen, M.D., Julius H. Corpening, B.D., Jane Ann Eppinger, M.S.W., John A. Fowler, M.D., Ihla H. Gehman, Ed.D., W. Scott Gehman, Ph.D., Maurice Hyman, M.D., J. David Jones, M.D., and Bailey Webb, M.D.

having trouble with school work. Larry, age 12, was quite bright yet unable to read; nor were we able to teach him to read. So we failed with him. It is such children as these that we aspire to help. To call them all "emotionally disturbed" is clearly to use language to obscure rather than to clarify. Nonetheless, they are all children who are in serious trouble, for whom the Re-ED idea was developed.

During the past summer, under the direction of William and Dianne Bricker and Charles McDonald, we have been working at Cumberland House with six of the most severely disturbed children we could find, mostly custodial cases from state institutions. Regular Re-ED activities are supplemented by a 24-hour schedule of planned behaviors and contingent rewards, the staff being augmented to make such individualized programming possible, but still using inexpensive and available personnel, such as college students. While it is too early to assess the effectiveness of this effort, we are pleased with the progress that most of the children are making, and we are certain we are giving them more of a chance than they had when their principal challenge was to learn how to live in an institution.

ECOLOGICAL CONCEPTS

Let us turn now to an examination of the theoretical assumptions and operational procedures involved in the process of reeducation. We do not, of course, make use of the principles involved in traditional psychotherapy; transference, regression, the promotion of insight through an exploration of inner dynamics and their origins are not a part of the picture. The teacher-counselor is not a psychotherapist, nor does he aspire to be one.

We have become increasingly convinced that a major barrier to effective national planning for emotionally disturbed children is the professional's enchantment with psychotherapy. Everything in most model institutions revolves around getting the child to his therapist one, two, or maybe three hours a week. A few superb treatment centers combine psychotherapy with a program of daily activities conducive to personal growth and integration. But these are rare indeed. It is not uncommon to find children locked 15 stories high in steel and glass, with a caged roof to play on, drugged to keep them from doing too

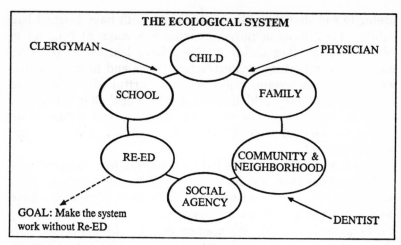

FIGURE 1　Chart of ecological system, the smallest unit in a systems approach to working with a disturbed child.

much damage to the light fixtures and air conditioning, while they await their precious hour, guarded by attendants who think disturbed children must scream, fight, climb walls, cower in a corner. Most frequently, of course, therapy is not available; most hospitals hold children hoping somehow they will get better.

An overcommitment to individual psychotherapy seems to us to stem from an uncritical acceptance of "cure" as the goal in working with a child, a consequence of defining the problem initially as one of "illness." That some disturbed children are "ill" in the usual sense may be accepted, but to define them all as such leads, we think, to a host of unvalidated and unquestioned assumptions; to a preoccupation with the intrapsychic life of the child, with what goes on inside his skull; to an easy use of drugs without knowledge of their long-term effects on character development; to the extended isolation of children from their families, the presumed source of contagion; to a limitation of professional roles; to the neglect of schools and of schooling; and so on. The preemptive character of a definition and the semantic sets that ensue are major barriers to innovation in working with disturbed children.

Of course we have our own ways of talking about the problem, and our metaphors are no less preemptive, making it all the more important for us to be explicit about definitions. We prefer to say that the children we work with have learned bad habits. They have acquired nonadaptive ways of relating to adults and to other children. They have learned to perceive themselves in limiting or destructive terms and to construe the world as an uncertain, rejecting, and hurtful place. We also recognize that the child lives in a real world that often falls short in giving him the affection, support, and guidance he needs. So we deal directly with social realities as well as with private perceptions.

This kind of thinking has led us gradually to a different way of defining our task, a definition of considerable heuristic merit (see Figure 1). For want of a more felicitous phrase, we have been calling it a systems approach to the problem of working with a disturbed child. We assume that the child is an inseparable part of a small social system, of an ecological unit made up of the child, his family, his school, his neighborhood and community. A social agency is often a part of the picture when a child has been designated emotionally disturbed, and other people—a physician, a clergyman—may be brought in as needed. The system may become "go" as a result of marked improvement in any component (the father stops drinking and goes back to work, a superb teacher becomes available, the child improves dramatically), or it may work as a result of modest improvement in all components. The effort is to get each component of the system above threshold with respect to the requirements of the other components. The Re-ED school becomes a part of the ecological unit for as brief a period of time as possible, withdrawing when the probability that the system will function appears to exceed the probability that it will not. We used to speak of putting the child back into the system, but we have come to recognize the erroneous assumptions involved; the child defines the system, and all we can do is withdraw from it at a propitious moment.

Once we abandoned cure as a goal and defined our problem as doing what we can to make a small social system work in a reasonably satisfactory manner, there ensued a number of operational patterns that contrast sharply with the practices of existing residential treatment centers for children.

For one thing, parents are no longer viewed as sources of contagion but as responsible collaborators in making the system work. Parents are involved in discussion groups and are helped to get assistance from mental health centers. They actively participate in the ongoing program of the school. They organize an annual reunion, publish a parent's manual, sew for the children, and in many ways assume responsibility for reestablishing the child as quickly as possible in his own home, school, and community.

The children go home on weekends to keep families and children belonging to each other, to avoid the estrangement that can come from prolonged separation, and to give the child and his parents and brothers and sisters an opportunity to learn new and more effective ways of living together. Visitors ask "Aren't your Mondays awful?" They are, indeed, but we cherish their chaos as a source of new instruction; we try to keep in mind that our goal is not to run a tranquil school but to return the child as quickly as possible to his own home and regular school.

The ecological model requires new strategies to involve home, neighborhood, school, agency, and community in a contract with us to help a child. It requires new patterns for the deployment of personnel, and it has led to the development of a new kind of mental health worker: the liaison teacher. The liaison teacher is responsible for maintaining communication with the child's regular school, again to prevent alienation and to arrange optimum conditions for the child's early return to a regular classroom. For example a liaison teacher may personally accompany a child to a new school to which he has been transferred in order to increase the probability that that component of the ecological system will function effectively.

The social worker in Re-ED honors an early heritage of his profession, before the lamentable sit-behind-the-desk-and-do-psychotherapy era got established. He reaches out to the family, to community agencies, and to individuals—to any reasonable source of help for a child in trouble. Again, the goal is to make the system work, not simply to adjust something inside the head of the child.

THE PROCESS OF REEDUCATION

Now, let us turn to the child himself, to our relationships with him, and to what is meant operationally by the process of reeducation. Here are an even dozen underlying concepts that have come to seem important to us as we try to talk about what goes on in a Re-ED school.

Item 1: Life is to be lived, now. We start with the assumption that each day, that every hour in every day, is of great importance to a child, and that when an hour is neglected, allowed to pass without reason and intent, teaching and learning go on nonetheless, and the child may be the loser. In Re-ED, no one waits for a special hour. We try, as best we can, to make all hours special. We strive for immediate and sustained involvement in purposive and consequential living. We constantly test the optimistic hypothesis that if children are challenged to live constructively, that if they are given an opportunity for a constructive encounter with other children and with decent adults, they will come off well—and they do, most of the time. They learn, here and now, that life can be lived on terms satisfactory to society and satisfying to themselves. Our task is to contrive each day so that the probability of success in this encounter clearly outweigh the probability of failure. I paraphrase Jessie Taft when I say, in the mastery of this day the child learns, in principle, the mastery of all days.

Item 2: Time is an ally. We became convinced, in the early stages of planning the project, that children are kept too long in most traditional treatment programs. The reasons for this are many. The abstract goal of cure through psychotherapy leads to expectations of extensive personality reorganization, of the achievement of adequacy in a wide array of possible life roles. It thus takes a long time either to succeed in this ambitious endeavor or to become aware that one has failed. Staff and children become fond of each other, making separation difficult. The widespread practice of removing the child from his home for extended periods of time causes a sometimes irreparable estrangement; the family closes ranks against the absent member. While everyone recognizes the importance of school in the life of the child, mental health programs have neither operational concepts nor specialized personnel necessary to effect an easy transition for the child from the institution back to his own school. Furthermore, the expectation of a prolonged stay in a treatment center becomes a self-validating hypothesis. A newly admitted child asks "How long do kids stay here?" He is told "about two years," and he settles down to do what is expected of him, with full support of staff and parents who also "know" that it takes two years to help a disturbed child. Myriad other constraints get established; for example, the treatment center hires just enough secretaries to move children in and out of a two-year cycle, and it is not possible to speed the process without hiring more secretaries, a restraint on therapeutic progress that is seldom identified. So before we admitted the first child, we set six months as the expected, average period of stay, a goal we have now achieved.

Time is an issue of importance in the process of reeducation in yet another way. We work with children during years when life has a tremendous forward thrust. Several studies suggest that therapeutic intervention is not demonstrably superior to the passage of time without treatment in the subsequent adjustment of children diagnosed as emotionally disturbed (Lewis, 1965). Treatment may simply speed up a process that would occur in an unknown percentage of children anyway. There is a real possibility that a long stay in a treatment center may actually slow down this process. Furthermore, in ecological perspective, it is clear that children tend to get ejected from families at low points in family organization and integrity. Most families get better after such periods; there is only one direction for them to go, and that is up. The systems concept may entail simply observing when the family has regained sufficient stability to sustain a previously ejected child. The great tragedy is that children can get caught up in institutional arrangements that must inexorably run their course. In Re-ED we claim time is an ally and try to avoid getting in the way of the normal restorative processes of life.

Item 3: Trust is essential. The development of trust is the first step in reeducation of the emotionally disturbed child. The disturbed child is conspicuously impaired in his ability to learn from adults. The mediation process is blocked or distorted by the child's experience-based hypothesis that adults are deceptive, that they are an unpredictable source of hurt and help. He faces each adult with a predominant anticipation of punishment, rejection, derision, or withdrawal of love. He is acutely impaired in the very process by which more mature ways of living may be acquired A first step, then, in the reeducation process, is the development of trust. Trust, coupled with understanding, is the beginning point of a new learning experience, an experience that helps a child know that he can use an adult to learn many things: how to read, how to be affectionate, how to be oneself without fear or guilt.

We are intrigued by the possibility, indeed are almost sure the thesis is true, that no amount of professional training can make an adult worthy of the trust of a child or capable of generating it. This ability is prior to technique, to theory, to technical knowledge. After seeing the difference that teacher-counselors in our two schools have made in the lives of children, I am confident of the soundness of the idea that some adults know, without knowing how they know, the way to inspire trust in children and to teach them to begin to use adults as mediators of new learning.

Item 4: Competence makes a difference. The ability to do something well gives a child confidence and self-respect and gains for him acceptance by other children, by teachers, and, unnecessary as it might seem, even by his parents. In a society as achievement-oriented as ours, a person's worth is established in substantial measure by his ability to produce or perform. Acceptance without productivity is a beginning point in the process of reeducation, but an early goal and a continuing challenge is to help the child get good at something.

What, then, in the process of reeducation, does the acquisition of competence mean? It means first and foremost the gaining of competence in school skills, in reading and arithmetic most frequently, and occasionally in other subjects as well. If a child feels that he is inadequate in school, inadequacy can become a pervasive theme in his life, leading to a consistent pattern of failure to work up to his level of ability. Underachievement in school is the single most common characteristic of emotionally disturbed children. We regard it as sound strategy to attack directly the problem of adequacy in school, for its intrinsic value as well as for its indirect effect on the child's perception of his worth and his acceptance by people who are important in his world. A direct attack on the problem of school skills does not mean a gross assault in some area of deficiency. On the contrary, it requires utmost skill and finesse on the part of the teacher-counselor to help a disturbed child move into an area where he has so often known defeat, where failure is a well-rooted expectancy, where a printed page can evoke flight or protest or crippling anxiety. The teacher-counselor need make no apologies to the psychotherapist with reference to the level of skill required to help a disturbed child learn.

So, in Re-ED, school keeps. It is not regarded, as it is in many mental health programs, as something that can wait until the child gets better, as though he were recovering from measles or a broken leg. School is the very stuff of a child's problems, and consequently, a primary source of instruction in living. Special therapy rooms are not needed; the classroom is a natural setting for a constructive relationship between a disturbed child and a competent, concerned adult.

Much of the teaching, incidentally, is through the unit or enterprise method. For example, a group of boys at Cumberland House was invited to go camping with some Cherokee Indian children on their reservation. The trip provided a unifying theme for three months' instruction in American history, geography, arithmetic, writing, and arts and crafts. At Wright School, rocketry has provided high motivation and an entrée to mathematics, aerodynamics, and politics. The groups are small enough to make individualized instruction possible, even to the point of preparing special programmed materials for an individual child, a method that has been remarkably effective with children with seemingly intractable learning disorders. The residential character of the Re-ED school means that the acquisition of competence does not have to be limited to increased skill in school subjects. It may mean learning to swim, to draw, to sing; it may mean learning to cook on a Dakota hole, to lash together a table, to handle a canoe, to build a shelter in the woods; it may mean learning to talk at council ring, to assert one's rights, to give of one's possessions, to risk friendship, to see parents as people and teachers as friends.

Item 5: Symptoms can and should be controlled. It is standard doctrine in psychotherapeutic practice that symptoms should not be treated, that the one symptom removed will simply be replaced by another, and that the task of the therapist is to uncover underlying conflicts against which the symptom is a defense, thus eliminating the need for any symptom at all. In Re-ED we contend, on the other hand, that symptoms are important in their own right and deserve direct attention. We are impressed that some symptoms are better to have than other symptoms. The bad symptoms are those that alienate the child from other children or from the adults he needs as a source of security or a source of learning. There is much to be gained then from identifying symptoms that are standing in the way of normal development and working out specific plans for removing or altering the symptoms if possible. The problem is to help the child make effective contact with normal sources of affection, support, instruction, and discipline. We also work on a principle of parsimony that instructs us to give first preference to explanations involving the assumption of minimum pathology, as contrasted to professional preference for deep explanations and the derogation of all else as superficial.

Item 6: Cognitive control can be taught. Though little emphasis is placed on the acquisition of insight as a source of therapeutic gain, there is a lot of talking in Re-ED about personal problems and how they can be managed better. The teacher-counselor relies primarily on immediate experience, on the day-by-day, hour-by-hour, moment-by-moment relationship between himself and the child; he relies on specific events that can be discussed to increase the child's ability to manage his own life. The emotionally disturbed child has fewer degrees of freedom in behavior than the normal child, yet he is not without the ability to shape his own behavior by self-administered verbal instruction. He can signal to himself if he can learn what the useful signals are. The teacher-counselor works constantly to help a child learn the right signals. The focus of this effort is on today and tomorrow, not on the past or the future, and on ways for the child to signal to himself to make each day a source of instruction for the living of the next. At the council ring at night, at a place set apart from the business of living, children in a group are helped to consider what was good about the day just past, what went wrong that might be handled better tomorrow, and what was learned, especially in successes and failures in relationships among themselves. Possibly more important than the solving of particular problems is the acquisition of the habit of talking things over for the purpose of getting better control over events, a habit that can frequently be carried over into the child's home and become a new source of strength for his family.

Item 7: Feelings should be nurtured. We are very interested in the nurturance and expression of feeling, to help a child own all of himself without guilt. Children have a way of showing up with animals, and we are glad for this. A child who has known the rejection of adults may find it safest, at first, to express affection to a dog. And a pet can be a source of pride and of sense of responsibility. Anger, resentment, hostility are commonplace, of course, and their expression is used in various ways: to help some children learn to control their violent impulses and to help others give vent to feelings too long repressed. In Re-ED schools one finds the familiar ratio of four or five boys to one girl, a consequence in part, we believe, of a lack of masculine challenge in school and community today. Thus we contrive situations of controlled danger in which children can test themselves, can know fear and become the master of it. The simple joy of companionship is encouraged. We are impressed by the meaningfulness of friendships and how long they endure. The annual homecoming is anticipated by many youngsters as an opportunity to walk arm-in-arm with an old friend associated with a period of special significance in their lives. And we respect the need to be alone, to work things through without intrusion, and to have a private purpose. Feelings also get expressed through many kinds of creative activities that are woven into the fabric of life in a Re-ED school. Throwing clay on a potter's wheel gives a child a first sense of his potential for shaping his world. A puppet show written by the children may permit freer expression than is ordinarily tolerable. Drawing and painting can be fun for a whole group. And an object to mold gives something to do to make it safe for an adult and child to be close together.

Item 8: The group is important to children. Children are organized in groups of eight, with two teacher-counselors in charge. The group is kept intact for nearly all activities and becomes an important source of motivation, instruction, and control. When a group is functioning well, it is extremely difficult for an individual child to behave in a disturbed way. Even when the group is functioning poorly, the frictions and the failures can be used constructively. The council ring, or pow-wow, involving discussion of difficulties or planning of activities can be a most maturing experience. And the sharing of adventure, of vicissitudes, and of victories, provides an experience in human relatedness to which most of our children have been alien.

Item 9: Ceremony and ritual give order, stability, and confidence. Many Re-ED children have lived chaotic lives, even in their brief compass. They may come from homes where interpersonal disarray is endemic. We have stumbled upon and been impressed by the beneficence of ceremony, ritual, and metaphor for children and have come to plan for their inclusion in the program. The nightly backrub is an established institution with the Whippoorwills, a time of important confidences. Being a Bobcat brings a special sense of camaraderie and has its own metaphorical obligations. And a Christmas pageant can effect angelic transformation of boys whose ordinary conduct is far from seraphic.

Item 10: The body is the armature of the self. We are intrigued by the idea that the physical self is the armature around which the psychological self is constructed and that a clearer experiencing of the potential and the boundaries of the body should lead to a clearer definition of the self, and thus to greater psychological fitness and more effective functioning. The Outward Bound schools in England, developed as an experience for young men to overcome the anomie that is the product of an industrial civilization, are built around the concept. Austin Des Lauriers' ideas about treatment of schizophrenia in children emphasize differentiating the body from the rest of the world. Programmatically, in Re-ED, the idea has been realized in such activities as swimming, climbing, dancing, tumbling, clay modelling, canoeing, building a tree house, and walking a monkey bridge.

Item 11: Communities are important. The systems concept in Re-ED leads to an examination of the relationship of the child to his home community. Many children who are referred to our schools come from families that are alienated or detached from community life or that are not sufficiently well organized or purposeful to help the child develop a sense of identity with his neighborhood, his town or city. He has little opportunity to discover that communities exist for people and, while the goodness of fit between the two may often leave much to be desired, an important part of a child's education is to learn that community agencies and institutions exist for his welfare and that he has an obligation as a citizen to contribute to their effective functioning. This is especially true for many of the boys referred to Re-ED, whose energy, aggressiveness, lack of control, and resentment of authority will predispose them to delinquent behavior when they are a few years older and gain in independence and mobility. This idea has a number of implications for program planning. Field trips to the fire, police, and health departments are useful. Memberships in the YMCA, a children's museum, a playground group, or a community center may be worked out for a child. Church attendance may be encouraged and a clergyman persuaded to take special interest in a family, and a library card can be a proud possession and a tangible community tie.

Item 12: Finally, a child should know joy. We have often speculated about our lack of a psychology of well-being. There is an extensive literature on anxiety, guilt, and dread, but little that is well developed on joy. Most psychological experiments rely for motivation on avoidance of pain or hunger or some other aversive stimuli; positive motivations are limited to the pleasure that comes from minute, discrete rewards. This poverty with respect to the most richly human of motivations leads to anaemic programming for children. We thus go beyond contemporary psychology to touch one of the most vital areas of human experiencing. We try to develop skill in developing joy in children. We believe that it is immensely important, that it is immediately therapeutic if further justification is required, for a child to know some joy in each day and to look forward with eagerness to at least some joy-giving event that is planned for tomorrow.

COSTS AND EFFECTIVENESS

Now, let us turn to the practical questions of cost and of effectiveness.

A Re-ED school costs about $20 to $25 per child per day to operate. Thus the per-day cost is about one-third the cost of the most widely accepted model and perhaps four times the cost of custodial care. Cost per day, however, is not the best index to use, for the purpose of a mental health program is not to keep children cheaply but to restore them to home, school, and community as economically as possible. In terms of cost per child served, the cost of a Re-ED program is equivalent to or less than the cost of custodial care. The cost per child served is approximately $4,000. If Re-ED can prevent longer periods of institutionalization, this is a modest investment indeed.

Appropriate to the systems analysis of the problem, most of our studies of effectiveness of Re-ED schools have employed ratings by concerned observers: mother, father, teacher, our own staff, and agency staffs, all important persons in the ecological space of the child. However, Laura Weinstein (1965) has been interested in the way normal and disturbed children construct interpersonal space, as illustrated by the accompanying representations of felt board figures. She used two techniques. In the first (the replacement technique), each of two

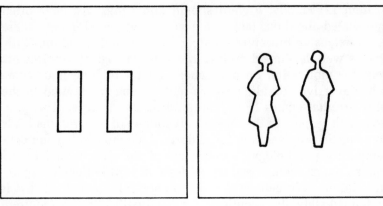

FIGURE 2 Geometric felt figures used in replacement technique (after Weinstein, 1965).

FIGURE 3 Human felt figures used in replacement technique (after Weinstein, 1965).

figure pairs—a pair of human figures and a pair of rectangles—is present on a different board and equally far apart (Figures 2 and 3). The child is asked to replace the felt figures "exactly as far apart as they are now." Normal and disturbed children make systematic errors, but in opposite directions: normal chil-

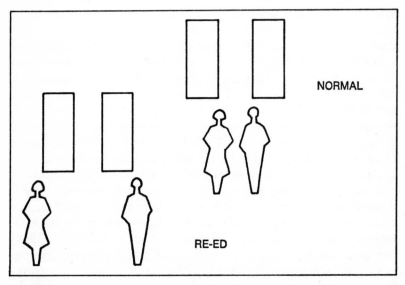

FIGURE 4 Placement of geometric and human felt figures by normal and disturbed children (after Weinstein, 1965).

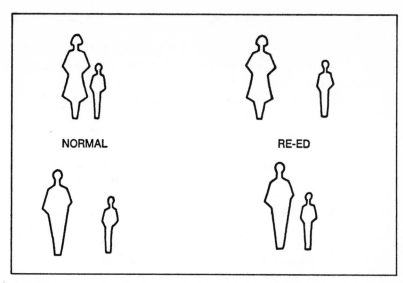

FIGURE 5 Mother, father, and child felt figures as placed by normal and disturbed children (after Weinstein, 1965).

dren replace human figures closer together while Re-ED children replace human figures farther apart (Figure 4). In the second technique (the free placement technique), human figures are used, representing mothers, fathers, and children. The children are asked to place the figures on the board "any way you like." Again systematic differences occur. Normal children place the child very close to the mother. Re-ED children place greater distance between the mother and the child than between any other human pair (Figure 5). The mother-child relationship is clearly crucial in the life space of the 6- to 12-year-old children with whom we work. It is gratifying to report that children after the Re-ED experience put the child figure closer to the mother than they did before; that is, they structure interpersonal space as normal children do.

The basic design for evaluating the effectiveness of the Re-ED schools involves observations taken at time of enrollment and repeated six months after discharge. Preliminary results present an encouraging picture. A composite rating of improvement, based on follow-up information on 93 graduates provided by all evaluators, gives a success rate of approximately 80 percent. We are in process of obtaining comparison data from control groups to determine the extent to which the reeducation effort is superior to changes that occur with the passage of time.

Detailed analyses show that mothers and fathers independently report a decrease in symptoms such as bedwetting, tantrums, nightmares, and school fears, and an increase in social maturity on a Vineland type checklist. School adjustment as rated by teachers shows the same favorable trends. On a semantic differential measure of discrepancy between how the child is seen and parental standards for him, there is an interesting and dynamically significant difference between fathers and mothers. Both see the child as having improved. For fathers the perceived improvement results in lower discrepancy scores between the child as seen and a standard held for him. For some mothers, however, improvement results in a raising of standards so that discrepancy scores frequently remain high. This is not true of all mothers, but it is more frequently true of mothers than of fathers.

But *T* tests seldom determine the fate of institutions; public and professional acceptance is crucial.

To obtain an informed and mature professional appraisal of Re-ED, we have established a panel of visitors composed of men whose judgment is held in high esteem: Eli M. Bower, psychologist; Reginald S. Lourie, psychiatrist; Charles R. Strother, psychologist; and Robert L. Sutherland, sociologist. Members of the panel have been visiting the schools regularly since their inception and will make public their final appraisal at the end of the project period. It is enough to say now that they are all strong supporters of the Re-ED idea.

A test of public support of the Re-ED idea was adventitiously obtained when the legislature of the state of North Carolina in June, 1966, terminated state funds for the support of Wright School after July 1, 1966. Protest from all over the state was immediate and strong; in less than three years of operation the school had won impressive public support. Funds have been raised to continue Wright School in operation until the legislature convenes again.[3] The governor has assured the mental

---

[3] Among the major contributors are the Wright Refuge Board, the Sarah Graham Kenan Fund, the Mary Duke Biddle Foundation, the Hillsdale Fund, and the Stanley County Mental Health Association. Many gifts have come from churches, mental health associations, civic organizations, and individuals. We gratefully acknowledge their help in keeping Wright School in operation.

health officials of North Carolina that he will support legislative measures to restore state funds for the operation of Wright School. Fortunately the Tennessee school has not been put to such public test, but professional and political endorsement is evident in the decision to build two new schools, one in Memphis and one in Chattanooga, that will be operated as reeducation centers. Finally, it is encouraging that several other states have committees working to establish Re-ED schools.

Our aspiration and our growing confidence are that the Re-ED model will be replicated in many states, that it will have its influence on the character of more traditional treatment programs, and that the beneficiaries will be the disturbed children of America.

We further think of Re-ED as an institution that exemplifies, in its development, the contemporary challenge to psychologists to concern themselves with the invention of social arrangements that put psychological knowledge to use to improve the quality of human life.

REFERENCES

Hobbs, N. 1964. Mental health's third revolution. *American Journal of Orthopsychiatry* 34:822–833.

Lewis, W. W. 1965. Continuity and intervention in emotional disturbance: A review. *Exceptional Children* 31 (9):465–475.

Weinstein, L. 1965. Social schemata of emotionally disturbed boys. *Journal of Abnormal Psychology* 70:457–461.

Reducing the Effects of Restricted Environments

16

By HERBERT YAHRAES

At first glance, this selection may not appear to deal with behavior disorders because there is heavy emphasis upon intellectual development and measurement of intellectual functioning. It has been included, however, because the study reached a group of children who are ignored ordinarily. Furthermore, while the children were not labeled as such, many of them certainly exhibited problem behavior. This study also reflects an increasing flexibility in ways of providing help for children. In this instance, nonprofessionals visited homes regularly, in contrast to the usual approach of having a child brought to a center. One of the reasons for doing so was that of promoting family involvement, especially that of the mother. As you read some of the descriptions of the homes, it will be easy to understand why these children were exhibiting developmental difficulties.

INTRODUCTION AND SUMMARY

DURING THE FIRST 15 or 18 months of life, a number of investigators have reported, children from one racial or socioeconomic group score about the same in tests of intellectual functioning as those from another. By school time, though, different groups have reached different levels; in particular, children from families of low socioeconomic status have a lower

From *Mental Health Reports*, vol. 4 (January, 1970). National Clearinghouse for Mental Health Information, publication no. 5026. This article was originally entitled "Reducing the Effects of Cultural Deprivation," and appeared as part of a series edited by Dr. Julius Segal.

This research was planned by Earl S. Schaefer of the National Institute of Mental Health and carried out in consultation with him. Doctor Paul H. Furfey, project director, and Thomas J. Harte, both of the Catholic University of America, were the investigators.

average IQ than children from families of higher status. The schools do not change this difference.

Other studies have shown that intellectual level, as measured by mental tests, is closely related to verbal ability, as measured by tests of vocabulary and information, and that disadvantaged groups score lower on these verbal tests than on others. It has also been shown that the children in these groups receive less verbal stimulation from parents—through being talked to, read to, taken on trips, etc.—than children in middle-class groups, and that the parents are usually not very good examples for children to follow in learning language.

These findings suggest that:

Children from low socioeconomic groups develop deficits in intellectual functioning because they lack adequate intellectual, particularly verbal, stimulation.

One reason many disadvantaged families remain disadvantaged, generation after generation, is the lower ability of their children to profit from our educational system and, therefore, a lower ability as adults to compete in our economic system.

If adequate stimulation can be provided early enough, it should prevent deficits in intellectual functioning and thereby help break the cycle of poverty and cultural deprivation.

To test one means of providing such stimulation, Earl Schaefer, Ph.D., of NIMH's Center for Studies of Children and Family Mental Health, initiated the Infant Education Research project in 1965. This is a project guided and financed by the Institute but carried out by a staff directed by Msgr. Paul H. Furfey, Ph.D., research associate, Bureau of Social Research, Catholic University. Under it individual tutoring—an hour a day, five days a week—was provided to a group of 28 Negro boys from slum areas of Washington, D.C.. . . .

TRAINING THE TUTORS

The tutors were chosen because they were intelligent, outgoing women interested in working with children. All had had experience in jobs—teaching, social work, nursing—that brought them in touch with children. A few were mothers. With the exception of a woman who was still in college, all were college graduates. Five were black and four white. They worked together beautifully, a project official reports, and those of one color seemed to get along with the children as well as those of the other. (Each child had two tutors—generally one of them black, the other white—who alternated weekly in working with him. This arrangement was intended to lessen disruptive effects in case a tutor left or was changed, to reduce any feeling on the part of the mother that the tutor was competing for the child's affection, and to provide two different observers of the child and his family.)

During the initial training period, which ran for about two months, half-time, the tutors heard and discussed lectures by Schaefer, Furfey, and others on child development, the special problems of the disadvantaged child, and means of overcoming those problems. The need to develop and maintain a relationship that would foster the child's interest, happiness, and success in his new experience was emphasized. If this need were to be met, the tutors were told they would have to accept the child's interests, praise his achievements, and enthusiastically explore new learning opportunities with him. The interaction between tutor and child was to be playful, spontaneous, and pleasant; formal instruction would be avoided. A tutor must be aware that a child's early learning involves a great deal of looking, listening, tasting, smelling, and feeling. She must also be aware that she is a model for the child—and the mother—to imitate. She will name things casually but often—toys, household objects, pictures in books, events, clothes, the child's body.

"We are all investigators, researchers, experimenters together," Schaefer told the tutors. "We are searching for a method of early education which will raise the intellectual functioning of children and increase their ability to do well in our American school system. We think we know some of the characteristics which help children to succeed in school. We think it helps a child to be cooperative, outgoing, verbal, friendly, helpful to others, resourceful, curious, attentive, to have goal-directed behavior and be able to concentrate and persevere. It helps if he has developed a feeling of competence and of human worth, if he is able to assert himself in a positive way and make a worthwhile contribution to a group. It is of great value that he have good comprehension and a good vocabulary. We hope to find ways of developing at least some of those characteristics."

Examples of a number of specific activities that might be used during the tutoring sessions were discussed—among them, blowing bubbles, playing with beads, making things with pipe cleaners, playing a guessing game, making a pull toy, having fun with paper plates, and playing a sorting game. The tutors were asked to encourage the child to participate in any activity as much as possible and to talk to him about what was going on. If tutor and child were making a bean bag, for example, the talk might go something like this:

We will make a bean bag.
Please hold the cloth for me.
I will cut it.
Be careful. The scissors is sharp.
Move your hands.
That's it.
Now we can sew it.
Look at this needle.
See the tiny hole.
We have to get the thread in this tiny hole—the eye of the needle.
Look at my thimble.
Try it on your finger.
See how it fits on mine.
Please hold the cloth while I thread the needle.
Watch me thread it.
You can string beads. Some day you will be able to thread a needle.
Now. I will hold the bag open while you put the pebbles in.
Put in one; now one more.
Put a whole bunch in at once if you can.
Now we will sew up the last side.
We must sew it so no pebbles will fall out.
See. It's all done.
Thanks for helping, Johnny. Johnny helped to make a bean bag.
See. Isn't it pretty. We're all finished.
Now move back, so I can throw it to you, etc.
Now let's try throwing it into that pail. Let's take turns, etc.

Making a bean bag would be fun. It would also help the child build his vocabulary. And it would help him in learning to count, learning goal-directed activity, learning that a combination of materials can make something different from the original materials, and learning that a person can create something and then have fun with it.

Emphasis throughout was placed on language stimulation. Schaefer urged the tutors to get the children "hooked on books."

The technique of *transfer*, too, was emphasized. "Children are happier and more comfortable with the familiar," Schaefer pointed out. "They can even become frightened by something entirely novel. Begin work with something familiar to the child. If it is something he likes and enjoys you will soon be able to transfer to a slightly different use or activity and thus capitalize on the child's initial interest and pleasure.

"For example, if he finds it fun to shake jingle bells because he enjoys the sound, you may later be able to transfer to sorting jingle bells according to size or color, counting them, making things with them, etc., and still maintain his interest and joy, while at the same time stimulating new learning."

As part of their training, the tutors observed the activities of children in day centers, an orphanage, an institution for delinquent children, and the homes of middle-class families having children of roughly the same age as those in the project. The tutors also recruited the families for the research program, by knocking on almost 200 doors in several of Washington's worst slum areas, and thus became acquainted with the types of homes they would be going into. And each worked for two weeks with a pilot case, a child who was a little too old to be chosen for the project.

There was in-service training, too. Each tutor discussed cases frequently with the leader of the tutoring team (in the beginning a speech therapist who had been a teacher of preschool deaf children, and since mid-1967 Mrs. Lillie Davidson, formerly a nursery school teacher, a supervisor of teachers, and a supervisor of children's counselors in a center for homeless children). Case conferences involving Schaefer, Furfey, the head of the tutoring group, the tutors, and sometimes a mother and her child were held frequently. All the tutors met weekly with other staff members to discuss problems and to give and receive suggestions about educational materials and techniques.

THE CHILDREN AND THEIR FAMILIES

The effect of certain environmental factors upon intellectual functioning has been found to differ according to sex.[1] Since the project could not afford a large enough sample to study both sexes, it limited itself to boys because lower-class black boys and men seem to have a more difficult time in school and society than girls and women.

The subjects were chosen from census tracts selected because they had high rates of crime, delinquency, infant mortality, joblessness, dilapidated housing, and families on welfare. The neighborhood environment as well as the typical home environment was deprived. Though the experimentals lived in a slightly worse neighborhood than the controls, the children from one area had been scoring much the same as those from the other on the Metropolitan Readiness Test, given to children on entering school. The median scores were approximately at the twentieth percentile on national norms, meaning that they fell in the lowest fifth.

Families having a boy of the right age were invited to participate if the home situation was relatively stable—that is, if it did not look too chaotic for daily tutoring session—and if the family met two of three other qualifications: its yearly income was less than $5,000; the mother had not finished high school; the mother had never been employed as a skilled worker.

Among the 98 homes the tutors visited to select the experimental group, 12 were rejected by the staff as unsuitable (because they were considered unsafe for the tutors or too crowded to work in, or because the family's attitude was judged likely to present unduly severe problems). Five other homes were ruled out because either the income or the mother's education was too high. Most of the other rejections were made because the children were not of the right age. Four families refused to participate.

The control group was selected from 89 homes in a slightly better area. Ten were rejected by the staff as unsuitable, and 12 were ruled out because the economic or educational level was too high.

---

[1] "The Effect of Childhood Influences upon Intelligence, Personality, and Mental Health," in *Mental Health Program Reports*, 3.

Stipends—$10 for each testing session and $1 for each tutoring session—were offered primarily in the hope of reducing losses from the sample, particularly losses of children with poorly motivated mothers. Since losses were expected to be high in any case, and the project wanted to retain at least 20 in each group, 31 children were chosen to be tutored and 33 to serve as controls. A number of the families have broken up, and some have moved, as many as five times. But only three in each group have been lost. (Among the experimental families, one moved out of town; one placed the baby in a day center so the mother could take a job, and the center refused to admit the tutors; and one notified the project that the tutors would no longer be safe: the wife's mother had moved in and she liked to throw things.) This unusual record is attributed both to the interest of most of the mothers in having something done for their children and to the tutors' persistence in following families and staying on the job in spite of any unpleasant circumstances. The staff now thinks that without the financial inducement, no more than three or four of the families in each group would have been lost.

The homes as a rule had neither toys nor books, and the mothers at first seemed to think it a joke to suppose that anything could be taught to a child as young as 15 months. Some of the parents, even some of those on welfare and with half a dozen children, were well organized. The families always had food; the children were sent to school daily; the mother knew how to go to second-hand stores and buy clothes. Other parents seemed overwhelmed by their problems.

The following quick sketches of representative cases are drawn from tutors' reports:

W. lived with his parents, a brother, a sister, an uncle, and an aunt—seven persons in all—in a three-room apartment on the third floor of a rapidly deteriorating house. The rats were so bad, his mother said, that she had to beat on a pan to frighten them away before she entered the kitchen. They had chewed the nose off a doll. The father had a steady job as a truck driver, and the mother worked part-time as a counter girl in a nearby drugstore. She kept the apartment tidy, showed her love for her children, and participated in the tutoring sessions.

At 15 months, J. was a shy, neglected, poorly dressed child who lived with his baby sister and his 17-year-old mother in a dingy six-room apartment, part of an old house. It was occupied by his grandmother, who worked as a domestic, an unemployed uncle, and the uncle's four-year-old daughter. J.'s father was in jail. The apartment was uncrowded but unpleasant. Fumes from an oil stove, which supplied inadequate heat, made the eyes smart. Chunks of plaster had fallen from the walls. The bedroom floors were littered with soiled clothing. Cockroaches crawled all around. There were no toys or books, but there were newspapers, a television, a radio, and three telephones which had been disconnected. The mother, a high school dropout, was quiet and timid, knew little about raising her children, and was apparently unable to show affection for them. She was interested mainly in going to school and getting a job. J. was cared for by the grandmother, a warm and friendly person and apparently the only member of the household bringing in money, and a baby-sitter.

When the tutoring began, V. lived with his parents in a spacious one-bedroom apartment and slept with them in a double bed. His father had a steady job, and his mother worked in the afternoon until her husband asked her to quit so she could spend more time with the boy. This was one of the few homes with books and toys. V. was as spoiled as any middle-class only child could be. When the tutor and he went for a walk and passed a store without going in and buying something, he had a temper tantrum. One night some men came to the apartment, threatened V.'s father with a gun, and chased him out. The next day the family moved to another section of the city. This was near the end of the tutoring program. The mother seemed despondent over the course of events, and the boy showed hostility toward the tutors.

A. and his mother, brother, and sister lived in a two-bedroom basement apartment that reeked with the odor of urine because the mother washed clothes and diapers together and did not properly rinse them. Sometimes the odor was so bad that the tutor had to take the boy outside. Cockroaches added to the discomfort. The mother, strict and brutal, would punish the children either by striking them or locking them up in a room.

E. was a happy, sociable child who readily sought and gave affection. He lived with his five brothers and sisters and his parents in a two-room apartment, which needed repairs but was kept in reasonable order. His mother worked nights in a carryout restaurant. She loved him and did a good job of caring for him. E.'s parents separated during the first year of tutoring, and the mother moved with all the children to another two-room apartment. When E. entered nursery school, she began going to night high school so she could get a better job.

R.'s mother showed the tutor a scar on the boy's upper thigh that had come from a rat bite. She had four other children but managed to sit in on many of the tutoring sessions, often went along on trips, and was proud of R.'s accomplishments. There were books in the house. The family seemed to pay little attention to R.'s father, who did not work regularly. When the mother got a job as a teacher's aide in a Head Start center, the children were sent to a baby-sitter's home, and the tutoring continued there.

T.'s mother separated from her husband during the course of the project and moved with her six children into a one-bedroom apartment. Three boys and their eight-year-old sister slept in a double bed, another boy in a crib, the newest baby in a bassinet, and the mother in a single bed in the same room. A bed in the living room was often used by overnight guests. The mother, who seemed disturbed as a result of problems first with her husband and then with a new man, constantly screamed at the children and threatened them with belts but got no response. The toilet was usually broken. Some of the children had ringworm. T. kept complaining of being hungry. The tutors found it difficult to get him to concentrate.

WORKING WITH THE CHILDREN

The tutors set out to build friendly, easy relationships with the children by playing with them and talking to them—activities in which some of the mothers had engaged only rarely. Some children made friends almost immediately. Others hung back. With one boy, shy almost to the point of being withdrawn, the tutors had to work almost a year to establish rapport. In other cases, productive relationships developed only after the tutors had worked to change maternal attitudes and behavior.

At the start, the children were given manipulative toys—blocks, pop beads, nesting sets—which they learned to put together and to separate. One toy would lead to a number of activities. Given pop beads, for example, a child would feel them, swing them in the air, and chew or suck on them. Perhaps he would learn by accident that they could be pulled apart.

This delighted him. Putting them together was too difficult for most of the children at 15 months, so the tutor would show how to do it and then guide the child's hands till he could do it himself. Other activities with beads included hiding some of them around the room for the child to find and add to the string, using a long string of them as a pull toy, counting, naming colors, and matching according to color or shape. Along with the simple manipulative toys, the child was given opportunities to play with balls of various sizes, a kiddie-car, a pounding bench, and other toys that helped develop the larger muscles.

Always the tutor talked to him about what was going on. When a new toy—for instance a ball—was presented, she would name it. The games that could be played with the toy gave the child opportunities to hear, imitate, and learn other new words—for instance, *roll, throw, catch,* and *kick.* As the child matured, the tutor would talk about the different sizes, kinds, colors, and number of balls.

If a boy liked a toy car, the tutor would talk about that car and other cars. Then she would get a book containing pictures of cars and talk with the child about what he saw on each page. When tutor and child went for a walk, they would talk about the cars seen. Looking at pictures of cars in a book helped develop an interest in books, too. One tutor was surprised and pleased to find the children associating one make of automobile with her. When they saw this auto in a book or on the street, the response would be, "Tha' teacher's car!"

Toys were used not only to aid physical development and to teach language but also to develop two of the characteristics essential to the mastery of schoolwork—attentiveness and perception. Here puzzles were considered especially valuable. First came simple, isolated-object puzzles—for example, a board containing pictures of three kinds of fruit, to be taken out and put back in—which were introduced between the ages of 15 months and two years. More difficult puzzles followed. One tutor, Betty Pair, describing her experiences for the benefit of other persons working with children, wrote:

"We talk about the puzzle while it is still intact; then dump out the pieces (this act I leave to the child, because he seems to derive great pleasure from the dumping); then talk about the side with colors on its and the dark, rough side; then trace with our fingers around the inside of the puzzle; then attempt to fit the pieces in the puzzle.

"It is important that the child complete the task, but it is imperative that he not become so frustrated in his attempt to do so that he sets up a negative block against the activity. For this reason, I initially put the pieces back slowly in the puzzle so that the child can observe me. This is the 'I Can Do It' part. We then see if he can do it, with the assistance he may require to prevent overt frustration. When there are signals that assistance is required, I put my hand over the child's hand on the puzzle piece, and I explain, 'Turn it around,' or 'Turn it over,' or 'Try another space,' as we do what each command directs.'"

Another tutor, Lucile Banks, offered these suggestions:

1. Present puzzles as enjoyable games.
2. Demonstrate how pieces are placed.
3. Give each piece a name.
4. Begin by taking only one piece out of the board at a time.
5. Finish one puzzle before starting another.
6. If frustration persists, direct the child to a more relaxing activity—such as painting or a favorite toy.
7. Praise the child.
8. Present puzzles already mastered for relaxation and reinforcement.

Through playtime activities, the tutors also worked to modify undesirable behavior. If a child were hyperactive, the tutor would try to get him interested in one activity—like putting rings on a stick, arranging animals, building a wagon—and would work with him to see it completed. "Well, Bobby," she'd say, "let's finish this. I will help you. . . . No, we aren't going to play with that until we've finished this" or "until we've picked this up and put it away."

Toys are credited with having aided social development, because they usually had to be shared with other children in the house, either during the tutoring sessions or between them. Generally a toy was left in the home for several weeks. If it became a favorite it might be left longer, or one like it bought as a birthday or Christmas present.

Tutors and mothers worked together to make toys. Milk cartons—cut into squares and the squares covered with paper—became blocks; oatmeal boxes, drums; pierced bottle caps on a string, a tambourine. Bleaching compound bottles were shaped for use as dolls' cribs. A roll of shelf paper filled with sketches

("This is Jim . . . he lives in a house . . . he has 3 brothers. . . .")
became, as it was slowly unwound, a movie. Two cans and
string made a walkie-talkie. Tutors and mothers also spray-
painted cartons for use in storing toys, and they cut down large
soap-powder boxes to make cases for children's books.

Books were introduced early in the project, though the attention span of these 15-month-olds was very short. To win the
children's interest, the tutors tried to relate things seen in books
to things known in daily life. Sometimes they would carry
books with them on walks and point to a picture of a dog or a
tree, bird, truck, and then to the real thing. Adults and children
in illustrations showing family groups would be named after
the persons in the child's family. Books that a child found
especially appealing would be presented again and again, unless
he showed boredom; books that had no attraction for him
would be taken away but might be introduced again later.

One boy clearly preferred books about horses. So his tutors
dug up as many horse books as they could find, and they took
him on trips to see horses and to ride ponies. Whenever a tutor
showed him a picture of a horse, he would tell her about these
trips. Sometimes he would sit for an hour looking at a book
with pictures of horses in it. A boy who preferred books about
animals in general was taken not only to the zoo several times,
but also to the Rock Creek Park Nature Center, the natural
history exhibits at the Smithsonian, and the circus. And his
mother took him to the country.

With the child, and sometimes his mother, watching and
helping, the tutors made books by cutting pictures from magazines and pasting them in scrapbooks. Some of the books were
concerned with a single subject—babies, for example, or automobiles. Others had pictures chosen because they would
remind the child of things he and the tutor had seen at the zoo,
or in a store, or during a walk around the block. Scrapbooks
were also made to illustrate such concepts as big and little (an
elephant and a mouse), one and many (automobile tires), old
and new (shoes), and circle and square. Other scrapbooks were
used to teach numbers. A picture of one sheep would be
headed, "This is 1"; of two donkeys, "This is 2," and so on.
The numerals were cut out of sandpaper so the child could
feel as well as see them. The homemade books were left in the
home for use whenever the child liked. So were some of the
others, particularly the cloth ones.

The tutors also told stories, read stories, and used the combination of story book and record player.

During their third year, most of the children went to the library a number of times and checked out, carried home, and kept for a few days a book of their own choosing. The children by this time had come to expect the presentation of at least one book, old or new, during each session, and books often took up more of the session than toys. "Hey, Teach," some of the children would say as the tutor entered, "I wanna book."

Music, too, was part of the curriculum. The tutors would sing to the children, play songs and other music on a record player, and use homemade or inexpensive children's instruments—drum, tambourine, bells, xylophone—to help the youngsters express rhythm and time.

"When the babies were young (15–18 months)," reports one of the tutors, Patricia Chernoff, "I held them in my lap or arms, facing me, and moved my body or knees to the rhythm of the song, at the same time articulating the words carefully and drawing the child's attention to my singing by holding him close and using exaggerated facial expression. I repeated the same songs until eventually the child attempted to sing. At this point, I simplified the words, concentrating on those which were repeated most often in the song and therefore easiest to perceive and repeat. For example, in presenting "Shoo, Fly, Don't Bother Me," I sang *Shoo Fly* with greater emphasis and volume than the rest of the words, expecting the child to repeat only those two words. Gradually, when he was able to sing *Shoo Fly* in the correct places throughout the song, I encouraged him to add the remainder of the phrase, *don't bother me.* The phrase, for *I belong to somebody,* because of its length and the rhythm with which it is sung, comes much later. When the child is unable to perceive the words from the recorded presentation, I have repeated them more slowly, later without the recording.

"Once the child has become interested in the actual singing of the songs, I have lessened body contact and emphasized the rhythm, concentrating only on the words. When the child becomes tired of singing, I terminate the music session rather than changing the emphasis to clapping, etc.

"I have found that the length of time required to learn a song has lessened considerably (in some cases, the child enters in during the first presentation) as the children become able to focus their attention on the words and as I continually reinforce with praise and enthusiasm their attempts to sing the words."

A child's birthday was always recognized, usually by a party and a book or a toy from the tutor. If a party could not be arranged, tutor and child would walk to a store to pick out a present.

INFLUENCE ON THE MOTHERS

The tutors believe that they have reached each family to some degree. One mother related with pride that whenever she took her boy to the store, he dragged her over to the display of books, and she sometimes bought him one. Another would sit in on the tutoring sessions and often ask questions about aims and techniques. Though she herself could not read, she took out a library card at the tutors' suggestion, and began borrowing books for her three youngest.

At the start, one mother kept screaming at her 15-month-old, who liked to get into things: "You are bad—I'm going to beat you." Her attitude was hostile, almost rejecting. As she watched the boy's progress under the tutors, though, she came to recognize his inquisitiveness as a mark of intelligence, and her attitude turned to one of acceptance and even pride. Another woman frequently made out-of-town visits, leaving her boy with a relative. During these absences he was obviously upset; even when the mother was at home he seemed to feel insecure. He became a happy, interested youngster only after the tutors persuaded the mother that he loved and needed her, and she began staying home. Under the influence of the tutors, A.'s mother, mentioned earlier, eased her harsh discipline and became so interested in learning how to help children that she took a volunteer job in a nursery school. A.'s IQ, which had dropped from 116 at 21 months to 89 at 36 months, rose to 102 at four years.

Some of the women would buy a toy or a book like one brought in by the tutor, or they would ask what they ought to buy. One displayed a 28-piece puzzle she had bought as a Christmas present. Since the boy in the program was only two and a half, the tutor supposed it was for the older children. "No, it's for him," said the mother. She dumped the pieces on the floor, and the youngster put them together in a few minutes. The boy's older sister found it difficult at times to keep up with him. The mother called her silly or dumb, till the tutor explained that the girl was smart enough—she just had not had her brother's training.

A number of the families began taking more trips with their children. Some mothers had not known that such resources as libraries, museums, and a zoo existed; others had not known how to get to them. A few mothers hadn't even known what bus to take to go downtown, and one never left the house to go anywhere unless one of the children went along: she didn't think she could find her way back.

The tutors often encountered problems that were outside their province as tutors but not as human beings. For instance, they would find a family sitting around in winter coats because the heat had been turned off. Or the mother would be distraught because the family faced eviction. Or the mother and father had quarreled, and the mother had gone off to visit relatives. The children in such cases would be upset—fearful, or apathetic, or quarrelsome; one child kept asking his tutor to take him with her.

One woman with half a dozen children had an especially difficult time with her money. (Says a tutor: "To budget welfare money—which is too low anyway—for a month is really a challenge even to someone who has taken a home economics course in college. When the welfare checks come out, food stores raise their prices, and people go around in cars trying to get you to buy nice looking but flimsy clothes that won't last over a month.") After the first two or three weeks of the month, this woman would run out of both food and money. Several times a tutor found the children picking crumbs from the floor and eating them. The project had no funds to feed the family, but the tutors sent the mother to agencies that could give her emergency help. They also went shopping with her and showed her how to choose economical foods, and they brought in snacks for the children.

When the children were three, the tutoring ended, except for twice-a-month visits, and the project tried to place them in nursery schools. It succeeded in all but two cases, where the family situation was particularly unstable. (An effort to place children from the control group succeeded in only half a dozen cases, partly because the effort was less intensive and partly because the families were little motivated to send their children to nursery school.)

At the same time the mothers were invited to meet once a month, in groups of four or five, for a planned program of discussions of subjects in which they were interested as well as subjects about which the project thought they needed to be informed. Most were pleased to accept, and one was delighted: she had always wanted, she said, to belong to something.

All kinds of problems have been discussed—for example, how to tell older children about sex (some of the women said that their own mothers had been too shy to talk to them, so they hadn't known about having a baby until they'd had it); what to do about a child who is having trouble in school or refuses to go to school; how to cope with poor health, bad housing, marital problems. The tutors conducting the meetings have felt equipped to answer some of the questions themselves. They have handled the others by giving out pamphlets on the subject or suggesting that the mother talk with her child's counselor at the school. Movies have been shown—about differences between children at different ages, about sibling rivalry, and about how parents are teachers, too. Mothers with jobs have told how they went about getting them, what training they took, and how they met the transportation problem. Only two mothers have failed to attend any of the meetings.

As one result of the project, at least in part, a number of the mothers are trying to better themselves economically and socially. Using skills learned largely from the tutors, one is working in a parent and child center setup under an Office of Economic Opportunity program, and several as aides in nursery schools. With advice and encouragement from the tutors, others have gone back to school or have entered training programs, in order to get better jobs. Some have sent their children off to school or a day care center, traveled an hour or an hour and a half to attend a training program across town, and hurried home late in the afternoon. After the children entered nursery school, several of the mothers coupled an all-day job with a training program at night. They would leave their children at a sitter's home five days a week, picking them up on Friday night and returning them on Sunday.

During the kindergarten year, the homes of working mothers will be visited on Saturdays, and the children of these mothers will be seen at the baby-sitter's during the week.

IMPLICATIONS FOR EDUCATIONAL POLICIES

To summarize, the Infant Education Research Project found that:

1. A tutoring program beginning at the age of 15 months for Negro boys from disadvantaged families and continuing, one hour a day, for 21 months significantly raised their level of intelligence until they were four years old, at least.
2. The average reached at the end of the third year, 106, dropped six points during the next year but was still significantly higher than the control group's average.
3. When maternal interest was high, a child's IQ was likely also to be high.

How long the benefits from the additional stimulation will continue remains to be seen. But the drop in the peak IQ level after the tutoring stopped, at three, suggests to Schaefer that short-term programs of early education are not sufficient to develop and sustain the child's potential over the long run. Other studies using different programs of stimulation point to the same conclusion.

The investigator thinks the answer lies in both early and continued education. "Genetics may determine the potential range of a child's intellectual level," he points out, "but the quality of the environment determines the actual level. Evidence is accumulating rapidly that because of physical, social and emotional, and cultural deprivations, many children are not developing their genetic potential, and therefore do not function effectively in school and in society."

Physical deprivations include inadequate medical care, insufficient and low-quality food, poor housing, and inadequate clothing. Social and emotional deprivations stem from the lack of stable and supporting relationships with the mother and father or their substitutes. Cultural deprivation occurs when parents fail to provide a stimulating environment. Children who lack pencils, paper, crayons, books, games, and other educational materials do not receive enough training in certain qualities and abilities—such as attention, concentration, perseverance, and perceptual-motor skills—that make for success in school. Children who are not encouraged to talk about their experiences, who do not have models of good language use to follow in their early years, and who have little or no opportunity to make visits beyond their immediate neighborhood are likely to reach school age lacking the language skills, the interest, and the knowledge of more fortunate children.

As Schaefer sees it, the intellectual development of the typical child can be viewed as having four basic stages. In the first, the parent develops a loving acceptance of the child and a positive involvement with him. In the second, this involvement elicits from the child the development of a positive relationship with the parent. In the third, the parent and the child engage together in activities, such as piling up blocks, rolling a ball, looking at a picture book, and the parent by word and by example teaches the child language, skills, and task-oriented behavior. From this early experience with the parent, the child reaches the fourth basic stage—he has acquired the interests and the skills that enable him to learn on his own. "Successful achievement of these early developmental stages in the home," says Schaefer, "may be a necessary basis for a successful education in the school. But deprivation during their own childhood may leave parents without the personal resources to support the optimal development of their children."

Do we then need more nursery schools? More child-care centers that will take children at 15 months and even younger? A spread of tutoring programs, like the one in Washington but lasting longer and made part of the public education system so that every child will be reached?

"We do need to recognize that education goes on from birth," Schaefer answers, "but I think it would be more fruitful in most instances to support parents in their educational role than to set up educational institutions to supplant them. Parents, or at least the mother, are there early and continue to be there. This study found that both tutoring and the quality of maternal care were related to the children's intellectual development at three and four. Tutoring can be thought of as supplementary maternal, or parental, care because in the middle class a good mother, and a good father, does what the tutors have done."

As one hopeful development, Schaefer points to a new Institute-supported project in Prince Georges County, Maryland, that seeks to integrate the educational efforts of home and school. When children are infants, teachers will go into the home to work with the parents; later on the parents will go into the school. But he thinks we ought to look even farther ahead. "If you assume that almost everyone becomes a parent and that one of the most important jobs for each generation is to rear the next generation," he says, "it follows that we should be giving children, beginning in kindergarten and running through the twelfth grade, some of the skills needed if they are to be competent as parents. We should have programs for future parents."

The Washington project has demonstrated that lower-class black infants can benefit from additional stimulation. Could other infants also benefit? Schaefer answers that we cannot be sure until programs of stimulation are tested with other ethnic and socioeconomic groups. "Some people say that middle-class parents are doing as well as they can with their children—that nothing else they could do would lead to higher levels of intelligence and achievement. I don't believe that, but it needs to be tested.

"Many parents—and I think they can be found in all social classes—don't have the skills to be effective in their roles as teachers. We need to develop methods of improving the education of young children, and we also need to develop better ways of communicating what we learn—and what we already know, for that matter—to all parents and future parents. If the whole culture became aware of the importance of parents as teachers, I believe it would lead to an educational revolution, and to a better adjusted, more competent, and more intelligent population."

REFERENCES

Bayley, N., and Schaefer, E. S. 1964. Correlations of maternal and child behaviors with the development of mental abilities: Data from the Berkeley Growth Study. Monographs of the Society for Research in Child Development 29:6.

Schaefer, E. S. 1969. Home tutoring program. Children 16:2.

Skeels, H. M. 1966. Adult status of children with contrasting early life experiences. Monographs of the Society for Research in Child Development 31:3.

U.S. Office of Education, Department of Health, Education, and Welfare. Infant education research project. Washington, D.C.: Superintendent of Documents, U.S. Government Printing Office.

U.S. Department of Health, Education, and Welfare. PHS Health Services and Mental Health Administration. 1969. The edge of education. HSMHA World 4 (1): 18–23.

Self-Support, Wholeness, and Gestalt Therapy

By STEPHAN A. TOBIN

17

The reader may recall from selection 1 that both behaviorism and humanism focus on man's relationship to his present environment. Neither approach finds much utility in exploring the past or, for that matter, speculating about the future. The here and now is of primary interest to both approaches.

Dr. Stephan Tobin of Encino, California, discusses this issue as it applies to one of the humanistic approaches to behavior disorders, namely, Gestalt therapy. Dr. Tobin argues that man is capable of experiencing and responding to the complete array of feelings, thoughts, and external events that are present at any point in time. This capability is another way of saying that man has an enormous range of possible behaviors available to him. He is potentially free to be what *he* wants to be, not what others want him to be. In order, however, to experience such freedom, man must become aware of what is happening around him and inside him. He must then accept complete responsibility for the ways he responds to the events. Gestalt therapy is one way in which this kind of personal autonomy can be achieved.

"TIME'S UP," I SAID. JIM HESITATED a moment, then slowly got up. I also stood. Instead of moving toward the door, Jim looked at me. Then he smiled, walked over to me, and hugged me rather stiffly. He then stepped back and said, "I've been thinking of going to Colorado for a while." He looked at me searchingly and I felt uncomfortable. I imagined he was waiting for me to give my opinion about his going to Colorado. "Are you asking me if I think you should go?"

"Yeah, I guess I am."

"Jim, it doesn't matter to me if you go to Colorado or not."

"Yeah, well . . . you know, I don't think I *really* want to go to Colorado at all. I feel more like going to the beach right now." Another searching look.

From *Voices*, Winter-Spring, 1969-1970. Reprinted by permission of the author and the American Academy of Psychotherapists.

"I don't care if you go to the beach either."

A disappointed look now. He backed away, said he had to be going. He wasn't through yet, though.

"You know, I just about decided to stop screwing around. I have been thinking about going back to college, maybe medical school."

"Look Jim, I really don't give a damn what you do; it just doesn't make any difference to me if you go to Colorado, medical school, or Disneyland. You're still trying to get me to approve of your decisions, to support. . . ."

"Yeah, yeah, you're right," he interrupted. "Well, guess I'll be going." He again started edging towards the door. "Oh, look, I hate to ask you, but I'm broke and don't have enough gas to get home. Could you lend me a buck?"

This dialogue is from a recent session with a young man I have been seeing in group therapy and infrequent individual sessions for about a year. He had a great deal of previous therapy before coming to me, about ten years of analysis and analytically oriented therapy. Despite all the "insight" he has obtained, he still regards himself as "sick" and leads a chaotic, unrewarding existence. Instead of making his own decisions and supporting himself emotionally, he continually attempts to manipulate others into taking responsibility for his life.

Although the analysts could make a convincing case for unresolved oedipal conflicts within Jim, I feel that such an explanation is irrelevant to Jim's major problems, which are existential. Underlying his continual need for validation from others are feelings of incompleteness, of being split-up into many parts, and inadequacy.

I believe that the desperate search outside oneself for self-esteem gratifications seen in Jim is also the major symptom of our culture, affecting the successful and well-functioning as well as the failures and "mentally ill." The basic feeling of worthlessness found in most people much of the time is, I believe, the motivating force behind the politician's striving for power, the businessman's dishonest practices, the black militant's hatred of "whitey," and the welfare recipient's attempts to cheat a humiliating, infantilizing Establishment.

As Fritz Perls has pointed out (Perls, 1965), any system of therapy that does not result in the patient's being able to provide his own validation as a human being is incomplete. The purpose of this paper is to discuss certain features of this ubiquitous problem of our times. I shall discuss its phenomenology, its causes, how it is maintained in our culture, and how the ability to validate oneself can be attained in therapy.

THE PHENOMENOLOGY OF INCOMPLETENESS

The emotional state of one who needs to manipulate others into validating him can best be described as a feeling of incompleteness. I find that when I myself am unable to provide my own self-esteem supports, I feel empty, worthless, tense, and vaguely dissatisfied. I am partially unaware of what is going on around me, and have fleeting, scattered thoughts about things I "should do." I sense that I am *missing* something and feel I must search outside myself for it. In the past I attempted to fill myself up with material objects, with praise from others, or by doing work I imagined would bring me prestige or power. Even major achievements, however, only made me feel worthwhile for a very brief time, and then I usually became depressed.

This pattern I have noticed in my own life has been reported to me by many other people. For example, a physician I know imagined that he would feel complete when he had established a successful practice. After eleven years of college and specialized medical training, and another four years of building up his practice, he had achieved his dream. He had "arrived," but, as you may have already guessed, his achievement left him feeling empty and despairing.

A sixty-five-year-old patient of mine had come to me after fifteen years of analytically oriented therapy. She had hung on to unsatisfactory relationships with her therapist and her husband because she felt basically worthless and empty, and believed that someday they would give her what they had previously been withholding. She would then, she imagined, feel complete and whole. When I spoke with the ex-therapist, I learned of his part in this neurotic relationship; as he spoke of her, his pessimism and despair and his opinion that she could never stand on her own came through his technical description of her "case."

Jim, the patient I described earlier, is luckier than the physician and the elderly patient, for he is dealing with this existential problem while still young. If he were unfortunate enough to be "well adjusted" to our psychotic society, he would probably have started on the same path as the physician, only to realize years later that what he was searching for all that time was something that only he could give himself.

CULTURAL CAUSES OF INCOMPLETENESS AND OTHER-SUPPORT

1. *The view that man is basically evil.* Because of the Judeo-Christian concept of original sin and the continuing influence of Puritanism, most people in our culture have an underlying attitude that man is innately bad. This attitude is revealed in the way we regard being itself: a person is worthless just existing; he must *do* something to be worthwhile. This attitude is also revealed in the great emphasis we place upon "self-control" and in our glorification of the mind and ignoring of the body. This lack of trust of man's free use of his body, with all its drives and functions, is related to a second aspect of American culture, its pervasive authoritarianism.

2. *Authoritarianism in major institutions.* The family, the school, the armed forces, the athletic team, the business, and almost all other major institutions in our culture are structured in an authoritarian fashion. The infant is viewed as an impulse-ridden, megalomanic little monster who would destroy everything in sight when frustrated had he the power to do so. Therefore, the child is supposed to need a great deal of "socialization" before he can be trusted to make any decisions on his own. In contrast, as Lee points out (Lee, 1959), the Navajo Indians see the child as having complete autonomy. An adult never speaks for a child or forces an idea or an act on him. Personal autonomy and freedom are so much a part of the Navajo culture that their language does not even contain words of ownership or coercion. An adult will speak of "going with" a child someplace, not "taking" him, and of "the child I live with" rather than "my child."

In most of the Western institutions mentioned above, the individual, whether he be an adult or a child, is treated in a dictatorial, authoritarian manner. Workers must punch time clocks because their bosses are certain they would not come in or leave on time were they not treated like irresponsible idiots.

The whole system of grading in our schools is predicated on the notion that people will not want to learn anything unless they are forced to.

Our institutional dictators—parents, team coaches, teachers, etc.—dole out the rewards as well as punishments. Since a member of American culture has lost all feelings of intrinsic self-worth by the time he is three years old, he is dependent on his dictators to validate him as a worthwhile human being for the rest of his life. To be approved or loved he must accomplish or achieve something.

3. *Thinking, achievement, and future-orientation.* In order to gratify himself fully in any situation, a person must be totally *in* the situation cognitively, emotionally, and sensorily. Unfortunately, however, most people tend to be only partially in the here-and-now, and partially in the there-and-then. That is, instead of attending fully to the situation at hand, they are partially aware of it and are thinking about the past or the future. There are a number of reasons for this inability to exist in the present.

First, a normal person in our culture is never to rest on his laurels. He is supposed to present himself with a new goal immediately after one is reached. To like oneself just for being human and alive is simply un-American. Thus, since the new goal can exist only in the individual's fantasy about the future, he must tear part of himself away from the present and put this part into the future.

Second, the complexity of our culture makes it virtually impossible to stay in the here-and-now. I find that I must remind myself of things I "should" do in the future or I forget them, e.g., people to call, letters to write, a loaf of bread to pick up on my way home. While reminding myself of these chores, however, I am not really involved in the present and thus am not getting complete fulfillment from the current stimulus situation.

Third, we are continually making comparisons between what is immediately present to us and something that is present in fantasy, e.g., an ideal.

4. *Playing comparison games.* In order to evaluate someone, one must use a standard. The standard can be an absolute one existing in the evaluator's mind, or it can be another person; in either case, the individual to be evaluated is placed on a scale and compared with the standard.

Making comparisons is so much a part of our culture that it is almost impossible for most people to talk without continually using words such as "better than," "worse than," "bigger," "older," etc. As soon as a person is born in the United States, he becomes involved in comparisons, i.e., adults evaluate him with respect to his weight, his looks, which parent he most resembles, etc. As he grows older, he is placed in a great many situations in which he is in competitive and comparative relationships with others. Unless he is extremely lucky, his approval events are likely to be few in number. This is particularly true in school, for there are only a limited number of "winners" allowed. Even the extremely bright and "well-behaved" child is apt to feel anxious and incomplete much of the time, for there is always the possibility that some other competitor will get a higher grade on the next test. The child's top dog[1] usually plays a major role in preventing him from feeling good about his achievements by torturing him with catastrophic expectations about failure if he does not continue to drive himself.

As the child gets older, the competition for self-esteem rewards becomes greater, and the things he must do to get approval become more complicated and difficult. No longer does he get praised for doing things like brushing his teeth and taking out the trash. He has to play ball well, be popular with girls, be "tactful" (i.e., dishonest and indirect), and not antagonize authorities while presenting a facade of self-assertiveness and aggressiveness. Even if he involves himself in a creative activity, he is not left to his own devices, but must seek approval from others for his creations.

By the time he reaches adulthood, he is almost totally unable to provide any of his own self-esteem rewards, for he now has a rigid, authoritarian, irrational top dog. The top dog is insatiable, and he can never attain a feeling of self-worth that lasts more than a brief period of time. If he manages to achieve excellency (e.g., all grades of 'A' except one 'B' in school), his top dog is likely to say, "That's pretty good, but what about that 'B'?" If he achieves perfection (e.g., all 'A's), the top dog says,

---

[1] The top dog is a Gestalt therapy concept; it is the self-righteous, demanding, perfectionistic part of the person. While similar to the concepts of conscience and superego, it is closest to Berne's concept of parent (Berne, 1964).

"Good, now keep up the good work and get the same grades next semester." If, however, he then repeats his success (all 'A's the next semester), the top dog says, "That's not so great; getting good grades is easy for you."

Many persons assume incorrectly that making comparisons is a universal trait and that man can never be satisfied with what he is. In many "primitive" cultures the individual is valued for being himself, a unique part of the universe, and is not compared to anyone or anything else. The Trobriand Islanders, for example, do not even have comparatives or superlatives in their language. Words equivalent to "better," "worse," "the most," and "younger" just do not exist (Lee, 1959).

The Hopi Indians, another supposedly primitive people, regard each person, animal, plant, and inanimate object as unique and as having an essential place in the universe. The idea of splitting people up into abstract attributes and then placing them on a scale to compare them would seem ridiculous and shameful to a Hopi. Anglo-American schoolteachers who have attempted to teach Hopi children have found that a Hopi child feels humiliated when he is singled out and praised in the classroom (Lee, 1959).

5. *Duplicity in interpersonal relationships*. Another custom of our culture that leads to incompleteness and low self-esteem is the ritual of attempting to get others to gratify one's need for self-esteem without asking for it directly. This is done by tricking the other into praising one or approving of a decision that has already been made. One technique I find college students using on me is to ask questions in class instead of stating their own opinions. If I answer their "questions" the way they want, they feel pleased because I "agreed" with them. If I don't answer the way they want, they are safe because they haven't committed themselves to an opinion.

The drawback with this technique (as with all indirect methods of trying to raise one's self-esteem) is that it's simply difficult to get what one wants when the other person does not know what's being requested. In addition, when two people are playing this game with each other at the same time, it is generally impossible for either one to get anything, for they're not really listening to each other. When their attempts to get support from the other are frustrated, the duplicity game is likely to degenerate into the blame game.

6. *Blame games and incompleteness.* I have found that the blame game starts when A makes an indirect request for a self-esteem present, and B fails to meet the request. A then feels hurt and worthless, blames B, and then B feels worthless. B then attacks back and, by this time, both parties are deliberately attacking each other's most vulnerable spots. This game is played endlessly by married couples. For example:

Wife: "Do you like the dinner tonight, dear?" (Translation: Tell me I'm a good cook, i.e., a worthwhile person.)

Husband: (He either thinks she wants to know about the dinner or really knows what she wants but is feeling resentful because of an esteem-attack he got from her recently.) "No, I don't care for it."

Wife: "Well! That's a *rotten* thing to say after I spent hours cooking. You're *always* criticizing me; nothing I ever do is good enough for you." (Translation: I'm hurt, but I won't give you the satisfaction of knowing that because I think you'll gloat. Instead, I'll get you!)

Husband: "Nag, nag, nag. If you spent as much time cooking as you say you do, your food wouldn't taste like you got it from the neighbor's garbage pails. Or maybe you do spend that much time, but you're too stupid to put a decent meal on the table." (Translation: I feel guilty and resentful because I also see myself as a critical grouch.)

And so they're off on another endless cycle of brutal, cutting attacks on each other's self-worth. What makes this type of game so difficult to stop is that they are unaware of their wishes, feelings, and intentions.

UNAWARENESS AND INCOMPLETENESS

To summarize, self-esteem is intimately related to awareness of the here-and-now. Unfortunately, however, most Americans spend most of their time fantasizing about the past or the future. They do not make use of their own resources. They don't trust their eyes and ears, their sense of touch, and the kinesthetic sensations from their own bodies that would tell them what they are feeling. Without sensory awareness, they are unable to express themselves and get what they want from the world. This inability to use one's own resources for self-fulfillment makes it necessary to look outside for these resources.

As an example of what I mean about awareness and completeness, I shall discuss something that happened to me when I first started teaching at San Fernando Valley State College about a year ago. After a class in which I had discussed and criticized the scientific and cultural assumptions underlying contemporary psychology, I noticed I was feeling tense and anxious. The class had been very exciting to me, and, as I was driving back to my office, I was having fantasy conversations with a few students who had argued with me in class. I noticed that I was constricting my breathing; when I deepened it, I became aware that I had been suppressing the excited joy that had been aroused in class. I stopped my fantasies at this point and began singing at the top of my lungs. Not only did I fully enjoy myself, but my anxiety left me. I also experienced a sense of wonder at my own potential for achieving a deep sense of fulfillment in life. Without awareness of my physical sensations, I would have continued to feel tense.

I also became aware that I had prevented myself from expressing my joy in the classroom by telling myself it would be unseemly for a professor to show too much excitement. Like most people, I had accepted my top dog's prohibition about expressing excitement without really examining this prohibition. This relative unawareness of the absurdity of the top dog's threats and "shoulds" is characteristic of most people with whom I have contact and is another barrier to achieving a feeling of wholeness.

I have also found, however, that most people are even less aware of their under dogs.[2] They usually have little sense of the under dog as a subself that is *actively* sabotaging, making excuses, and generally conning their top dogs. They describe themselves as "lazy," not being aware just how much active effort the under dog is putting into creating what superficially appears to be inertness.

I have an idea that people have less awareness of the under dog than they do of the top dog because the former tends to

---

[2] The under dog is, in Gestalt therapy, the guilty, "bad," rebellious part of the person. It rebels however, in subtle, indirect ways against the top dog's demands, saying, e.g., "I can't do it, I'm too sick" (rather than "I won't"). It is similar to Berne's concept of child (Berne, 1964).

be less verbal. Many of the dogmatic, dictatorial, and persecutory aspects of the top dog are introjected by persons from their parents when they are very young and had a limited vocabulary. Since language helps to create one's picture of "reality," the top dog *seems* to have a more accurate and well-defined picture of the world. The child, however, rebels even without having words to express his rebellion, e.g., the two-year-old who refuses to eat but can't tell his parents why.

Finally, most people have experienced feelings of wholeness so infrequently that they are unaware that incompleteness is not the natural state of man.

THE ATTAINMENT OF WHOLENESS IN THERAPY

In order to create a climate in which a patient can achieve a sense of wholeness and the ability to provide his own support, the therapist should be able to support himself or at least be aware of how he is incomplete. Without awareness of his own incompleteness, a therapist is apt to become involved in a variety of mutual manipulation games with patients.

For example, therapists who view themselves as "healers" of sick persons tend to be vulnerable to patients who play the sick role as a way of manipulating the environment. These patients never really want to "get well," even though they pretend to put complete faith in the "doctor."

The therapist who needs to have his patients admire him, agree with him, and ape him is easily trapped by the person who plays the "good patient." The "good patient" picks up the therapist's jargon very quickly. He is particularly obvious in group therapy, where he plays the role of assistant therapist. If the therapist happens to stress honesty and self-expression, the patient gets the idea that the quickest way to get the magical goodies the therapist has hidden is to play bad patient. So he becomes nasty, obstinate, and argumentative. If the therapist does not approve of his change in behavior, he will revert back to playing good patient. In neither role is he doing what he wants; he is doing what he thinks the therapist wants.

The therapist who does not *need* anything from his patients realizes the patient is just as autonomous as he is and therefore is just as responsible for his behavior. Not needing anything, he sets the patient free. He is only responsible to himself, not the patient. In a very fundamental sense, he doesn't care *about* the patient, although he may care *for* him. He responds to the patient as he is right there in front of him, not as the patient says he is outside the office or as he intends to be in the future.

I feel that the self-esteem problem is fundamental to the entire progress of therapy, that a lack of wholeness and an intrinsic feeling of worthlessness are the real "ultimate symptoms" (to use Helmut Kaiser's phrase) of Western man. Consequently, I focus much of my therapeutic effort on communicating to patients that "I don't care." Eventually the patient may come to the awesome realization that neither I nor anyone else has any magical goodies for him, no fountain of chicken soup, no giant penis, no immortality pills.

PHENOMENOLOGY OF WHOLENESS

I shall conclude this paper with a brief discussion of how I experience wholeness on the infrequent occasions that I do.

I am sensorially aware of the present; I see, hear, smell, touch, and feel without the intrusion of thoughts. I use thinking only when a conflict is experienced and for the purpose of considering various alternatives for resolving the conflict. I know when I have found the best solution: my feeling of completeness returns.

I am aware that, as Steve Tobin, I am alone in the universe. I am not *lonely*, but realize the inevitability of my death in a much more profound way than I do when I am feeling incomplete. (In fact, I would say that I don't really believe I shall die when I am feeling split, even though I "know" it intellectually.) I realize that no one is more of an expert about what is right for me than I myself am. I also realize that I don't need power, prestige, love, or lots of money; these things will not make me feel any more worthwhile as a person.

Paradoxically, I feel a sense of community, of being a part of the entire universe. Since I am not observing myself, I have no sense of "I" as separate from the universe. I have a sense of the unity of the universe, but see myself as neither more nor less important than any other part of the universe. This feeling of no sense of self seems to contradict the feeling of aloneness

I described in the preceding paragraph, but I do not experience any contradiction when I feel whole.

Freedom is a very important part of the experience for me. I realize that I had innumerable invisible, enslaving bonds between myself and others that I have broken, at least for the time being. I am also free in the sense that I know I can make my own decisions, that I am not enslaved to the past, to expectations of the future, or to any other person.

I also feel very much alive and am in touch with all my emotions. Sometimes these are painful, sometimes they are joyful, but, whatever the emotions, I have no need to avoid them. Experiencing "pleasure" is unimportant to me, and I find myself becoming annoyed at anyone attempting to attenuate my painful feelings by comforting me.

Finally, and most importantly, I find I can really become involved with people in a nondefensive way. Since *I don't need* anything from them, I can risk asking directly for *what I want* from them, even though refusal might hurt me. I find I can really see people at these times, instead of viewing them as potential enemies or as potential ass-wipers.

REFERENCES

Berne, E. 1964. *Games people play.* New York: Grove Press.

Lee, D. 1959. *Freedom and culture.* Spectrum Books.

Perls, F. S. 1965. Gestalt therapy and human potentialities. Esalen paper no. 1. Big Sur: Esalen Institute. Mimeographed.

Misconceptions about Behavior Therapy: A Point of View

18

By AUBREY J. YATES

Dr. Aubrey Yates of the University of Western Australia clarifies the behavioristic position on behavior disorders and treatment. In following Dr. Yates's description of common misconceptions about behavior therapy, particular attention should be paid to Yates's conclusions. Yates views these misconceptions as largely due to the continuing influential medical model of behavior disorders. In addition, he expresses his concern that behavior therapy may follow in the footsteps of medical model approaches if its proponents are guided by such misconceptions.

According to Yates, behavior therapy is a strategy—a way of approaching behavior disorders. As such, the strategy bears no allegiance to theory or technique. In essence, it represents the ground rules of experimental psychology as applied to individual behavior disorders. The word *individual* is important because it exemplifies the notion that people *are* different; we cannot meaningfully group them as far as which type or technique of therapy will be most appropriate. Ideally, each individual should be considered without reference to what therapy has "worked" in the past. The clinician must experiment; he must attempt to discover factors that maintain the individual's behavior problem and design the therapy accordingly.

The term *experiment* refers not only to the searching efforts of the therapist; it has reference also to experimental psychology. That is, the therapist must be concerned about the reliability of his observations and the validity of his treatment techniques. Thus, each clinical case is a carefully designed encounter between therapist and client. The outcome should not only benefit the client; the therapist will have gathered data that might advance our understanding of human behavior.

From *Behavior Therapy*, vol. 1 (1970), pp. 92–107. Reprinted by permission of the author and Academic Press, Inc. © by Academic Press, Inc. Revised and expanded version of a paper presented at the annual conference of the Australian Psychological Society, Melbourne, August, 1965.

IN RECENT YEARS A NUMBER of empirical and critical papers relating to behavior therapy which have appeared have demonstrated quite clearly the existence of several rather serious misconceptions concerning the nature and purpose of what has come to be called "behavior therapy." These misconceptions appear to have been accepted uncritically by the majority of behavior therapists even though their perpetuation will, in this author's view, rapidly eliminate the special defining characteristics of behavior therapy which distinguish it from other forms of therapy. It is the purpose of this paper to point out the nature of these misconceptions. Since they arise largely from ignorance of the historical development of behavior therapy (particularly in the United Kingdom), some account of how behavior therapy developed in England will be necessary. Attention will be concentrated on five major misconceptions: the existence of so-called "schools" of behavior therapy; the definition of behavior therapy; the identification of abnormality of behavior with neurosis or psychosis; the alleged peripheral nature of behavior therapy; and the appropriate techniques for establishing the "validity" of behavior therapy. The five misconceptions will be stated first; then a brief account of the history of the development of behavior therapy will be given. The "essential" nature of behavior therapy will be elucidated by providing a definition of behavior therapy. Finally, the nature of the misconceptions will be discussed in the light of the development and revised definition.

FIVE MISCONCEPTIONS ABOUT BEHAVIOR THERAPY

Misconception 1: "Schools" of behavior therapy. Breger and McGaugh (1965) identify three different approaches within the general framework of behavior therapy: Dollard and Miller, Wolpe and Eysenck, and Skinner (as represented by Krasner). The basic misconception here is the identification of Wolpe with Eysenck, which appears to have resulted from ignorance of the history of the development of behavior therapy in South Africa and England.

Misconception 2: The definition of behavior therapy. Eysenck (1964, p. 1) has defined behavior therapy as "the attempt to alter human behavior and emotion in a beneficial manner according to the laws of modern learning theory." Since, in other places, Eysenck has correctly identified the *essential* features of behavior therapy, it must be presumed he formulated this definition in a moment of forgetfulness since, at least as it applies to the development of behavior therapy at his own institute, it is incorrect. Unfortunately, the identification of learning theory as the *sine qua non* of behavior therapy is by now widely accepted, as instanced, for example, in the critique of Breger and McGaugh (1964).

Misconception 3: That behavior therapy is peripheral in nature and ignores intraorganismic variables. There is probably some justification for this assertion (Murray, 1963; Bookbinder, 1962) insofar as it is directed against the behavior modification approach of the American operant psychologists (Goldiamond, Ferster, Krasner, Ullmann, etc.) since the Skinnerian approach avowedly eschews the postulation of intervening constructs. It remains a misconception, however, when directed against other behavior therapy approaches. The present author must accept some responsibility for the appearance of this misconception, which appears to have been derived from a misreading of the paper on symptoms and symptom substitution (Yates, 1958*a*) and to have gained substance from Eysenck's equally misinterpreted dictum: Get rid of the symptom and you have eliminated the neurosis (Eysenck, 1959).

Misconception 4: The identification of abnormality of behavior with neurosis and psychosis. Although this misconception is absent from the definition of behavior therapy by Eysenck, it is clearly present in the titles of two of his books (Eysenck, 1960; Eysenck and Rachman, 1965), in which it is implied that behavior therapy is concerned with the "causes and cures" of neuroses (and psychoses, though this term is not used in either title). This error is also implicit in the work of Wolpe, where neurotic behavior is defined as "any persistent habit of unadaptive behavior acquired by learning in a physiologically normal organism" (Wolpe, 1958, p. 32). It will be noted that Wolpe's definition also contains misconception 2.

Misconception 5: That the validity of behavior therapy may be established by controlled group comparisons. This misconception is clearly exemplified in recent studies which attempt to compare the effects of particular techniques of behavior therapy with the effects of various psychodynamic techniques by using the matched group method with pre- and posttreatment assessment (Cooper, 1963; Cooper, Gelder, and Marks, 1965; Gelder and Marks, 1966, 1968; Gelder, Marks, and Wolff, 1967; Marks and Gelder, 1965). These studies led to some rather sharp exchanges between Eysenck and the authors of these papers, with none of the protagonists apparently realizing that these techniques, at the present time, are fundamentally irrelevant to the assessment of the validity of behavior therapy.

The nature of these misconceptions can be adumbrated by presenting a brief account of the history of the development of behavior therapy. Since this history, in relation to the development of behavior therapy in England, has not been given before, it is pertinent to state that the author was student, research assistant, and then lecturer in the clinical-teaching section at the Maudsley Hospital during the critical period 1951 to 1957.

THE DEVELOPMENT OF BEHAVIOR THERAPY, 1950–1960

Behavior therapy did not, of course, spring full-fledged into existence in 1950; it was, in fact, the end product of a long history of behavior modification techniques. Since this historical framework is reported elsewhere in detail (Yates, 1969), and since it is not directly relevant to the present misconceptions, it will not be detailed here.

DEVELOPMENT OF BEHAVIOR THERAPY IN ENGLAND

By 1950 considerable dissatisfaction with the usual role of the clinical psychologist in a psychiatric setting had developed in the clinical-teaching section at the Maudsley Hospital. This dissatisfaction derived from a large number of sources, of which the most significant were the following: the futility of attempting to answer diagnostic questions posed by the psychiatrist (e.g., is this patient a hysteric or a schizophrenic; is this patient brain-damaged or deteriorated intellectually, and so on) when a diagnostic decision usually had neither etiological nor treatment implications; the futility of the "battery" approach to the psychological assessment of the patient, as exemplified by the work of Rappaport and Schaffer; the demonstrated lack of validity (for diagnostic or personality descriptive purposes) of the projective techniques; and the futility of routine testing (e.g., assessing the intelligence of all child patients, whatever the nature of their disorder). In brief, the dissatisfaction in general related to two closely related points. First, the tendency of the clinical psychologist to behave like a "pseudopsychiatrist," attempting to use the same language as the psychiatrist (and falsely believing that he had successfully communicated with the psychiatrist by, for example, labelling a patient as "schizophrenic" because of a high Sc score on the MMPI). Coupled with this was the failure to use the knowledge of behavior which was peculiarly his by virtue of his training as a psychologist. Second, the growing belief that the psychiatrist, because of his comparative lack of knowledge of psychology, and particularly because of his tendency to transfer concepts acquired during his training in medicine to the field of abnormal behavior, was unable to ask the psychologist the right kind of questions. These negative factors were buttressed by an increasing conviction that the fundamental role of the clinical psychologist should be that of basic research worker, either in relation to basic theoretical questions (such as those investigated by Eysenck and his colleagues, using large groups of patients), or in relation to the clinical study of the individual patient.

As these considerations crystallized, important changes began to appear in the kind of work that was performed at the individual level in the clinical-teaching section. These changes in orientation and method were largely due to the influence of the head of the clinical-teaching section, M. B. Shapiro. He stressed three points. First, that the psychologist should formulate the problem of an individual patient in terms of questions such as: What precisely are the characteristics of the behavior of the patient which have, in effect, made it impossible for him to maintain his place in society (and hence brought him into a psychiatric hospital; that is, excluded him temporarily or permanently from society)? Second, in terms of that body of empirical and theoretical knowledge which the psychologist, qua psychologist, possesses, what explanation(s) can we advance to account for the genesis and maintenance of this behavior? The third point developed by Shapiro, however, was the most crucial one. He argued that it should be possible to investigate the first two points by the rigorous application of the experimental method (that is, the setting up of hypotheses which are then tested by experimental methods) to the study of the individual case. As a corollary of this viewpoint, he argued that the validity of the results of the application of the experimental method could be determined by establishing control conditions within the behavior of the individual patient (though he did not rule out the use of standardized data where this was appropriate, and stressed particularly the frequent need to collect new standardized data for a particular purpose). In summary, Shapiro believed that it was possible to investigate and account for abnormalities of behavior by treating the patient as the object of a rigorous experimental investigation.

The development of this approach was slow and painful and occupied a period of some five years (1950–1955). Much of the experimental work of this period remained unpublished,[1] though some pertinent studies did appear in print (e.g., Bartlett and Shapiro, 1956). Shapiro himself has described his approach in detail in a long series of papers (Shapiro, 1951, 1961a, 1961b, 1963, 1966; Shapiro, Marks, and Fox, 1963; Shapiro and Nelson, 1955; Shapiro and Ravenette, 1959).

To this point, attention had been directed mainly to the formulation and experimental testing of hypotheses concerning the description, measurement, and explanation of the disability of the patient. From this point, however, it was but a small step to the further question: If we can use the experimental method to describe, measure, and explain the genesis and maintenance of the disability of an individual patient, why should not the same approach be utilized to modify this abnormal behavior? The posing of this question very rapidly led to the attempt to apply this approach to the treatment of the individual patient (e.g., Jones, 1956; Meyer, 1957; Yates, 1958b). The critical assumption underlying these studies was that each individual patient presented a new problem for which standardized methods of investigation and treatment were not available. Investigation and treatment therefore became essentially a matter of treating the patient as an object of experimental investigation.

With all of these considerations in mind, we may now proceed to a definition of behavior therapy as this term was understood at the Maudsley during the period 1955–1960:

Behavior therapy is the attempt to utilize systematically that body of empirical and theoretical knowledge which has resulted

---

[1] Jones (1960, pp. 766–773) has described some of the unpublished studies carried out during this period.

from the application of the experimental method in psychology and its closely related disciplines (physiology and neurophysiology) in order to explain the genesis and maintenance of abnormal patterns of behavior and to apply that knowledge to the treatment or prevention of those abnormalities by means of controlled experimental studies carried out on the individual patient.

DEVELOPMENT OF BEHAVIOR THERAPY IN SOUTH AFRICA

Parallel with (but to a considerable extent uninfluenced by, and uninfluencing) these developments in England was the work of Wolpe (1958) and his colleagues (especially Lazarus and Rachman) in South Africa (and later in the U.S.A. and England) in developing the technique of systematic desensitization therapy. This need not be reviewed in detail here except to note several critical points of difference between the two approaches. First, Wolpe's techniques were developed as a result of theoretical considerations derived from a neurophysiological model. Second, the techniques used by Wolpe were very rapidly standardized. Thus, systematic desensitization involves three basic stages: training the patient in relaxation (with or without the use of hypnosis); constructing anxiety hierarchies; and applying desensitization procedures by combining relaxation with presentation of graded anxiety-arousing stimuli. Third, during this period (up to 1960) the assessment of the results of treatment was achieved by assessment of the status of the patient after treatment as compared with before treatment by the use of questionnaires, real-life testing (e.g., of phobic reactions), and so on in the case of individual patients; and by comparing group percentages of "improvement" in patients treated by Wolpe's techniques with results obtained by other techniques.

DEVELOPMENT OF BEHAVIOR MODIFICATION TECHNIQUES IN THE U.S.A.

Parallel with (and, again, largely independently of) these two developments was the growth of behavior modification techniques in the U.S.A., derived from the atheoretical approach of Lindsley, which in turn was a direct translation of Skinner's operant conditioning techniques. Lindsley's pioneering work was quickly taken up (particularly in relation to the modification of psychotic behavior) by Goldiamond, Ferster, Azrin,

Krasner, and many others, resulting in the publication of a volume of studies carried out within the operant procedure framework (Ullmann and Krasner, 1965).

With this brief historical review in mind, we are now in a position to consider the misconceptions listed earlier and see why they are regarded as such by the present author.

THE FIVE MISCONCEPTIONS CONSIDERED

MISCONCEPTION 1

The first misconception stated that Breger and McGaugh were in error in identifying a Wolpe/Eysenck "school" or "position." That this is so can clearly be seen from the historical account given above. First, the development of behavior therapy in England was largely uninfluenced during its critical developmental period by the ideas of Wolpe, although there were isolated cases where his influence was manifest (e.g., Meyer, 1957). Second, there were crucial differences between the approach of Wolpe and that of the English behavior therapists. In fact, it can be argued that Wolpe, during this period at least (1950–1960), should be linked with Dollard and Miller's approach rather than with that of the English behavior therapists. Dollard and Miller (1950) first translated Freudian theory into learning theory terms, as far as possible, and then attempted to apply the theory in the clinical situation. But this attempt remained clinical rather than experimental in nature. At no time did Dollard and Miller carry out experimental investigations or treatment of their patients. Wolpe's approach at this time was essentially similar. On the basis of a general neurophysiological model of learning he attempted to apply the theory of reciprocal inhibition (particularly via the technique of systematic desensitization) in the clinical situation. As in the case of Dollard and Miller, however, the approach to the individual patient was quite different from that applied at the Maudsley Hospital. For he applied a *standard technique* (with variations from patient to patient, of course, to suit individual cases) to a patient with a given disorder and then assessed the results in terms of "improvement" of varying degrees. But he did not carry out experimental studies on his individual patients at this time in the sense in which this term was used by the Maudsley workers. His technique was, of course, a marked advance on the purely clinical procedures of Dollard and Miller, but was fundamentally different from that utilized in England. It seems that behavior therapy, as it developed in England, was in large part a product of the work and inspiration of Shapiro. That Shapiro has not thus far received the recognition due him is perhaps one result of the fact that Shapiro has not, in general, himself applied his principles to the treatment of disorders of behavior.

Thus, instead of the three "positions" described by Breger and McGaugh (1965) we may conclude that the three parallel developments which occurred between 1950 and 1960 were: the approach of Wolpe, Lazarus, and Rachman in South Africa; the approach of Lindsley, Goldiamond, Ferster, and others in America; and the "experimental investigation of the single case" derived from the work of Shapiro in England. Since 1960, of course, a considerable degree of cross-fertilization and amalgamation between these three approaches has taken place. It may be noted in this connection that originally the approach of behavior therapists in England differed in two important respects from the approach of the American behavior modifiers. First, the former tended to deal with neurotic behavior whereas the latter tended to deal with psychotic behavior (this difference, of course, has now entirely disappeared). Second, the former tended to make much greater use of theoretical constructs (e.g., habit strength, reactive inhibition) and neurological models (e.g., feedback control models for speech) than the latter (this difference remains, though in somewhat attenuated form).

It is also important to note that the approach stressing the experimental investigation of the single case should not be confused with, nor identified with, the classical clinical approach as exemplified, for example, in the clinical investigation in medicine or the neurologist's bedside examination. Neither of these activities has, as its distinguishing mark, the experimental investigation of the single case, even though many tests may be applied to the patient. The aim of the clinical or neurological approach remains, of course, that of diagnosis with a view to a standard form of treatment.

MISCONCEPTION 2

This misconception relates to the linking of behavior therapy with the application of learning theory to the modification of behavior. It follows directly from the historical account and revised definition that, in relation to its development in England, behavior therapy is not the application of learning theory or any other kind of theory to the modification of behavior. Behavior therapy as it developed in England was the application of a particular approach (the use of the experimental method in the individual case). The distinction is important because it implies that disabilities may arise from causes other than those relating to learning factors, and that theoretical models for explanation and treatment may meaningfully be derived from any part of the body of psychological knowledge. A classic instance of this is the feedback control model for stuttering. This, of course, is not to deny that learning theory has played a major role in behavior therapy thus far. But this may well be a historical accident resulting from the fact that empirical knowledge in the area of learning, and theories of learning themselves, are at present more readily utilized for explanatory and treatment purposes than other areas of experimental psychology. To identify behavior therapy with learning theory, however, is to commit an error of judgment which, if perpetuated, may seriously retard the utilization of other equally important areas of knowledge from experimental psychology and the theoretical models derived therefrom.

MISCONCEPTION 3

The alleged peripheral nature of behavior therapy is a justified comment (though by no means necessarily a valid criticism) insofar as it relates to the behavior modification techniques of the operant approach, since this approach avowedly rejects the use of postulated, not directly observable and measurable, intervening variables such as habit strength, reactive inhibition, and so forth. Insofar as it is directed against Wolpe's approach or the Maudsley approach, it is both misconceived and factually inaccurate. The present author's original paper on symptoms and symptom substitution was not intended to deny the importance of "organismic" variables but to highlight the distinction between the behavioral approach [which stresses a sequential or "horizontal" linking of chains of stimulus-response (internal or peripheral) events without assigning priority to either in treatment] and the psychodynamic approach (which stresses a "vertical" approach in which the overt behavior or symptom is unimportant or even irrelevant as compared with the "underlying" conflict which must have priority in treatment). That this is so is clearly seen in the study by Yates (1958b) which utilized the theoretical constructs of Hull's basic equation (drive, habit strength, reactive and conditioned inhibition), none of which are directly observable or measurable. Similarly, the feedback-control model of stuttering (Yates, 1963) postulates internal cortical events which are not directly observable. Allied with this misconception is the belief that behavior therapists deal only with relatively straightforward, "uncomplicated" abnormal responses, such as tics, bed-wetting, simple phobias, etc. Such an approach *could* be justified on the grounds that, if we are unable to account for and modify such "simple" forms of behavior, we are unlikely to make much progress in handling more complex disorders, such as "free-floating" anxiety, and that theory and technique are likely to develop more rapidly by initially dealing with situations in which the responses and the change in responses can be accurately measured. In fact, of course, behavior therapists (especially Wolpe) have dealt right from the start with more complex forms of disturbance.[2]

MISCONCEPTION 4

The tendency to identify behavior therapy with the modification of neurotic or psychotic behavior is unfortunate, since it can be argued that the terms *neurosis* and *psychosis* should be applied only to certain forms of abnormality (if indeed these terms are necessary at all) and that abnormalities of behavior can occur in individuals who are neither neurotic nor psychotic. Thus, there is no evidence whatever that enuretics or stutterers are neurotic, and to label them as such is quite misleading. To put it another way, while neurotic behavior is abnormal, not all forms of abnormal behavior are neurotic.

The distinction is important because, taken in conjunction with other considerations, it leads to significant differential conclusions regarding both the explanation of the genesis and maintenance of various kinds of abnormalities and of their

---

[2] The whole problem of symptom substitution has recently been considered in much greater detail resulting in a more sophisticated approach to the question (Ayllon, Haughton, and Hughes, 1965; Cahoon, 1968; Crisp, 1966; Weitzman, 1967; Yates, 1969).

treatment. This theme cannot be developed in detail here, but briefly let us begin with the distinction (implicit in all of Eysenck's work) between neuroticism and neurosis. Neuroticism may be regarded as an inherited predisposition to develop a neurosis (or, more accurately, neurotic forms of behavior) under certain specifiable conditions. Let us also accept Eysenck's contention that the dimension of neuroticism is normally distributed in the population. Let us further postulate that a person high in neuroticism is characterized by extreme lability of the autonomic nervous system (ANS). This means in effect that a stimulus which is neutral or nonthreatening to a person low in neuroticism will be perceived as threatening by a person high in neuroticism, that is, his autonomic reactivity will be triggered off at much lower intensities of stimulation than is the case for the normal person. On this basis, it may be argued that early in childhood (since neuroticism is conceived as a basic inborn property of the ANS) the person high in neuroticism will learn a wide range of conditioned avoidance behaviors (CARs), the content and direction of which will depend on the specific environmental experiences to which he is subjected. The person low in neuroticism, on the other hand, will develop CARs only if he is subjected to unusually high degrees of threatening stimulation and will tend, in these circumstances, to develop highly specific CARs. One immediate consequence of this distinction is that persons high in neuroticism will tend to develop polysymptomatic abnormalities in conditions of objectively low stress, whereas persons low in neuroticism will tend to develop monosymptomatic abnormalities in conditions only of very high specific stress such as exposure to a highly traumatic situation from which escape by direct means is impossible. Furthermore, it would follow directly from the model that it would be much more difficult to treat the person high in neuroticism successfully and that, even where success were attained, since the neuroticism variable by definition is not amenable to psychological forms of treatment, the ready development of new abnormalities would be expected, though it should be carefully noted that this would not represent an instance of symptom substitution in the psychodynamic sense. In the light of this discussion, the term *neurosis* would seem to be better reserved for those disorders of behavior which are generalized and widespread and derived from a high degree of neuroticism.[3] It should further be pointed out that certain disorders of behavior have been clearly shown to be unrelated to the presence of high degrees of neuroticism (e.g., enuresis), while other disorders are not only not related to neuroticism but are evidently better conceptualized in terms other than as representing deficient or surplus forms of learning (e.g., stuttering).

MISCONCEPTION 5

In order to explain misconceptions concerning the assessment of the validity of behavior therapy as evidenced in several recent studies, it is necessary to introduce a little more history. In Eysenck's paper on the effects of psychotherapy (Eysenck, 1952), it was clearly shown that the conclusion that changes following psychotherapy were causally produced by factors in the psychotherapeutic situation was a logical *non sequitur*. Since the changes which followed psychotherapy could have been produced to an equal degree by extra-therapeutic factors in the absence of psychotherapy (usually referred to as the "spontaneous recovery rate," a term which merely indicates ignorance of the factors producing the change), Eysenck argued that, as a minimum requirement, an untreated control group (and preferably other groups treated by other means) was required. Now, the misconception which is being considered here is simply that it has been assumed that the effects of behavior therapy could be compared with the effects of no treatment or alternative methods of treatment (usually individual or group psychotherapy) in exactly the same way. Such a conclusion is implicit in much of the earlier work of Wolpe and his colleagues (e.g., Lazarus, 1963; Wolpe, 1961) and is explicit in the more recent studies referred to above. Let us consider a recent study of Gelder, Marks, and Wolff (1967) as an example. They matched three groups of patients with a main complaint of one or more phobias as carefully as possible on variables which might confound differential results (age; sex; duration of illness; verbal IQ; severity of main and other phobias, anxiety, depression, obsessions; and Cornell score). Each group was then subjected to a different form of treatment (imaginative desensitization, individual psychotherapy, group

---

[3] Yates (1969), in fact, has devoted an entire chapter to the "normal" disorders of "normal" people.

psychotherapy). The groups were then compared with respect to pre- and post-treatment changes in symptoms, social adjustment, and interpersonal relations. The design of the experiment seems to be exemplary in terms of Eysenck's critique, and this and other studies of a similar kind have consistently shown a slight, but probably significant, superiority of behavior therapy over alternative forms of therapy. Why then should any objection be raised against this method of validating behavior therapy?

The answer lies, of course, in the historical account and definition of behavior therapy given earlier in this paper. Consideration of the experimental design of the study of Gelder et al. reveals at once that it is another example of the persistence of the medical model and that it violates practically all of the assumptions on which behavior therapy, as it developed in England, was based. First, it assumes that standard techniques of behavior therapy exist which may be applied in a routine fashion. Thus, systematic desensitization is regarded as a technique in which the patient is taught relaxation by a standard method, anxiety or fear hierarchies are constructed by standard procedures, and then systematic desensitization is proceeded with in a standard way [Wolpe (1961) has, in fact, published detailed instructions for the application of this technique]. The patient is then assessed as being improved to a greater or lesser degree at the end of the treatment. The overall efficacy of the technique is assessed by comparison of groups of patients. It will be at once apparent that this whole procedure is at complete variance with the basic assumption of behavior therapy as it developed at the Maudsley, namely, that *each patient is to be investigated as an experimental problem in his own right* and not as a particular case to whom a standard set of procedures is applied, with the patient being changed or unchanged at the end of the procedures. The fundamental assumption of the English behavior therapists from 1950 to 1960 was that there are no standard methods of treatment which can be routinely applied.[4] It is here argued that this premature

---

[4] It may be noted that Gelder, Marks, and Wolff (1967) state that behavior therapy in their study was carried out by five psychiatrists, four of whom had no previous experience with behavior therapy. Apparently, however, the "therapists found the deconditioning techniques easy to learn." This, of course, is not surprising if behavior therapy is regarded as the application of a standard technique rather than as the application of the experimental method.

crystallization of behavior therapy into sets of standardized techniques is the most dangerous development of the past five years; if not corrected, it will almost certainly lead to the early encapsulation and mummification of behavior therapy and reduce it to the same degree of impotence and frustration which is one of the major complaints behavior therapists bring against classical psychotherapy.

Second, this approach to assessing the validity of behavior therapy violates a further fundamental tenet of the English behavior therapists in that it assumes that validity can best be established by group comparisons of the kind described. But the English behavior therapists argued quite differently, namely, that the validity of behavior therapy was not an either/or matter but was a continuing process to be established experimentally. Put another way, it was assumed that validity could best be established by the interaction of theory and empirical data in a continuing experiment on single cases. An example from the writer's own work will clarify the point. In treating a patient with multiple tics (Yates, 1958b) a theoretical model was first constructed, utilizing Hull's notions of drive, habit strength, and reactive and conditioned inhibition. From this theoretical model (and in conjunction with the results of empirical studies), it was predicted that massed practice would lead to a permanent reduction in the ability of the patient to perform the tic, due to the growth of conditioned inhibition. A long series of experiments was then carried out on the patient with a view both to establishing whether the theoretical model were valid and, if so, to establish the optimal conditions for the growth of conditioned inhibition. Two points should be particularly noted. First, the interaction of theory and technique constituted the validation of the experimental procedures, and this was so whether or not the patient was clinically "improved." For a therapeutic "failure," within this framework, might yield information relevant to future studies and treatment that was just as important as if therapeutic "success" was achieved. Second, although not actually achieved (for various reasons) in this study, an example of internal control (and validation) would have been not to apply massed practice to one of the tics and thus predict no decline in ability to reproduce this tic as compared with the others. Furthermore, although a very substantial reduction in the patient's capacity to reproduce the tics voluntarily was achieved, it was not assumed that a standard technique for the treatment of tics had been devised [a caution well justified in the light of more recent results by Feldman and Werry (1966)].

The desire to demonstrate that behavior therapy "works" (or not) and, particularly, the desire to derive and utilize standard methods of treatment (which "work" for some patients, but not for others) is natural in a field in which so many need help and so few techniques are available. To suppose, however, that it is at all likely that such standard techniques (with a high success rate) will be forthcoming in the immediate (or even perhaps distant) future in behavior pathology is simply to fly in the face of the evidence of history. The development of even a moderately satisfactory (valid and reliable) method of measuring temperature took over 100 years to achieve; the discovery of the molecular structure of morphine was achieved only after 120 years of unremitting experimental effort. To suppose that behavior therapy can be assessed as to its validity by the group comparison method of various "standard" techniques less than fifteen years after its inception is quite unwarranted.

It is not intended to deny in any way the importance or interest of the papers criticized here. Indeed, it is meaningfully possible to propose a dimension along which experimental studies of various kinds may be ordered, from those which are furthest removed from the individual patient at one extreme to those which analyze and attempt to modify experimentally the behavior of the individual patient in the clinical situation at the other extreme. Thus at the one extreme we have the corpus of experiments (e.g., those on partial reinforcement) which are not performed with treatment in mind at all, but the results of which may be highly relevant to clinical experimental investigations (as has been shown in the case of enuresis). Then we have those kinds of experiments which are concerned with attempts to provide a framework of laboratory-based knowledge for the treatment of specific abnormalities of behavior, or which are intended to explore particular techniques (e.g., desensitization) in order either to demonstrate their validity or to improve them and specify limiting conditions for their application.[5] This work may still be restricted to normal subjects, or it may involve normal subjects with various abnormalities. Shading into this part of the dimension is work of the kind

---

[5] The recent review of the experimental work on systematic desensitization by Rachman (1967) is an excellent example of this kind of work.

criticized in this paper, where the interest is a combination of the assessment of both individual and group changes in abnormal patients, utilizing experimental methods, but where the individual patient is treated in a standard fashion, according to some rules. Finally, there are the studies which, in this writer's view, constitute behavior therapy properly so called, where the individual patient is treated as an individual, as the object of a controlled experiment. While all of the other procedures contribute indirectly to the validation of behavior therapy, the essence of validating behavior therapy lies in the production of meaningful, predicted changes following the experimental manipulation of the single case.[6]

Nor is it intended to deny that standard techniques may ultimately be devised for limited purposes, such as facilitating the start of an experimental investigation. In this author's view, however, the essence of behavior therapy should involve the controlled experimental investigation of the single case along the lines so clearly indicated by the work of Shapiro. One final example will suffice. It appeared for more than 20 years that a rational theory for the treatment of enuresis had been developed and from that theory a rational method of treatment had been derived (Mowrer and Mowrer, 1938). Yet Lovibond (1964), by a careful reexamination, was able to show conclusively that Mowrer's theory must be incorrect, was then able to formulate an alternative theory, and from that theory was able to derive a modified method of treatment. Not only that, but knowledge of a highly specialized area of experimental psychology (partial reinforcement) has recently indicated clearly ways in which the technique can be modified further so as to reduce very significantly the probability of relapse. The technique of systematic desensitization is in grave danger of becoming as standardized and routine a procedure as the Mowrer technique for enuresis, that is, the patient is treated in a standard fashion and he either recovers or he does not. It would appear that the only safeguard against this danger lies in an insistence on the "controlled investigation of the single case."

---

[6] Methodological problems associated with "intensive" (as opposed to "extensive") design and analysis of experiments have been discussed generally by Chassan (1967); and in relation to particular studies by Dukes (1965), Edgington (1966, 1967), and Revusky (1967).

CONCLUSION

The misconceptions criticized here derived in large part from the perpetuation of the insidious influence of the medical model. The essential distinguishing feature of behavior therapy, the feature which makes it fundamentally different from other forms of therapy, is the stress on the experimental investigation of the single case. If this distinction is lost, there seems little doubt that behavior therapy will follow the same path and suffer the same fate as other therapies.

REFERENCES

Ayllon, T.; Haughton, E.; and Hughes, H. B. 1965. Interpretation of symptoms: Fact or fiction? *Behaviour Research and Therapy* 3:1–7.

Bartlett, D., and Shapiro, M. B. 1956. Investigation and treatment of a reading disability in a dull child with severe psychiatric disturbances. *British Journal of Educational Psychology* 26:180–190.

Bookbinder, L. J. 1962. Simple conditioning versus the dynamic approach to symptoms and symptom substitution: A reply to Yates. *Psychological Reports* 10:71–77.

Breger, L., and McGaugh, J. L. 1965. Critique and reformulation of "learning-theory" approaches to psychotherapy and neurosis. *Psychological Bulletin* 63:338–358.

Cahoon, D. D. 1968. Symptom substitution and the behavior therapies: Reappraisal. *Psychological Bulletin* 69:149–156.

Chassan, J. B. 1967. *Research design in clinical psychology and psychiatry.* New York: Appleton-Century-Crofts.

Cooper, J. E. 1963. A study of behavior therapy in thirty psychiatric patients. *Lancet* 1:411–415.

Cooper, J. E.; Gelder, M. G.; and Marks, I. M. 1965. Results of behavior therapy on 77 psychiatric patients. *British Medical Journal* 1:1222–1225.

Crisp, A. H. 1966. "Transference," "symptom emergence," and "social repercussion" in behavior therapy: A study of fifty-four treated patients. *British Journal of Medical Psychology* 39:179–196.

Dollard, J., and Miller, N. E. 1950. *Personality and psychotherapy.* New York: McGraw-Hill.

Dukes, W. F. 1965. *N*=1. *Psychological Bulletin* 64:74–79.

Edgington, E. S. 1966. Statistical inference and nonrandom samples. *Psychological Bulletin* 66:485–487.

Edgington, E. S. 1967. Statistical inference from *N*=1 experiments. *Journal of Psychology* 65:195–199.

Eysenck, H. J. 1952. The effects of psychotherapy: An evaluation. *Journal of Consulting Psychology* 16:319–324.

Eysenck, H. J. 1959. Learning theory and behavior therapy. *Journal of Mental Science* 105:61–75.

Eysenck, H. J., ed. 1960. *Behavior therapy and the neuroses.* London: Pergamon.

Eysenck, H. J. 1964. The nature of behavior therapy. In *Experiments in behavior therapy,* ed. H. J. Eysenck, pp. 1–15. Oxford: Pergamon.

Eysenck, H. J., and Rachman, S. 1965. *The causes and cures of neurosis.* London: Routledge and Kegan Paul.

Feldman, H. B., and Werry, J. S. 1966. An unsuccessful attempt to treat a tiqueur by massed practice. *Behaviour Research and Therapy* 4:111–117.

Gelder, M. G., and Marks, I. M. 1966. Severe agoraphobia: A controlled prospective trial of behavior therapy. *British Journal of Psychiatry* 112:309–320.

Gelder, M. G., and Marks, I. M. 1968. Desensitization and phobias: A crossover study. *British Journal of Psychiatry* 114:323–328.

Gelder, M. G.; Marks, I. M.; and Wolff, H. H. 1967. Desensitization and psychotherapy in the treatment of phobic states: A controlled inquiry. *British Journal of Psychiatry* 113:53–73.

Jones, H. G. 1956. The application of conditioning and learning techniques to the treatment of a psychiatric patient. *Journal of Abnormal and Social Psychology* 52:414–420.

Jones, H. G. 1960. Applied abnormal psychology: The experimental approach. In *Handbook of abnormal psychology,* ed. H. J. Eysenck, pp. 764–781. London: Pitman.

Lazarus, A. A. 1963. The results of behavior therapy in 126 cases of severe neurosis. *Behaviour Research and Therapy* 1:69–79.

Lovibond, S. H. 1964. *Conditioning and enuresis.* Oxford: Pergamon.

Marks, I. M., and Gelder, M. G. 1965. A controlled retrospective study of behavior therapy in phobic patients. *British Journal of Psychiatry* 111:561–573.

Meyer, V. 1957. The treatment of two phobic patients on the basis of learning principles. *Journal of Abnormal and Social Psychology* 55:261–266.

Mowrer, O. H., and Mowrer, W. A. 1938. Enuresis: A method for its study and treatment. *American Journal of Orthopsychiatry* 8:436–447.

Murray, E. J. 1963. Learning theory and psychotherapy: Biotropic versus sociotropic approaches. *Journal of Counseling Psychology* 10:250–255.

Rachman, S. 1967. Systematic desensitization. *Psychological Bulletin* 67:93–103.

Revusky, S. H. 1967. Some statistical treatments compatible with individual organism methodology. *Journal of the Experimental Analysis of Behavior* 10:319–330.

Shapiro, M. B. 1951. An experimental approach to diagnostic psychological testing. *Journal of Mental Science* 97:748–764.

Shapiro, M. B. 1961a. A method of measuring psychological changes specific to the individual psychiatric patient. *British Journal of Medical Psychology* 34:151–155.

Shapiro, M. B. 1961b. The single case in fundamental clinical psychological research. *British Journal of Medical Psychology* 34:255–262.

Shapiro, M. B. 1963. Clinical approach to fundamental research with special reference to the study of the single patient. In *Methods of psychiatric research,* ed. P. Sainsbury and N. Kreitman, pp. 123–149. London: Oxford University Press.

Shapiro, M. B. 1966. The single case in clinical-psychological research. *Journal of General Psychology* 74:3–23.

Shapiro, M. B.; Marks, I. M.; and Fox, B. 1963. A therapeutic experiment on phobic and affective symptoms in an individual psychiatric patient. *British Journal of Social and Clinical Psychology* 2:81–93.

Shapiro, M. B., and Nelson, E. H. 1955. An investigation of an abnormality of cognitive functioning in a cooperative young psychotic: An example of the application of experimental method to the single case. *Journal of Clinical Psychology* 11:344–351.

Shapiro, M. B., and Ravenette, A. T. 1959. A preliminary experiment of paranoid delusions. *Journal of Mental Science* 105:295-312.

Ullmann, L. B., and Krasner, L., eds. 1965. *Case studies in behavior modification.* New York: Holt.

Weitzman, B. 1967. Behavior therapy and psychotherapy. *Psychological Review* 74:300-317.

Wolpe, J. 1958. *Psychotherapy by reciprocal inhibition.* Stanford: Stanford University Press.

Wolpe, J. 1961. The systematic desensitization treatment of neuroses. *Journal of Nervous and Mental Disease* 132:189-203.

Yates, A. J. 1958a. Symptoms and symptom substitution. *Psychological Review* 65:371-374.

Yates, A. J. 1958b. The application of learning theory to the treatment of tics. *Journal of Abnormal and Social Psychology* 56:175-182.

Yates, A. J. 1963. Recent empirical and theoretical approaches to the experimental manipulation of speech in normal subjects and in stammerers. *Behaviour Research and Therapy* 1:95-119.

Yates, A. J. 1969. *Behavior therapy.* New York: Wiley.

In Defense of Operant Conditioning Programs in Mental Institutions

By ROGER E. VOGLER and PATRICK L. MARTIN

19

Roger Vogler of Pomona College and Patrick Martin of Patton State Hospital discuss some central features of behavioristic treatment programs in mental institutions. In addition, the authors respond to some often voiced criticisms of these programs.

It is unfortunate that humanistic approaches to behavior disorders are called by that name. Such labeling implies that behavioristic approaches are somehow less humane, less concerned with human dignity and suffering. As Vogler and Martin point out, nothing could be further from the truth. Behavioristic techniques of treatment are designed to modify behavior; it is the *intent* of the therapist that classifies a treatment as humane or inhumane. Certainly it is possible that some therapists (behavioristic or humanistic) might not value other humans. But, as Vogler and Martin emphasize, "any operant conditioner worth his salt would deplore such a state of affairs."

CRITICISM OF OPERANT conditioning programs in mental institutions has focused on the potentially immoral, unethical, and "dehumanizing" use of operant conditioning techniques (e.g., Lucero, Vail, and Scherber, 1968).

These critics imply that certain programs labeled "operant conditioning" have employed essentially punitive methods or deprivations which "can be dehumanizing and can at times lead to a total loss of human values [Lucero et al.]." Lucero et al. (1968) have made recommendations on the use of operant techniques which have subsequently been made standard policy for all of Minnesota's state mental institutions. These recommendations are as follows:

1. Aversive reinforcement is never to be used in a general program for groups of patients. However, in unusual indi-

---

From *Psychological Record*, vol. 19 (1969), pp. 59–64. Reprinted by permission of the authors and the *Psychological Record*.

vidual cases in which physical abuse of self or others is otherwise unchangeable, aversive reinforcement methods may be used.

2. Deprivation is never to be used.
3. Positive reinforcement is the only conditioning technique to be used with the exception of aversive methods in the approved individual cases noted above.

Humane treatment for the mentally ill is a concern most certainly shared by laymen and mental health professionals alike, including those employing operant conditioning methods. Just why programs using operant techniques have been singled out as the target for criticism is not altogether clear, but unless such criticism is evaluated, the result might be the spread of erroneous information, serious misunderstandings, and eventual curtailment of the development and use of some of the most powerful therapeutic techniques for helping the mentally ill.

Perhaps one reason for the criticism is the actual effectiveness of operant methods in a field where results are hard to come by. Often it is only when techniques which work are developed that society becomes concerned about regulating their use. Another possible reason is the image of the operant conditioner as researcher and cold scientist, a role repeatedly impressed upon the public by our communication media as generally incompatible with the role of humanist. Not only is the "incompatibility" questionable, but actually unlikely in the case of the behavior therapist, whose aim is to help restore to the institutionalized those skills which he needs to regain his human dignity as a productive citizen living in the community.

Whatever the reasons for the attack on operant conditioning programs, some form of regulation of their use seems not only desirable, but needed. One does not expect surgery to be performed by anyone but a trained person, nor should his professional activities escape evaluation by the public. Not uncommon among programs labeled "operant conditioning" are those which are developed and/or implemented by individuals who are essentially ignorant of the principles of operant conditioning, the systematic use of the techniques derived from them, and the experimental paradigm upon which the techniques are based. It is, of course, inaccurate to label such programs "operant conditioning" or "behavior modification."

Mislabeling, whether intentional, out of ignorance, to confer respectability, or for whatever reason, leads to confusion in communication. This confusion apparently includes Lucero et al., who have recommended that "deprivation" should never be used in operant conditioning programs and that only positive reinforcement be used. The contradiction between these two recommendations is obvious. A stimulus does not have positively reinforcing properties unless some state of deprivation exists at the time of its presentation. For example, food is not reinforcing to a man who has just finished an ample and delicious meal. Thus, these critics must be using the term *deprivation* to mean something else, possibly to mean the prolonged absence of basic necessities of life. This, of course, is not what the behavior therapist means by the term *deprivation*, nor does it resemble what he does in practice. Nowhere does the theory prescribe the use of deprivation in this extreme sense.

One gets the impression that many individuals unfamiliar with the use of deprivation in operant methodology believe that it is used to "starve" the patient into submission, that is, as a way to motivate. However, this belief is a misconception simply because such a statement entirely ignores the major purpose of operant techniques, what they involve, and how they are implemented. The manipulation of states of deprivation is not solely a matter of inducing activity. Most experimental psychologists have long realized that very little increase in constructive activity develops simply as a function of hunger. The manipulation of deprivation states is a matter of developing effectiveness for stimuli so that they can be used to guide (reinforce) the patient toward more acceptable modes of functioning. The operant conditioner is interested in reinforcers, not in so-called drive states. He knows full well that reinforcers are not particularly effective when there is no state of deprivation, but that is where his interest in deprivation ends. In fact, if someone proposed to starve a patient into submission, he would object because the highest level of motivation one can produce in a patient is rather pointless unless the behavior which results can be shaped to conform to acceptable standards.

But this perhaps does not allay the concern of those individuals who believe that deprivation is potentially harmful to the patient. However, one might well ask what is meant by the statement that deprivation "can be dehumanizing and at times leads to a total loss of human values"? What must be meant is that enforcing a state of deprivation—regardless of its severity—causes the individual to adopt forms of behavior which are at variance with social values and mores. For example, a hungry person might beg and whine (dehumanization) or might attempt to steal food if all other alternatives are frustrated. Yet, any operant conditioner worth his salt would deplore such a state of affairs. In fact, he would predict an undesirable outcome so long as attention is fixed solely upon deprivation. Rather than manifest an unusual amount of interest in the operation of deprivation the competent behavior therapist would insist that any treatment involving deprivation provide the patient with alternatives which are quite in line with social mores and values. If he is especially competent, he would also insure that those alternatives are well within the patient's current level of capability. His requirements of the patient would always be adjusted in terms of how the patient is doing in working towards a clearly defined goal: a patient whose behavioral capacity allows him to take the responsibility for satisfying the deprivation states which are a natural consequence of living, in ways which our society deems appropriate.

The use of aversive stimulation ("aversive reinforcement" in Lucero et al.), except in "unusual individual cases in which physical abuse of self or others is otherwise unchangeable," has also been questioned. In evaluating this criticism one must consider two points: voluntary submission to painful procedures and long-range benefits from short-term unpleasantness. One readily submits to the pain of having a tooth drilled by a dentist in order to maintain the use of the tooth, or willingly volunteers for the pain and discomfort of surgery if the alternative is imminent death. These temporary submissions to pain generally result in obvious subsequent benefits. The problem becomes one of proving that particular techniques of aversive stimulation do, indeed, result in sufficient benefit to warrant their application. The use of aversive conditioning techniques with humans is much like the field of surgery was a century ago—initial work (e.g., Blake, 1965, 1967; James, 1962; Kushner, 1965; Lavin, Thorpe, Barker, Blakemore, and Conway, 1961; Rachman, 1961; and Raymond, 1956, 1964) suggests immense potential for benefiting mankind with a strong need for research and development including refinement of existing techniques and methods. Safeguards to protect patients, such as insistence upon voluntarism, thorough examination of the technique with lower organisms before use with humans, etc., are certainly necessary. Yet to prevent their controlled usage and extension through research can only result in forestalling, or perhaps even preventing, the development of techniques which may be of immense benefit in helping alcoholics, sexual deviates, autistic children, or even people who would like to stop smoking.

Moreover, denying the use of any procedure which can be construed as "aversive reinforcement" as a method "in a general program for groups of patients" does not allow a treatment program to proceed in accordance with a realistic view of living. The world outside the hospital is a world in which aversive consequences abound. If any program, operantly oriented or not, does not in some way prepare some patients to cope with the possibility of such consequences, then it seems that the program is avoiding a serious responsibility. It is not enough to point out to these patients that we live in a "rough and tumble world" because this in no way provides them with a behavioral repertoire which is functional in situations offering an unpleasant outcome. It seems a much better procedure to present aversive consequences in a controlled situation which is designed to guide the patient toward learning behaviors which will enable him to cope successfully.

One must again consider that many concerned individuals do not fully understand the use of aversive techniques as they are properly applied in behavior modification programs. The application or programming of aversive consequences for a given behavior should always be used to increase the probability that a desirable alternative form of behavior shall or can be emitted. In this way, the use of aversive stimulation becomes instructive because the patient is encouraged to adopt a more desirable and socially acceptable method of satisfying his needs. This, of course, is quite different from the procedure of simple punishment.

With punishment the falsely labeled "behavior therapist" merely suppresses undesirable behavior, without providing opportunity for desirable alternative behavior to be emitted. Moreover, the unsophisticated punisher is often unaware of the many behaviors concomitantly elicited by a moderately severe punishing stimulus which may interfere with learning acceptable alternatives. Occasionally, too, one gets the impression that staff employ punishment for purposes of vengeance or to immediately (but only temporarily) eliminate an undesirable behavior. It is important that those who critically evaluate operant conditioning programs do not include as operant conditioners those individuals who use what the layman thinks of as "punishment" or "reward," and who equate them with "operant conditioning." Alternatives may be suggested for those who wish to acquaint themselves with some of the principles (e.g., Holland and Skinner, 1961; Schaefer and Martin, 1968; Ulrich, Stachnik, and Mabry, 1966).

Perhaps another reason for the criticism of operant conditioning programs is their attribution of responsibility for behavior to patients. From the traditional point of view, these persons are "mentally ill," i.e., "sick" in a manner similar to a heart or cancer patient and should not be held accountable for their actions. Behavioral accountability is viewed by the objectors as referring almost solely to inappropriate behavior, which implies untoward consequences. Actually, operant principles prescribe that for a change in behavior to occur, the patient must participate, i.e., engage in behaviors relevant to the learning task and experience the differential consequences of their behaviors. This includes both appropriate and inappropriate behavioral consequences, with emphasis on the use of positive reinforcement for appropriate behavior in gradually increasing steps of improvement (method of successive approximation). Extinction, or the withholding of positive reinforcement for a particular behavior when it occurs, is the procedure of choice for eliminating inappropriate behavior, and not solely the use of punitive consequences, as is sometimes incorrectly implied. The hospitalized mental patient is not treated as an infrahuman, bereft of the dignity of effecting some influence over his own actions and some control over his environment. In short, the institutionalized person is afforded the human dignity of responsibility and behavioral accountability, and this approach has been convincingly demonstrated in numerous settings to result in efficacious behavior changes (e.g., the 50 studies reported in Ullmann and Krasner, 1965).

The traditional "illness" model is, in fact, becoming viewed with suspicion by many mental health professionals as often maintaining the very problems which have resulted in institutionalization in the first place. This is done by providing a ready explanation for patients' problems as the result of some "sickness" or "disease process" which runs its course essentially independently of intervention. This approach fosters dependency upon the hospital and therapist and requires little or no patient participation in the "curative" or change process.

Criticism of operant conditioning programs can be healthy and promote the growth and development of a promising area of treatment. However, criticism from the unsophisticated, who do not understand the fundamentals of operant conditioning, is of questionable value and potential harm if it leads to misunderstandings among mental health professionals and hospital administrators and curtails development of the field. Safeguards are most certainly necessary for operant conditioning programs, or any kind of program for that matter. But at least some members of a team of evaluators should be knowledgeable of operant conditioning principles and techniques and the therapeutic rationale for such programs.

REFERENCES

Blake, B. G. 1965. Application of behavior therapy to the treatment of alcoholism. *Behavior Research and Therapy* 3:75–85.

Blake, B. G. 1967. A follow-up of alcoholics treated by behavior therapy. *Behavior Research and Therapy* 5:89–94.

Holland, J. G., and Skinner, B. F. 1961. *The analysis of behavior.* New York: McGraw-Hill.

James, B. 1962. Case of homosexuality treated by aversion therapy. *British Medical Journal* 1:768–770.

Kushner, M. 1965. The reduction of a long-standing fetish by means of aversive conditioning. In *Case studies in behavior modification,* ed. L. P. Ullmann and L. Krasner. New York: Holt, Rinehart, and Winston.

Lavin, N. I.; Thorpe, J. G.; Barker, J. C.; Blakemore, C. B.; and Conway, C. G. 1961. Behavior therapy in a case of transvestism. *Journal of Nervous and Mental Disease* 133:346–353.

Lucero, R. J.; Vail, D. J.; and Scherber, J. 1968. Regulating operant-conditioning programs. *Hospital and Community Psychiatry,* February, pp. 41–42.

Rachman, S. 1961. Sexual disorders and behavior therapy. *American Journal of Psychiatry* 118:235–240.

Raymond, M. J. 1956. Case of fetishism treated by aversion therapy. *British Medical Journal* 2:854–857.

Raymond, M. J. 1964. The treatment of addiction by aversion conditioning with apomorphine. *Behavior Research and Therapy* 1:287–291.

Schaefer, H. H., and Martin, P. L. 1969. *Behavioral therapy.* New York: McGraw-Hill.

Ullmann, L., and Krasner, L., eds. 1965. *Case studies in behavior modification.* Holt, Rinehart, and Winston.

Ulrich, R.; Stachnik, T.; and Mabry, J. 1966. *Control of human behavior.* Glenview, Ill.: Scott, Foresman.

Name Index

Rickels, K., 210
Ridley, D., 182
Riesman, D., 215, 230, 237
Ring, K., 183, 184, 191
Roberts, R. C., 40, 42
Rogers, C. R., 18, 23, 193, 228, 236, 237
Rogler, L. H., 12, 13, 23
Rose, A. J., 209
Rosenthal, M., 201
Ross, H. A., 46
Rowley, L. B., 242
Rubin, E., 210
Ruesch, J., 210, 232, 237
Ryan, W., 15, 23, 37, 42, 171–181

Sarbin, T. R., 2, 23
Sasaki, Y., 123–124, 130
Saslow, G., 209
Schaefer, E. S., 260, 261–278
Schaefer, H. H., 317, 319
Schaffer, L., 294
Scheff, T. J., 43–63
Scherber, J., 312–313, 318
Schermerhorn, R. A., 141, 147
Schofield, W., 33
Schooler, C., 183, 191
Schultes, R. E., 210
Schuster, C. R., 208
Schwartz, M. S., 163, 170
Scott, J. M., 210
Searles, H. F., 183, 191
Seeley, J., 172, 181
Segal, I., 260
Seiler, D., 182
Selye, H., 232, 237
Selznick, D., 141–142, 147
Shapiro, M. B., 295–296, 299, 307, 308, 310, 311
Sharpless, S. K., 210
Shelly, J. A., 201, 210
Skeels, H. M., 278
Skinner, B. F., 16, 23, 234, 237, 292, 297, 317, 318
Smith, D. E., 209
Smythies, J. R., 210
Snygg, D., 235, 237
Solomon, H. C., 39, 42
Stachnik, T., 317, 319
Stanton, A. H., 163, 170
Sternfield, L. A., 35, 42

Szasz, T., 9, 23, 64–107, 116, 118, 183, 191

Taft, J., 248
Taylor, N., 211
Temerlin, M. K., 108–118
Thorpe, J. G., 315, 318
Tobin, S. A., 279, 289, 290
Torrey, E. F., 119–130
Tourney, G., 211
Towbin, A. P., 183, 191
Trippe, M. J., 239

Ullmann, L. P., 2, 21, 23, 293, 297, 311, 317, 318, 319
Ulrich, R., 317, 319

Vail, D. J., 312–313, 318
Vogler, R. E., 312–319

Wahler, R. G., 1–23, 202
Wallace, A., 128–129, 130
Warner, W. L., 176
Watson, J. B., 16, 23
Weber, M., 177, 181
Weinstein, L., 15, 23, 239, 255, 256, 257, 259
Weitzman, B., 301, 311
Werry, J. S., 306, 309
West, L. J., 209
Wheatley, D., 211
Wheelis, A., 215, 225
White, E. B., 192
Wiehofen, H., 7, 22
Wilcox, R., 192–211
Wilmer, H., 124, 130
Wittenborn, J. R., 210
Witter, C., 211
Wittkower, E., 128, 130
Wolfe, T., 197, 211
Wolff, H. H., 294, 303, 309
Wolpe, J., 16, 23, 292, 293, 297, 298, 299, 300, 303, 304, 311
Woodworth, R. S., 163, 170

Yahraes, H., 260–278
Yates, A. J., 291–311

Zeisset, R. M., 164, 170
Zimbardo, P. G., 151–161, 163, 168–169, 170

Subject Index

325